D1595351

Socializing Security

SOCIALIZING SECURITY

Progressive-Era Economists and the Origins of American Social Policy

DAVID A. MOSS

HARVARD UNIVERSITY PRESS
Cambridge, Massachusetts
London, England   1996

Library of Congress Cataloging-in-Publication Data

Moss, David A., 1964–
    Socializing security : progressive-era economists and the origins
of American social policy / David A. Moss.
        p.   cm.
Includes bibliographical references and index.
ISBN 0-674-81502-5 (alk. paper)
1. Industrial welfare—United States—History—20th
century.   2. Social security—Law and legislation—United
States—History—20th century.   3. Labor laws and legislation—
United States—History—20th century.   4. American Association
for Labor Legislation—History.   I. Title.
HD7654.M67   1996
331.25'5—dc20   95-20652

For Abby

Contents

Introduction

I n 1906, Adam Rogalas earned $1.60 a day working for the Iron City Grain Elevator Company of Pittsburgh. His wage roughly equaled the national average for manufacturing workers, and it was probably sufficient to support his wife and four young children at a minimal standard of living. No doubt, his income was considerably greater than it would have been had he not emigrated from Russia. And in America, there was every reason to believe that his wages would rise steadily over time. Had he continued to earn the national average a decade later, his take-home pay would have been about $2.10 a day.

Unfortunately, the American dream came crashing down on Adam Rogalas and his family on October 16, 1906. That day, Adam was at work in a grain-storage building when suddenly the floor above him gave way: an avalanche of grain crushed him to death. His pregnant wife and children were left without a provider and without any savings. Iron City's claim agent offered to settle the case for $400, but Mrs. Rogalas refused, preferring instead to engage a lawyer and sue the company for $20,000. As the case dragged on, the Rogalas family faced hard times. Mrs. Rogalas found some work as a washerwoman, but she depended as well on relief and charity. She received $6 worth of groceries each month from the city of Pittsburgh, and she collected a bit more by begging outside the Catholic church on Sundays. She also received occasional help from her sister, who had six children of her own, and from her lawyer. In the end, Mrs. Rogalas lost her case against Iron City.[1]

Stories like this one, and the conditions they epitomized, led a group of reform-minded academics to organize the American Association for Labor Legislation (AALL) in early 1906 and to launch a national movement for compulsory social insurance and protective labor legislation. The leaders of the AALL were motivated primarily by the problem of worker insecurity. They found it intolerable that hard-working Americans like Adam Rogalas should be faced with the constant threat of industrial hazards and the potentially catastrophic financial consequences. They were most concerned about on-the-job accidents, illness, and unemployment, which induced individual insecurity and sapped the vitality of the labor force. According to the Association's secretary, John B. Andrews, the enactment of legislation protecting workers against major industrial hazards would inaugurate "a social revolution such as is little dreamed of at present."[2]

Andrews grounded his prediction on the belief that security was beginning to rival growth as a cardinal economic issue. Although individuals had always sought to protect themselves and their families against pecuniary loss, at the turn of the century the importance of economic security rose sharply relative to other personal and social objectives. There are many reasons for its ascendance, but two byproducts of industrialization—rising incomes and the disintegration of tight-knit rural communities—stand out as particularly important.[3]

Industrialization precipitated an exodus from country to city. Between 1880 and 1920, the proportion of the U.S. population living in rural areas declined from 72 percent to just 49 percent. The resulting erosion of rural communities deprived many individuals and families of effective support networks, leaving them more vulnerable to a wide variety of hazards, including the death of a breadwinner. The process of urbanization also dramatically increased workers' dependence on monetary earnings, since they no longer enjoyed easy access to food on the farm. Meanwhile, as average incomes rose ever further above subsistence levels (another byproduct of industrialization), individuals increasingly valued the preservation of their living standards as much as or more than the potential elevation of those standards. John Kenneth Galbraith writes that in industrial nations "most people, when employed, are not primarily preoccupied with the size of their income. They seek to increase it . . . but inadequacy of income is not their first concern . . . Their principal worry is the danger of losing all or most of their income."[4]

The growing significance of economic security at the turn of the century was clearly reflected in the development and diffusion of insurance. Private insurance, though dating back to ancient times, barely touched the lives of ordinary people until the second half of the nineteenth century. In Britain, fire insurance contracts were not unknown in the seventeenth century, and marine insurance was already well developed by the sixteenth century. Crude forms of life insurance also emerged in the sixteenth century, but such early policies served mainly as vehicles for gambling and for circumventing usury laws. In all of these cases, formal insurance contracts remained the nearly exclusive domain of economic elites until well into the nineteenth century.

Industrial life insurance, which was marketed directly to workers, originated in Britain around 1850 and arrived in the United States (courtesy of the Prudential Insurance Company) in 1875. Covered workers typically paid 5¢ to 25¢ a week for policies valued in the vicinity of $100. The first private pension plan in the United States, established by the American Express Company, also dates from 1875. Indicative of the mounting demand for economic security, private insurance and pensions spread rapidly in the early twentieth century. Between 1900 and 1920 the number of life insurance policies in force in the United States increased nearly fivefold, from 14 to 65 million; and the number of workers covered by company pensions reached an estimated 3.7 million in 1929.[5]

The leaders of the American Association for Labor Legislation recognized the importance of these trends. Yet they adamantly insisted that private insurance failed to provide workers with adequate protection against industrial hazards. Andrews wrote in the mid-teens:

> Probably no human device has done more to substitute security for uncertainty in the economic affairs of our complex modern life than the device of insurance. Property is protected by insurance against fire, burglary, or loss at sea. Persons with comfortable incomes insure themselves or their dependents against the financial results of accident, ill health, or death. But wage-earners, who are largely without property and whose incomes are too small to provide for adequate insurance in a commercial company, have until recently been exposed without protection to the winds of adversity.[6]

The types of insurance accessible to wage earners at the turn of the century were remarkably limited. When Adam Rogalas died in 1906, it does not appear that he carried any life insurance. Industrial life insurance would have been available to him at that time, but the average death benefit was then only about $150, hardly enough to finance a funeral and support his family for more than a few months. Nor did he carry any accident insurance. Although coverage against industrial accidents was not unheard of, it was difficult to obtain and thus relatively rare.[7]

The apparent inadequacy of existing security institutions motivated the AALL reformers to champion protective labor legislation and compulsory social insurance. They believed that state intervention was necessary because workers and their families were unable to protect themselves against potentially devastating industrial hazards. "Since the efforts of individual workmen have proven so futile," Andrews wrote in 1915, "it seems time for the State to step in . . ."[8]

And step in it did. From the dawn of the progressive era to the end of the twentieth century, the state's role in guaranteeing economic security expanded enormously. Nearly every state government enacted a workers' compensation law (i.e. compulsory accident insurance) between 1911 and 1920; and many passed various forms of protective labor legislation, including safety standards for hazardous industries and minimum-wage and maximum-hours laws. President Franklin D. Roosevelt ushered in deposit insurance and implicit crop insurance in 1933, unemployment and old-age insurance in 1935, and federally mandated workplace standards in 1938. Even after the New Deal, federal policymakers created many new public insurance programs, including disability insurance, health insurance for the elderly, pension insurance, and implicit coverage against natural disasters. Over forty states adopted mandatory automobile insurance laws, while changes in the tort system rendered coverage against product liability and medical malpractice suits effectively compulsory. The most notable absence from this long list of security policies has been compulsory health insurance, which American reformers described as inevitable—the "next great step" in labor legislation—as early as 1916.

Although many of the nation's security institutions are commonly lumped together under the heading "welfare state," the term "security state" is probably more appropriate. After all, workers' compensation, unemployment insurance, and old-age insurance have much more in common with deposit insurance and pension insurance than they do with Aid to Families with Dependent Children (AFDC), commonly known as "welfare." Compulsory insurance programs differ from welfare programs in that they are intended to offer security to individuals who have something to lose rather than assistance to the needy, who have little or nothing to lose. Every year, the federal and state governments spend a great deal more on security programs than they do on welfare programs.[9]

Back in the progressive era, none of the AALL reformers predicted, or perhaps even desired, that the national appetite for economic security would ever become so voracious. Yet, by demanding public responses to risk-based insecurity, they laid the foundation for the modern security state. And this is why they are worthy of close study—because they inaugurated the American movement to socialize security.

The leading figures at the American Association for Labor Legislation, particularly in its early years, were nearly all economists. Richard T. Ely and John R. Commons were well-known institutional economists and professors of economics at the University of Wisconsin. Henry W. Farnam, Henry Rogers Seager, and William F. Willoughby were professors of economics at Yale, Columbia, and Princeton, respectively. Though less heterodox than their Wisconsin counterparts, all three easterners embraced elements of German historicism. In fact, Farnam and Seager, like Ely, had studied in Germany. John Andrews, who had a doctorate in economics, joined the AALL full-time in 1909, immediately after completing his graduate work at Wisconsin under Ely and Commons. Adna F. Weber, one of the original founders of the AALL, had a Ph.D. in political economy from Columbia and was the chief statistician at the New York State Department of Labor. Ely, Farnam, Seager, and Willoughby served as the Association's first four presidents; and Weber, Commons, and Andrews as the first three secretaries. Andrews became secretary in 1910 and held the position until he died in 1943. Although many other, more prominent individuals were associated with the organization as members and honorary vice-presidents—including Woodrow Wilson, Louis Brandeis, Samuel Gompers, and Jane Addams—the economists just mentioned comprised the organization's core.

The AALL was an offspring of the International Association for Labor Legislation (IALL), a scientific reform organization based in Europe which promoted uniform labor laws among industrial nations. Initially, the American Association functioned mainly as a research and publicity bureau under the direction of Ely and Commons. The two Wisconsin professors and their staff compiled summaries and comparative analyses of all types of protective labor legislation, focusing in particular on factory inspection and child labor laws. They sponsored studies of industrial diseases and poisons, and they distributed over a thousand copies of the famous Brandeis brief of 1908, which scrutinized the adverse effects of long hours on women workers.[10]

After a few years, the AALL leadership broadened its mandate to include policy advocacy as well as research and publicity. Andrews and Farnam actively promoted this organizational change against the advice of both Ely and Commons. Reflecting the shift in power, the Executive Committee decided in 1909 to move the Association's headquarters from Madison, Wisconsin, to New York City.[11] The following year, the AALL membership amended its constitution. The third statement of objective, which had read, "To encourage the study of labor legislation," was changed to read, "To encourage the study of labor conditions in the United States with a view to promoting desirable labor legislation."[12]

At the same time, the AALL leadership raised minimum annual dues from $1 to $3 and took steps to establish a permanent quarterly journal. The *American Labor Legislation Review* made its first appearance in January 1911. Even if part of the motivation for founding the journal was to secure reduced postage rates for AALL publications (as Andrews once acknowledged to Commons), Andrews and his colleagues viewed the inauguration of the journal as a symbol of the Association's health and maturation. Between 1908 and 1910, membership increased from about 300 to nearly 2,000 (a level maintained for many years), and annual contributions rose from under $2,000 to over $16,000. Farnam, the son of a prosperous railroad builder, alone contributed several thousand dollars each year, helping to finance Andrews' salary and also that of the permanent assistant secretary, Irene Osgood. Osgood, like Andrews, had studied economics as a graduate student at Wisconsin, and the two were married in August 1910.[13]

The increase in dues, the dramatic growth of contributions and membership, and the organization's constitutional amendment all signaled the Association's new ambitions and capacities to lead a legislative campaign for the reform of labor conditions in the United States. Although Commons initially sought to limit the AALL's role to scientific investigation and publication, he accepted the new mandate and remained a vital member of the Association. Ely, on the other hand, had already begun to withdraw from active participation by the time the shift toward policy promotion was underway in 1909 and 1910.[14]

Until about 1913, the leadership championed protective labor legislation as an effective means of minimizing the risks of industrial accidents and disease. They campaigned, for example, for a federal law that would protect match workers against the scourge of phosphorus poisoning by taxing phosphorus matches out of existence. Gradually, however, the AALL reformers shifted their primary focus from specific protective laws to social insurance. They began campaigning for workers' compensation laws in 1909, and they launched the American movement for unemployment and health insurance several years later.

T here is little disagreement among students of American social policy that AALL reformers played an important role in the progressive-era movement for social welfare reform. Although the organization is not yet familiar to most American historians, it has received considerable attention from several interested scholars.[15] Similarly, the origins of the so-called American welfare state is a subject that many scholars have addressed but that few have considered from the vantage point of the progressive era.[16] Those who have explored the first two decades of the twentieth century have generally focused on why the United States lagged more than a generation behind many of its European counterparts in enacting social insurance legislation. There are several schools of thought on why this was so, and all offer valuable conceptual frameworks.[17] But their common emphasis on failure—seeing the glass as half empty rather than half full—is nonetheless limiting.[18] Progressive-era reformers, for all their legislative failures, exerted enormous influence on the subsequent course of social legislation in the United States. The theories of John Commons alone helped to set the terms of debate for several generations.[19]

This book aims to explain not only why the AALL reformers failed in so many of their campaigns but also the ways in which, in spite of these setbacks, they succeeded in setting the trajectory for the development of American social policy. The following chapters address four basic questions. First, who were the AALL's leaders, and what motivated them to initiate a movement for social welfare reform in the early twentieth century? Second, what were their ideas about poverty, where did these ideas come from, and how did these ideas influence their reform agenda? Third, how did the AALL reformers structure their legislative campaigns, what obstacles did they face, and what factors distinguished success from failure? Finally, how did these reformers' ideas and policy initiatives influence the future course of social welfare policy in the United States?

Scholars differ sharply over the issue of what motivated the AALL reformers and what interests they served. James Weinstein, for example, has characterized the Association's leaders as servants of powerful capitalists, as "an organization of middle class reformers financed by such men as John D. Rockefeller, Elbert H. Gary, and V. Everitt Macy." Theda Skocpol, by contrast, regards the AALL reformers as independent, elite intellectuals who "rarely ventured beyond rational arguments meant to persuade other elites and voluntary organizations" and who "were not prepared to engage in popular political mobilization." Roy Lubove offers yet another view, portraying the Association reformers as aggressive and influential lobbyists, grounded in the discipline of social science. The AALL, he writes, "testified to the emergence of the social scientist as an influence in social legislation and reform."[20]

Although the interpretation presented in Chapters 1 and 2 draws on much of this work, it attempts to resolve differing views through a reexamination of the AALL reformers' writings and activities. This reexamination focuses particularly on how leaders of the Association identified and defined national problems, how they conceived of their role in solving them, and how they related to other interest groups. As has been mentioned, the organization's founders were mainly academic economists who shared a belief that the state could be employed to right social wrongs associated with industrial capitalism, especially the problem of worker insecurity. They viewed themselves as independent of both capital and labor. Although they accepted financial contributions from both sides (and undoubtedly much more from business people than from union officials), there is no evidence that they consciously catered their policy proposals to either interest. The leaders of the AALL believed that they functioned as mediators between capital and labor and, most important, as disinterested scientific stewards uniquely qualified to lead public opinion toward a more positive and constructive view of the state.

Confident of their purpose, they fashioned a policy agenda on the basis of a distinctive conception of poverty and social welfare. The best work examining views of poverty around the turn of the century is still Robert Bremner's *From the Depths,* first published in 1956. Bremner argues that a fundamental change from a moral to an environmental conception of poverty was underway in the United States by the end of the nineteenth century. By shifting attention from individual failings (such as laziness and drunkenness) to systemic risks (such as adverse economic conditions), this "new view of poverty" is supposed to have alerted reformers to the need for new social welfare institutions.[21]

While the "new view" was extremely important, it comprised but one piece of the AALL reformers' complex conception of the nation's social welfare problem. Just as important as their newfound environmentalist perspective were two enduring Anglo-American predilections. Like many generations of reformers before them, the leading figures of the AALL sought to differentiate the so-called worthy poor from the unworthy poor. They also exhibited the long-standing American preference for prevention over relief, always searching for measures that would help to prevent poverty rather than for ones that would merely relieve (and potentially demoralize) the poor.

The AALL reformers' policy agenda cannot be understood without first understanding this peculiar combination of new ideas and old values, the central subject of Chapters 3 and 4. Although they often spoke broadly about the need to address poverty, they focused almost exclusively on the problem of worker insecurity, not economic deprivation in general. They viewed regular workers as worthy individuals, who fell into poverty mainly as a result of environmental factors such as unemployment, industrial accidents, and illness. Poor people who were not members of the regular workforce presented a more difficult problem. They were not necessarily worthy since their poverty could not easily be ascribed to environmental factors. As a result, the Association's leaders mostly overlooked the very poor—the long-term poor—in formulating their agenda for reform.

Another consequence of the AALL's distinctive perspective on social welfare was its commitment to a strategy of prevention. European social reformers generally conceived of social insurance as a just, nonstigmatizing method of compensating the victims of major industrial hazards. Association reformers, by contrast, regarded it mainly as a vehicle for shifting the costs of industrial hazards from workers to employers, thus inducing the latter to focus on prevention. "The great object of social insurance is not to pay benefits," Commons explained in a 1916 address, "but to prevent sickness and accidents, and if it brings about that result it is well worth while."[22] As with their fixation on worker security, their commitment to utilizing social insurance as a preventive tool was the product of a new environmentalist view of poverty superimposed upon traditional beliefs about who the poor were and how they should be treated.

The AALL reformers would have been of less interest to historians had they not worked aggressively to transform their ideas into legislation. The existing literature on the Association's campaigns for social insurance identifies and tracks the major players and interest groups.[23] The literature is weaker in its coverage of the AALL's battles for protective labor legislation. It is weaker still in its treatment of basic institutions that imposed on the politics of both types of reform. In Chapters 5–8, therefore, I reexamine the Association's major legislative campaigns, focusing on issues and events that have received inadequate attention from other scholars. This requires covering some relatively new territory, such as the AALL's battle for federal legislation to abolish phosphorus matches. It also involves consideration of several important themes that social welfare historians have tended to understate, misconstrue, or overlook altogether. Two of the most critical themes pertain to institutional constraints—those imposed by representatives of capital and organized labor and those imposed by the constitution and the courts.

The influence of corporate capitalists on reform campaigns during the progressive era has received considerable scholarly attention, especially from proponents of the so-called corporate liberal thesis. The evidence presented here suggests a qualified (or weak) version of that thesis, one that confirms the importance of corporate elites in the process of social welfare reform but rejects the notion that they constituted the primary motive force. In most of the AALL's legislative campaigns, corporate capitalists tended to set the broad boundaries in which reform either did or did not occur. Organized labor, though less influential, often exercised veto power over particularly offensive proposals. Yet the Association reformers were neither politically impotent nor the mere servants of corporate elites. AALL strategists took control of the crucial agenda-setting process, deciding what types of policies to advance and when. They were also influential in defining the specific content of numerous pieces of reform legislation, sometimes to the great displeasure of captains of industry or labor who accepted a reform in principle but objected to the AALL's formulation of it. The leaders of the Association were thus independent agents who assumed a vital role in the early twentieth-century campaigns for social welfare reform. They met with success, however, only when they operated within the nebulous realm of acceptability established by capital and, to a lesser extent, by organized labor. When they moved outside that realm, they consistently failed to turn their model bills into law.

Another formidable obstacle to legislative success during the progressive era were the federal and state constitutions and the courts' interpretations of them. Progressive-era judges struck down many protective labor laws intended for male workers, while upholding numerous laws that protected female workers. A growing body of literature addresses the impact of these gender-biased rulings on women's reform organizations,[24] but little work has been done assessing their impact on the AALL. As described in Chapter 6, Association reformers gradually moved from supporting gender-neutral laws to endorsing gender-biased ones as a result of unyielding pressure from the courts.

An even more fundamental constitutional constraint was the doctrine of federalism and the related dynamic of competition among the states. As interpreted at the time, the doctrine prevented the federal government from regulating economic activity that did not involve interstate or foreign commerce. Progressive-era reformers therefore assumed that nearly all social insurance and protective labor laws would have to be enacted at the state level. State legislators, however, feared that such policies would place businesses in their states at a disadvantage relative to competitors in other states. In many cases, the fear of competitive disadvantage deterred legislators in every state from enacting otherwise desirable social reforms—a dynamic that will be referred to here as "degenerative competition." Although AALL reformers did not use the term, they certainly recognized the problem. The author of a 1906 article in the New York Department of Labor *Bulletin*, which described the Association's founding, explained:

> The greatest obstacle to protective labor legislation is always found in the fact that so much of this legislation, wise and salutary as it may be in the long run, acts temporarily at least as a handicap in the competition of one industrial community with another. Statesmen, for example, who are thoroughly convinced of the necessity of restricting child labor, in the interest of the state's future citizenship, have at times held back from such legislation through fear of handicapping even temporarily their own manufacturers in their rivalry with competitors not subject to similar restriction.[25]

To avoid the degenerative-competition trap, the leadership of the AALL attempted to introduce uniform model bills simultaneously in numerous states. But this strategy proved largely unsuccessful.[26] Only when the Association's leaders urged state reforms that did not introduce significant new costs, or when they found reasons to appeal to the federal government, did they obtain better results.

Several scholars have pointed to the role of federalism in impeding, or at least influencing, the enactment of social welfare reforms in the United States during the progressive era. Most notable is the work of William Graebner and David Brian Robertson, both of whom offer extremely important insights.[27] Yet none of the existing literature explores the dynamic of degenerative competition across multiple legislative campaigns or carefully assesses means for circumventing the federalism obstacle. As a result, federalism and degenerative competition have not become generally recognized as important factors in determining the United States' status as a social policy laggard—a significant historiographical blind spot that this book attempts to rectify.[28]

T he various themes highlighted in these pages derive from a close examination of the AALL. The Association was by no means the only influential organization devoted to social welfare reform during the early years of the twentieth century, but it was the most prominent one in the two critical areas of protective labor legislation for adult male workers and social insurance. As discussed in the final chapter, moreover, the AALL reformers' influence extended long beyond the progressive period, helping to shape much of the landmark social legislation enacted during the New Deal.

Because the leaders of the Association were mainly academic economists, their ideas and observations are particularly accessible to the historian. In both their published books and articles and their unpublished letters and manuscripts, they wrote extensively about their reasons for promoting reform as well as about many of the obstacles they faced in their political campaigns. The chapters that follow take advantage of these rich source materials to offer the story of the organization.

Like a spider's web, the story expands in many directions. Yet at the center of it all lies the AALL reformers' fundamental commitment to worker security—a commitment founded upon an intriguing mix of radicalism and conservatism. The leaders of the AALL, much like Karl Marx, focused on the adverse social consequences of industrial capitalism. But where Marx favored the socialization of capital as a remedy, these American economists advocated instead the socialization of risk. A more secure labor force, they believed, would exhibit less political volatility and greater economic efficiency. The strategic spreading (or socialization) of risk, therefore, promised not only to uplift the individual worker but also to strengthen the nation as a whole.[29] Whatever its limitations—and there were many—the AALL reformers' vision of an economically secure working class proved sufficiently attractive to future generations to become one of the pillars of American social policy in the twentieth century.

1

A Strategic Moment
in History

On a mild winter day in late December 1908, John Commons and
Henry Farnam fell into a conversation about the AALL as they
walked together taking in the sights of Atlantic City. The occasion
for their meeting was the Association's second annual conference, held in
conjunction with the annual sessions of the American Economic Association. Strolling down the boardwalk, Farnam announced that he was
excited about the AALL's work and was willing to put up $5,000 to bring
John Andrews and the organization's headquarters to New York City.
Then he said to Commons, "Curious isn't it, that you, a radical, and I, a
conservative, find ourselves working together." Reflecting on the incident
years later in his autobiography, Commons acknowledged that the relationship "was curious, but good for me during all the remaining years of
Farnam's life."[1]

The leaders of the AALL encompassed a wide arc in the middle of the
political spectrum. During the controversial presidential election of 1912,
AALL reformers cast votes for all three of the major candidates, Wilson,
Roosevelt, and Taft.[2] Farnam, a close friend of President Taft, was a pa-
trician, his views of social welfare grounded firmly in paternalism. Commons, by contrast, was a political eclectic who occasionally expressed
sympathy, even solidarity, with radical causes. Accepting a new academic
post in the spring of 1895, Commons facetiously described himself to the
chancellor of Syracuse University as "a socialist, a single-taxer, a free-
silverite, a greenbacker, a municipal-ownerist, a member of the Congre-
gational Church."[3]

What brought individuals like Farnam and Commons together was a
mutual recognition that the American social order was "somewhere badly

out of gear," the apparent victim of a vibrant but callous industrial economy.[4] "Even those [industrial] improvements which seem altogether good," Farnam explained in his 1909 presidential address to the Association, "may bring in some incidental evil, which, while not by any means counterbalancing the good, yet makes itself felt as something to be removed."[5] Although they sometimes disagreed over details, all of the leading AALL reformers believed that the state had a crucial role to play in removing the incidental evils of industrialism. William F. Willoughby, the organization's fourth president, attempted in 1913 to characterize the Association's philosophy. Individual freedom, he said, was inseparable from a minimum level of economic comfort; and it was the state's responsibility to guarantee that the minimum was never violated. Willoughby suggested that appropriate state action would help to conserve the labor force and thus advance not only individual liberty but national economic efficiency as well.[6]

The AALL reformers were not foes of industrialization. They were not academic Luddites seeking to employ the state as a constraint on industrial progress. Rather, they were socially minded defenders of capitalism, apprehensive about tensions they saw mounting between a rapidly developing industrial machine and woefully inadequate social and legal institutions. Farnam once used the metaphor of a locomotive pulling furiously against a braked train. A dislocation inevitably would ensue unless legislatures and especially the courts became more permissive of laws that offered security to laborers.[7]

Nearly all of the major figures who founded and ran the Association were born between 1845 and 1880, mainly in the midwest and the east. They were well positioned in both time and space to witness one of the most extraordinary periods of economic expansion in history. Between 1860 and 1900, the population of the United States more than doubled to about 76 million people, and real gross national product increased by almost fourfold. Meanwhile, the proportion of workers engaged in agriculture fell from 59 percent to under 40 percent. The United States surpassed Britain in iron production in the mid-1880s, in steel production a few years later, and in coal production less than a decade after that. The period is commonly referred to as the second industrial revolution. Like most revolutions, however, this one did not come without costs. The United States suffered two of its sharpest depressions during the second half of the nineteenth century—the first in the mid-1870s and next in the mid-1890s.[8]

It was within this dynamic but convulsive economic environment that most of the individuals who later led the AALL pursued the study of economics. Unsatisfied with orthodox theories of the market, many sought out alternative schools that seemed more consistent with economic reality. German historicism, emphasizing historical fact over theoretical abstraction, proved especially influential. Joseph Schumpeter wrote of historicism:

> the high level of historiography; the widespread respect for the historical fact; the low level of theoretical economics; the lack of respect for its values; the supreme importance attributed to the state; the small importance attributed to everything else—these points individualize the school and they were all of them typically German, in their strengths as well as in their weaknesses.[9]

The first three AALL presidents—Richard T. Ely, Henry W. Farnam, and Henry Rogers Seager—all undertook graduate study in Germany in the late nineteenth century, as did Adna Weber and Charles Henderson, two other key members of the Association. Neither Commons nor Andrews studied abroad, but each absorbed German influence indirectly through Ely, and each developed an institutionalist approach to economics. Commons studied under Ely at Johns Hopkins, and Andrews worked with both Ely and Commons at the University of Wisconsin.

German historicism represented a counterpoint to the English classical school of laissez-faire economics. Ely wrote in his autobiography that the classical school "held that natural laws established certain fundamental principles for all times and places. It was only necessary that we should study these natural laws and follow them to attain the highest state of economic felicity possible to mankind." By contrast, his German professor of political economy, Karl Knies, "conceived of economics as belonging neither to the natural nor to the mental sciences, but to the group of historical disciplines which have for their object the study of man in society in terms of its historical growth."[10]

Profoundly influenced by Knies, Ely worked to transplant and adapt the teachings of the German school to American soil. He helped to found the upstart American Economic Association in 1885, which originally served as both a refuge and a platform for opponents of the classical school in America. In his academic and popular writing, Ely described the economy as a living organism that matured and adapted to its environment. This marked a clear departure from the classical economists, who tended to characterize the economy as a machine with regular inputs and outputs. In his teaching, Ely encouraged students to engage in what he called the look-and-see method. When John Commons arrived as a graduate student at Johns Hopkins in 1888, Ely sent him off to investigate building and loan associations and to serve as a case worker for the Baltimore Charity Organization Society. Such field research, the professor thought, would foster a practical understanding of political economy. In

Commons' case, it inspired a lifelong commitment to improving the condition of the working classes—a result entirely consistent with the social predilections of the German historical school.[11]

Like Ely, Commons developed an evolutionary conception of economic activity and institutions, which helped inform his approach to policy. He exhibited particular fascination with the legal foundations of capitalism. Market transactions, and the institution of private property on which they are grounded, are not natural phenomena, Commons explained, but rather consequences of state action that created, defined, and defended property rights.[12] In his view, the classical economists had overlooked this critical insight. Commons wrote in 1893, in his first theoretical text:

> The place of law in Political Economy is a subject which has received from English economists no attention at all commensurate with its far-reaching importance. The reason for this is mainly a lack of historical investigation ... The English economists have taken the laws of private property for granted, assuming that they are fixed and immutable in the nature of things, and therefore needed no investigation. But such laws are changeable—they differ for different peoples and places, and they have profound influence upon the production and distribution of wealth.[13]

A year later, Commons suggested an intriguing connection between his legal conception of economic institutions and his commitment to social reform. "If the State creates corporations," he insisted, "it can determine the conditions of their existence." In other words, what the state gives, the state may take away or, better yet, regulate for the public good.[14]

Though it would be wrong to characterize all of the AALL economists as institutionalists like Ely and Commons, it is fair to describe all of them as more or less heterodox in their views. Farnam—the most conservative member of the group—took exception to the German historicists. In his words, they "not only did not expect to discover general economic laws by the historical method, but denied that such laws existed." Still, even Farnam recognized the value of historical investigation to the discipline of political economy, and he acknowledged and advertised the practical limits of laissez faire as an economic doctrine.[15]

In his 1910 presidential address to the AALL, Farnam developed an elaborate simile comparing social reform to surgery. Surgery had once been a primitive and, indeed, dangerous art, and most patients living then probably were wise to stay away from the surgeon altogether. "But increased knowledge," Farnam declared, "has made surgery bold. It is bold because it is instructed." The same held true for social legislation. Laws not based on careful scientific investigation were likely to do more harm than good. Notions of laissez faire, he suggested, made a good deal of sense before the advent of social science. But as in the case of surgery, scientific advance would render social legislation bold and beneficial. "Legislation is just beginning to pass out of the primitive stage in which surgery found itself a century ago," Farnam concluded, "and it is the purpose of such organizations as ours to try to point out the method by which its work may become more effective and less dangerous."[16]

Farnam's and Commons' agreement about the obsolescence of laissez-faire doctrinc was a necessary, but not a sufficient, condition for them to work together as members of the same reform organization in the early years of the twentieth century. In 1890, their ideas about the proper economic role of the state were so far apart that it is difficult to conceive of them forging a lasting political alliance. But a great deal happened between 1890 and the early 1900s. Although Farnam's views about political economy remained relatively stable, Commons' and Ely's changed dramatically. By moderating their radical positions, the two institutionalists allowed for an intellectual and political convergence with men like Farnam, which proved crucial for the formation of the AALL.

Ely's biographer wrote that in the book *Socialism and Social Reform* (1894), Ely "anticipated almost every reform of the Progressive and New Deal eras."[17] True enough, but many of Ely's recommendations for social reform, in that book and others, went far beyond what progressive or New Deal policymakers ever adopted. Over the last two decades of the nineteenth century, Ely suggested a wide array of radical proposals, ranging from the socialization of natural monopolies to the creation of a legal right to employment. He also urged far-reaching land reform; the expansion of public education; the establishment of postal savings banks, public credit bureaus, public employment agencies, and social insurance; tariff reform; tax reform; bimetallism and the establishment of a central bank.[18]

For an American in the late nineteenth century, Ely held an expansive view of the state. He was sympathetic to socialism and its critique of capitalist institutions. He insisted adamantly that he was not a socialist, but his rhetoric often seemed to suggest otherwise. "[Socialism] points out real defects in our present social order," he wrote in *Socialism and Social Reform.* "The wastes of the competitive system are so enormous as to be awful; its operations are as cruel as laws of nature. In its onward march it crushes and grinds to powder human existence by the million."[19] In reviewing Ely's *Labor Movement in America* eight years earlier, Henry Farnam had suggested that Ely's language "sounds so much like what a good many of the socialists say, that he ought hardly to complain, if people occasionally mistake him for one."[20]

In fact, Ely was not a socialist. He did not endorse the complete socialization of economic resources and means of production, and he was not willing to risk bringing down the middle and top of the social order in order to raise the bottom. He did believe, however, that the state had a large role to play in economic affairs because "private property has a social side." He explained that whenever the social side and the individual side of private property come into conflict, "the social side is dominant and the individual claims must be yielded." In other words, state action could be justified whenever the system of private ownership and market competition failed to deliver a socially beneficial outcome. Few socialists would disagree with this formulation, but they would contend that the capitalist system very frequently failed to deliver socially beneficial outcomes. Ely, by contrast, stressed not only the costs but also the important benefits of private property, especially the "incentives to thrift and industry." The trick was to find a "golden mean" between "rigid, obstructive . . . conservatism" and "reckless radicalism." Can we not, he asked, "conservatively add to our social order some of the strong features of socialism, and yet keep this social order intact?"[21]

Commons, too, held an expansive view of the state. (The only book-length biography of the man is entitled *John R. Commons: His Assault on Laissez-Faire*.[22]) Commons regarded private property as a product of state action and therefore always subject to state regulation. In the mid-1890s, he suggested that cities should own municipal monopolies, and he recommended that the government should guarantee a common-law right to employment.[23]

Commons' overall agenda for social and economic reform was neither as comprehensive nor as well-articulated as Ely's during this early period. Yet his penchant for challenging orthodoxy led many contemporaries to tag him as a radical. He noted in his autobiography that the first vote he ever cast was for the Prohibitionist candidate for president in 1884; and he claimed that about a decade later he voted for a Communist for governor of New York. Commons was ardently independent in his academic life as well. In 1898 he declared at the annual meetings of the American Economic Association that economists like Henry George and Karl Marx, representing the working classes, were beginning to displace the classical economists, who spoke for the capitalist and banking classes. The remark was not atypical. Three years earlier, Ely had felt compelled to warn his former student about the dangers of expressing radical ideas in public. Commons replied: "I believe fully in what you say regarding the *timeliness* of expressions of advanced views and I recognize that on some occasions I may have seemed to needlessly have aroused antagonism. It is difficult to combine opportuneness with exposures of injustice, but I believe I am getting more cautious."[24]

Ely's warning regarding expressions of radicalism was not simply a casual piece of advice. Many nonconformist (especially historical) economists had come under attack for their supposedly radical views beginning in the late 1880s. The historian Dorothy Ross observes that the leading historical economists—including John Bates Clark, Henry Carter Adams, and Richard Ely—faced intense challenges and began to retreat from radical theoretical and political positions after the Haymarket riot of 1886. Clark was the first to shift. After Arthur Hadley attacked him for spreading "socialist fallacies," Clark began to rethink his ideas regarding the distribution of wealth. He ultimately developed a sophisticated theoretical framework that, in many ways, justified the classical economists' free market system of distribution. Adams was next. He apparently infuriated Cornell patron and trustee Henry W. Sage when he spoke in 1886 about the need to reorganize society, and especially the wage system, upon a more just basis. At Sage's insistence, Adams' Cornell contract was not renewed. He subsequently accepted a position at the University of Michigan, where, notably, he exhibited a great deal more caution in his discussions of capitalism and the free market.[25]

Ely was initially defiant. Though concerned about criticism from friends like Adams and Clark, he continued into the early 1890s to champion a combination of socialism and individualism. In 1892 he resigned as secretary of the AEA because, he believed, conservatives had taken control of the organization. What finally muzzled him was a charge of socialism by a trustee at the University of Wisconsin in 1894. Ely faced a trial before the Board of Regents and ultimately was exonerated of academic subversion. Yet the experience seems to have overwhelmed him. He defended himself not by invoking the principle of academic freedom but by vigorously denying the charge that he had preached socialism. Were he a socialist, he said, he would not belong on the faculty of the university.

After the trial was over, Ely became more careful about what he said and wrote, and he withdrew from almost all of the reform organizations with which he had become associated. Writes Ross, "Ely, like Adams, gave up the effort to transform the national ideology to include some measure of socialism." By 1900 he had moved sufficiently far to the right to accept election to the presidency of the now much more conservative and professionally oriented AEA, the organization he had scorned for betraying him less than a decade before.[26]

Compared to Ely, John Commons faced an even greater challenge from conservatives: he was encouraged to leave one academic position and was dismissed from another. In 1895 Commons was a professor at the University of Indiana. Upon receiving an offer from Syracuse University to fill a new chair in sociology, he went to speak with Indiana's president. He had no interest in leaving Bloomington but hoped that he could use the offer to bargain for a bigger salary. To his surprise, President Swain refused to bargain and simply told him, "Accept the offer at once."

Aware that his poor treatment at Indiana was largely a consequence of his nonconformist views, Commons decided to level with the chancellor at Syracuse. He explained that he was not a mainstream academic; for effect, he boasted that he was, among other things, a socialist. The chancellor replied that this was fine so long as he was not an "obnoxious socialist," and Commons assured him that he was not. Five years later, however, Commons met with the chancellor again for a much less pleasant conversation. He learned that the trustees of the university had voted to discontinue his chair. Apparently a number of large contributors had refused to continue giving to the university as long as Commons continued to be affiliated with it. The economic historian Joseph Dorfman speculates that Commons' remark about George and Marx at the AEA conference in 1898 may have been the last straw for the university's patrons and trustees. Whatever the cause, Ely correctly summed up the result when he noted in a letter to Robert Hunter that his former student had been "practically blacklisted."[27]

Commons' experience at Syracuse, like Ely's at Wisconsin, affected both his scholarship and his reform activities. After 1900, he no longer wrote enthusiastically about the "right to employment" or about the "advantages of socialism."[28] Dorfman observes that as time passed "Commons became more cautious in desiring that the 'coercive' power of the State should operate in labor reform." He worked as Ralph Easley's general assistant at the National Civic Federation from 1902 to 1904.[29] Although he reentered academic life in 1904, accepting an offer from Ely to join the faculty at the University of Wisconsin, Commons never revisited his earlier radicalism. In 1915, as a member of the U.S. Commission on Industrial Relations, he dissented from the final report, insisting that it recommended too much remedial legislation. "One of the most important facts to be recognized," he wrote in his dissent, "is that governments, whether State or Federal, can not be looked to alone for remedying evil conditions." By 1916 Commons was actively warning labor to stay away from socialism. He suggested to the members of a prominent labor organization in Wisconsin that year that workers could rely on the state's police power to strengthen their bargaining position, but that a platform of "revolution or confiscation" was dangerous and unworkable. Commons' shift away from radicalism was perhaps best reflected, as Ely's was, in his election to the presidency of the American Economic Association in December 1917.[30]

In the aftermath of the politically charged 1890s, Ely and Commons increasingly saw protective labor legislation and social insurance as appealing and ideologically acceptable objectives of social reform. They remained decidedly to the left of Farnam but had shifted far enough right to create a practical basis for collaboration.

Over the first two decades of the twentieth century, the leading reformers of the AALL agreed, more or less, on three fundamental justifications for labor legislation. The first was moral: the state had a clear obligation to raise the ethical plane of competition among employers. The second was economic: because the free market failed to conserve the vitality of the labor force, the state would have to assume that responsibility to assure continued American competitiveness in the world economy. The third justification was institutional: it was necessary for the state to reduce the economic and social insecurity of labor because the problem of worker insecurity threatened the very existence of industrial capitalism.

AALL reformers regularly commented on the need to raise the ethical plane of competition through labor legislation. In describing workers' compensation, for example, Commons said in 1916 that it "equalizes competition, prevents the worst employers from dragging down the others." Henry Carter Adams first identified this rationale for state action in 1887, and Ely elaborated upon it seven years later in *Socialism and Social Reform*. To illustrate the principle, Ely told the story of a town with twenty barbers. Nineteen of the barbers were good Christians who wanted to close their shops on Sundays, but the twentieth chose to keep his shop open on the Sabbath to secure an advantage over his competitors. The nineteenth barber, afraid of losing market share to the "mean and unscrupulous" twentieth, felt compelled to give up his day of rest. The eighteenth followed, and then the seventeenth, and soon all the barber shops were open on Sundays. Ely's point was that competition drove ethical standards down to the level of the least ethical competitor, and he labeled this dilemma the "problem of the twentieth man." The solution was government regulation that raised the ethical plane of competition— one-day-rest-in-seven laws, minimum-wage and maximum-hours laws, safety and sanitation regulations, and so forth.[31]

The AALL reformers' second major justification for state action was that free competition often failed to conserve national resources. Inspired by the progressive-era movement for the conservation of forests and other environmental treasures, leading members of the AALL argued that the conservation of human resources was at least as vital as the conservation of natural resources. In 1909 the Association's General Administrative Council adopted a resolution declaring, "The fundamental purpose of labor legislation is the conservation of the human resources of the nation."[32] Soon the motto "Conservation of Human Resources" appeared atop all AALL letterhead and on most of the organization's publications.

The essential argument about human conservation was that, in the absence of legislation, employers would "waste" labor (through overwork and unnecessary exposure to hazards) because it was the least expensive thing for them to do. If a worker became sick or was injured on the job, his employer could easily replace him, with minimal or perhaps no costs showing up in the firm's financial accounts. There were two definite costs to society, however. First, communities and states often had to pick up the expense of supporting incapacitated workers and their families. Second, every case of worker injury and sickness constituted a weakening of the national labor force—a charge against the country's most valuable asset. Especially after the outbreak of World War I in 1914 and the entrance of the United States in 1917, reformers at the AALL were quick to highlight threats to national competitiveness. In 1918, for example, a new slogan appeared atop the AALL letterhead: "Conservation of the workers—sound policy for the state and nation in time of peace—becomes an imperative duty in meeting the acute strain of war."[33]

In employing the rhetoric of conservation, the reformers were making an economic argument as well as a moral one. Wasting labor was not only wrong but inefficient. And if the market could not utilize human resources efficiently, then the state would have to intervene. As will be seen in Chapter 4, this particular conception of the problem heavily influenced the types of solutions that the AALL reformers advanced in their legislative campaigns.

The third and final justification for state interference in the labor market was the most fundamental of the three: without such interference, capitalism might not survive. Many key figures associated with the AALL—especially John Commons—were enthralled by the prophecies of Karl Marx. For the most part, they accepted the diagnosis that worker insecurity was destabilizing. The unusual strength of the Socialist Party in presidential elections between 1904 and 1920, for example, seemed to corroborate this view. Commons wrote in 1922 that job insecurity "is the breeder of socialism, of anarchism, of the restrictions of trade unionism, and a menace to capitalism, the nation, and even civilization."[34] Unlike Marx, however, Commons and his colleagues did not believe that the collapse of capitalism was inevitable.

In *Socialism and Social Reform* Ely acknowledged that Marx and Engels' dire predictions about the demise of capitalism in England might have come to pass had laissez faire not been replaced by a more socially oriented regime:

> Had things been allowed to take their own course, the condition of the wage-earners would have grown more and more wretched, the concentration of wealth and the centralization of production would have been carried even further, and it is not improbable that the collapse in England would have taken place before this.

What saved England, in Ely's view, were "social efforts . . . put forth to guide social evolution."[35] Labor legislation was not the only necessary social effort, but it was an essential one. Said Commons at an address in 1916, "Karl Marx has but one remedy for the labor problem—public ownership. He has no place for an intermediary remedy—the police power." Under the heading of "police power," Commons included not only protective regulations (such as wages and hours laws) but also workers' compensation, the only form of compulsory social insurance then existing in the United States.[36]

Critics of the AALL frequently dismissed its reform agenda as socialistic. Naturally, the AALL reformers disagreed. With but a few exceptions—I. M. Rubinow, an avowed socialist, being the most prominent—most of the leading members of the Association believed that their proposals for reform would stand as crucial defenses against socialism. Henry Seager wrote that "the novel social policies which are being tried in this country . . . may prove not advances toward socialism, but rather bulwarks against the revolutionary changes in our fundamental institutions of private property and freedom of contract which socialists advocate."[37]

In contrast to Marx, who proposed the socialization of capital as the only possible solution to the problems of the proletariat, the AALL reformers proposed instead the socialization of risk. More specifically, they sought to socialize risks associated with a variety of industrial hazards, especially accidents, illness, and unemployment. There are two basic reasons for their departure from Marx. The most obvious one is that they had great faith in the productive power of capitalist institutions. Like most Americans, they assumed that the introduction of pure socialism would lower the living standards of nearly everyone. The other, less obvious reason is that the AALL reformers believed workers felt more threatened by uncertain incomes than by small incomes. Worker insecurity thus eclipsed extraction of surplus value as a critical concern at the AALL. Once again, Commons expressed this point most clearly:

> The principal underlying cause of social unrest is the uncertainty of income of wage earners and small producers. A steady, continuous income, even though it be small in amount, is of more importance than high wages or

earnings at certain times and no earnings at other times. This uncertainty of income is the main cause of dependence, inequality and oppression which produce conflicts between capital and labor.[38]

Given these assumptions, state intervention designed to socialize the most threatening forms of risk would go a long way toward satisfying the working classes and, consequently, preserving capitalism.

These three justifications for state action—raising the ethical plane of competition, conserving human resources, and removing threats to the capitalist system—together fix the ideological locus of the AALL. The economists who founded and ran the organization in the early years of the twentieth century converged toward a common, humanitarian vision of American society—essentially conservative in nature but with traces of radicalism, remnants of an earlier time. It was a vision of constructive change, but not of upheaval.

Significantly, their expectation that conservative reform could be transformative was grounded on the assumption that they were living at a strategic moment in history. This assumption was implicit in all of their planning and preaching. It was sometimes articulated explicitly. John Andrews once wrote in a membership letter, "At no previous time in the history of the country have the opportunities been so favorable for the enactment of progressive measures to promote the comfort, health and safety of [American workers]. We are morally bound to leave no single one of these opportunities neglected."[39] A number of years earlier, John Commons had offered an even more dramatic statement of the strategic-moment-in-history assumption. "The present is indeed a critical time," he wrote in 1898.

> We live at a new turning point of humanity. Old institutions are passing away. Society is again plastic and impressionable. The good work that is done now will multiply like the leaven indeed, and will set itself deep in the institutions of the future . . . But, on the other hand, just as surely does the evil work of the present have a deadlier opportunity than ever before. It too will multiply and will contaminate the coming centuries. The men of to-day are to decide.[40]

Like Commons and Andrews, all the leading members of the AALL believed they possessed a unique opportunity to transform society in a fundamental and positive way. Industrialism was still young, and the institutions associated with it remained malleable. If the reformers acted quickly and prudently, they might correct some of the most critical flaws that plagued this young but rapidly maturing economic order. As we shall see in the next chapter, they also believed that their academic training specially qualified them to spearhead such a movement for social reform.

2

Charging up the Middle

The most famous statement about the far-reaching influence of economic thinkers is that of John Maynard Keynes. In the last paragraph of *The General Theory,* he wrote, "Practical men, who believe themselves to be quite exempt from any intellectual influences, are usually the slaves of some defunct economist."[1] In the case of the AALL, however, the leading reformers served simultaneously as economists and "practical men"—as intellectual guides and political tacticians.

As we have seen, the economists who comprised the Association believed that certain types of social problems (especially those relating to worker insecurity) could best be solved through state action. These scholars might have been satisfied to author theoretical texts that would inspire future generations of policymakers; to publish popular articles justifying the enactment of specific reform legislation; or perhaps to attach themselves as advisers to sympathetic political officials. They did all of these things. Why did they choose, in addition, to enter the political arena as activists? And what were the consequences of this highly unusual choice?

Richard Hofstadter has suggested that many middle-class professionals became reformers during the progressive period out of a sense of status anxiety. Displaced from positions of power in their local communities by an emerging industrial plutocracy, they embraced reform as a way to reassert their social relevance and authority.[2] Hofstadter's analysis is not wholly applicable to the individuals who founded the AALL, but it does touch on one of their primary motivations.[3]

The Association's economists felt constrained within the walls of the academy. They believed that professors—and social scientists, in particular—had an obligation to involve themselves in practical affairs. In his autobiography Richard Ely explained that the culture at the University of Wisconsin proscribed intellectual isolationism: "The people of Wisconsin have never allowed their university to lose itself in academic unrealities."[4] Associated with their sense of social obligation were pangs of status anxiety. With the social order apparently undergoing a fundamental transformation, these economists were fearful of being rendered politically irrelevant as big business and big labor took the lead in defining the rules of a new industrial society. Charles Henderson, a sociologist at the University of Chicago, hinted at this concern while discussing the problem of unemployment at the Association's fifth annual meeting in 1911. "The business world has already gone in advance of us," he said, "when university men ought to have led."[5]

Key AALL reformers justified their activist political aspirations on the basis of two attributes, their ostensible neutrality between capital and labor and their rigorous training in the social sciences. They argued that because of their neutrality, they could serve the public as disinterested advisers. The legal scholar Ernst Freund wrote in a 1915 letter to John Andrews: "It is important that the public should receive information from a disinterested source. The A.A.L.L. claims to be disinterested and aims to supply such information."[6] The Association reformers laid equal emphasis on their academic credentials, asserting that their social scientific background specially qualified them to address social problems and to guide public opinion. The AALL, said one member of the organization's Executive Committee,

> was founded to apply scientific methods to the subject of labor legislation. That means that we endeavor, as far as is possible in so complex a subject, to base our action on a careful study of experience. It also implies that we must take into account the welfare of the whole country, for the future as well as for the present, and not merely what may seem to be at a given time the interests of a single class.[7]

Although they never used the phrase, these reform-minded economists conceived of themselves as scientific stewards. The doctrine of social and moral stewardship had deep roots in American history, dating back to the preachings of John Winthrop and Cotton Mather. Traditionally, stewardship had been the self-styled domain of the clergy, of prominent patricians, and (more recently) of master capitalists such as Andrew Carnegie.[8] The founders of the AALL refined the doctrine by claiming to derive their authority as stewards not from divine inspiration or enormous wealth but from science. The application of social science to problems involving industrial relations and labor conditions would expose critical flaws in the social order and point to promising remedies. No one, in their view, was better prepared to lead a movement for the reform of American institutions.[9]

In anointing themselves scientific stewards of the public interest, the AALL reformers accepted, perhaps unknowingly, a daunting political challenge. Employers and union leaders had little patience for "do-gooders." They viewed the world in bipolar terms—the only relevant interests being those of capital and labor—and generally resented interference from any third party. Labor issues, they believed, were best settled through private, bilateral negotiations. The prospect of a new player entering the field struck representatives of both capital and labor as highly suspicious.

The most obvious expression of distaste for the AALL came in the form of intellectual-bashing. One employer, the brother-in-law of the Association's fifth president, complained about the AALL's "theoretical economists who had no practical experience in handling numbers of employees." The president of the American Federation of Labor offered an even harsher assessment. "As these expert reformers—'intellectuals'—increase in number and zeal," Samuel Gompers wrote in the *American Federationist,* "they disclose plainly that their prototype is the ancient village busybody."[10]

Such attacks were common but not particularly damaging. More formidable were questions about the Association's political integrity. Individuals on both sides of the industrial bargaining table regularly challenged the AALL's assertions of neutrality. In fact, almost no one believed that these academic reformers were truly disinterested. Critics on the right claimed that the Association was allied with organized labor, while critics on the left dismissed the organization as a tool of the capitalist class.[11] Although John Andrews regularly denied these charges, insisting that the organization's activities "have always been prosecuted from the *general welfare* point of view," he could not make the accusations disappear. By 1918 he felt compelled to argue that the attacks themselves, coming from both sides, served as proof of the Association's neutrality.[12]

Notwithstanding his rhetoric, Andrews' experience in running the day-to-day operations of the AALL demonstrated that the principle of neutrality was more meaningful in theory than in practice. A good example involves the organization's handling of the union-label controversy. In preparing the Association's letterhead in 1909, Andrews and Farnam had to decide whether to display the union label. Anxious not to offend anyone, they agreed to produce two versions of the letterhead, one with the label and one without. Presumably, correspondents who were partial toward organized labor would receive the former, while manufacturers and others who opposed the closed shop would receive the latter. The Association followed the same policy in publishing its pamphlets and monographs, either using or not using the union label as seemed appropriate. In some cases, however, Andrews and his staff simply picked the most convenient printer, regardless of whether the establishment employed union or nonunion workers.[13]

Despite their best efforts, the AALL staff found it impossible to maintain the appearance of neutrality. Time and again, letters and literature with the label ended up on the desks of manufacturers, while material without the label found its way into the hands of union supporters. During the same week in June 1909, the AALL headquarters received two complaints—one from an organizer in Chicago, who said that no one would take his pamphlets because they lacked the union label, and another from an outraged employer in Boston, who discovered the label on a piece of Association literature. In responding to the employer, Commons explained, "I will say that the Association as such takes no position on this subject or upon the subject of trade unionism. Its object is solely that which comes under what is termed protective legislation." Significantly, Commons cleared his reply with both Farnam and union leader John Mitchell (an honorary vice-president of the AALL) before sending it.[14]

The Association's ambiguity on the union-label issue continued to provoke criticism throughout the progressive era. In one of his several letters of resignation to the AALL, a prominent official from the National Association of Manufacturers declared, "The progressive employers of the United States are quite as much interested in the subject [of constructive labor legislation] as any other faction, but you cannot hope to enlist their co-operation if you approach them with letters and literature carrying the union label."[15] Rebuffs from the other side continued as well. In 1916 the corresponding secretary of Brooklyn's Central Labor Union refused to accept Andrews' letters because they did not bear the label of the Bookkeepers, Stenographers, and Accountants Union. "If your Association is so much interested in labor legislation," he asked pointedly, "why does it not interest itself in Labor as well? And employ union people in their offices?"[16]

Buffeted by criticism, Andrews and his staff sometimes asserted their independence. "This is a scientific organization," Andrews once told a disgruntled employer, "and we allow no one to dictate to us either way with reference to the label."[17] At other times, he and his aides simply claimed that their printer had made a mistake.[18] It was a convenient and perhaps entirely truthful excuse, but it is doubtful that it proved very effective in calming angry correspondents.

The union label controversy illustrates one of the basic contradictions embedded in the AALL's approach to reform. Claims of neutrality were generally unconvincing because, given the polarized political environment, these claims had little practical meaning. Andrews and Farnam had worked out what they thought was the best possible compromise. If they had ignored the union-label issue altogether and left the symbol off all their letterhead and literature, the choice inevitably would have been interpreted by labor supporters as anti-union rather than as neutral. By producing two versions of the letterhead, they were attempting to remain even-handed. The result, however, was that they alienated potential supporters on both sides of the issue.

Even in a less polarized political environment, the AALL reformers' assertions of disinterestedness would probably have proved untenable, since they chose to utilize their academic training as active policy advocates rather than as passive expert witnesses. The distinction is important. As advocates, they were undeniably interested in the legislation they proposed. In many cases, enactment would offer not only psychic but also material payoffs on their investment of personal capital. The establishment of administrative and investigatory commissions, for example, often created positions for well-trained social scientists, including positions for the AALL reformers themselves.[19]

The leaders of the Association generally avoided acknowledging that they constituted an interested party. They preferred to cast themselves as experts rather than as lobbyists. In 1919 John Commons wrote that the "principals in industry are the associated employers and the associated employees. The expert's place is that of attorney, statistician, accountant, economist, mediator, adviser, agent, in short employee—of the principals. The principals determine what shall be done, their agents execute it."[20] Ironically, Commons' formulation left little if any room for the AALL.

Such contradictions only served to exacerbate distrust of the Association. Most employers and labor leaders were unsure exactly what the organization's interests were. More fundamentally, they were suspicious of any interference from outsiders. In 1915, for example, AALL reformers infuriated leaders of trade associations and labor unions in New York State by inserting themselves into a contentious political battle over a proposed industrial commission. Angry about the reformers' intervention, the editor of a prominent upstate trade-association journal, the *Monitor,* wrote a column touting the superiority of direct negotiations between employers and employees. The editor also emphasized the value of squeezing out the hard-to-pin-down AALL: "It makes it a clean fight between the two parties solely interested and shuts out the self-appointed third party whose interest frequently has been guessed at, but never satisfactorily defined."[21]

The controversy in New York began in March 1915, when State Senator George E. Spring introduced a bill to consolidate the Workmen's Compensation Commission and the Department of Labor into a single Industrial Commission. The bill had the support of the Associated Industries of New York State, the powerful organization of employers that published the *Monitor,* but it met with strong opposition from organized labor, the AALL, and other reform organizations. Labor representatives objected because prominent labor men already headed the Workmen's Compensation Commission and the Department of Labor. Any change, they thought, could reduce their political influence in the state. The *Legislative Labor News,* the political organ of the New York State Federation of Labor, reported on March 15 that the bill would "legislate out of office Labor Com. [James] Lynch . . . It also legislates Com. John Mitchell and his associates on the Compensation Commission and all deputy commissioners out of office."[22]

Although the AALL reformers opposed the Spring bill in its original form, they were not sympathetic to labor's objections. They detested cronyism in government and strongly supported both civil-service reform and consolidation in the name of public efficiency. They also regarded the proposed commission as an ideal forum for bringing capital and labor together to work out their differences. Their concern about the Spring bill was that it seemed poorly drafted for those purposes. At a public hearing in the New York senate chamber on April 6, three AALL representatives joined labor officials in opposing the bill. The three reformers made it clear, however, that they supported the concept of consolidation, and Republican senators encouraged the AALL to redraft the bill in a more acceptable form. The historian Irwin Yellowitz has suggested that the Republicans' invitation was intended to divide the bill's opponents. Whatever the case, Andrews and his colleagues accepted the challenge; they rewrote the bill and quickly sent it back to the state legislature.[23]

The revised bill, known as the second Spring bill, had essentially the same object as the first, the consolidation of labor administration in New York State. The size of the proposed commission was increased from three to five, which provided room for more than one labor representative. Even more important in the minds of the AALL reformers, the revised bill included provisions for an advisory council composed of five individuals to represent employers and five to represent employees. Andrews described the advisory council as "a practical method for introducing a greater degree of nonpartisanship, both political and industrial, into the administration of labor laws." Commons, likewise, regarded the council as an institutional affirmation of his concept of industrial government, which held that representatives of capital and labor were the parties best positioned to determine and negotiate improvements in employment conditions. "[I]ndustrial government should be separated from the political government," Commons wrote several years after this episode, "and . . . if legislation is necessary it should first be agreed upon by organized employers and employees and then presented to the legislatures for adoption without material change through political influence."[24]

The second Spring bill passed both houses of the New York State legislature and became law on May 22, 1915. Andrews noted to a correspondent, "We have had the fight of our lives for a big piece of legislation and fortunately we have won. It has involved extraordinary strain both upon our nervous systems and upon our treasury." Significantly, the bill was enacted over the objections of many vocal employers and union leaders. The latter continued to fear that consolidation would weaken labor's political influence. Employers, on the other hand, were frustrated because they recognized that the second bill was much less preferential to their interests than the first.[25]

The position of the AALL reformers can be described, at best, as puzzling and, at worst, as hypocritical. After justifying the proposed industrial commission on the grounds that it would bring representatives of capital and labor together in the administration of labor law, the Association's lobbyists went ahead and secured the enabling legislation without the support of either industrial party. Andrews and his colleagues were confident that, like children who ended up enjoying the water after being compelled to bathe, employers and employees would soon recognize the great advantages of the new Industrial Commission. Once they did, Andrews maintained, they would "not only withdraw their opposition . . . but at the same time forget their fears that the so-called disinterested third parties are aiming to get the official jobs for themselves."[26]

On one level, Andrews was correct. The New York Industrial Commission gradually gained acceptance, especially among labor leaders. Contrary to the expectations of most union officials, organized labor retained its influence on the new commission. The former commissioner of labor, James Lynch, became one of the Industrial Commission's five members, and the former workmen's compensation commissioner, John Mitchell, became its chairman.[27] On another level, however, Andrews and his colleagues proved naive. They failed to understand the inherent conflict between their own vision of scientific reform and the reality of interest-group politics.

The AALL reformers devoted themselves to creating institutions that would, in their view, serve labor, capital, and the public. They preferred to work with the established industrial interests but, when necessary, were willing to go it alone. In the case of the New York Industrial Commission, the reformers maintained that a consolidated administrative body would be more efficient and less subject to political influences than a decentralized network of agencies. They also insisted that it would link the task of accident compensation with that of accident prevention and that it would serve a harmonizing role, bringing employers and employees together under public auspices. The important point to recognize is that the AALL reformers' primary focus was on policy—scientifically engineered policy. Politics were merely a means to an end.

In the minds of many employers and labor leaders, however, policy and politics were inseparable. In fact, in New York both parties seemed to be more incensed about the AALL's willingness to cross them than about the particular policy outcome in question. The president of the Associated Manufacturers and Merchants of New York State (which had changed its name from the Associated Industries of New York State) scolded Andrews for opposing and rewriting the first Spring bill. "Now I am afraid of the general attitude of your organization toward industry," he wrote. "I am afraid that you would, in the matter of the administration of the law, give no quarter to industry."[28]

Even more disturbing was Samuel Gompers' reaction to the affair. Furious that the Association would support anything that labor so strongly opposed, he resigned from the AALL. He called on other labor leaders to do the same, and he facetiously renamed the AALL the "American Association for the Assassination of Labor Legislation."[29] Gompers had served as an honorary vice-president of the Association for many years, and his name was one of the more prominent ones on the Association's letterhead. Andrews later boasted to friends that only two other labor officials heeded Gompers' call for resignations. He noted as well that many labor officials had written to affirm their support for the organization. Still, Andrews knew that Gompers enjoyed widespread support. It seems unlikely that he convinced anyone, including himself, that Gompers' angry departure was anything but a sharp blow to the Association.[30]

T he Industrial Commission episode illustrates a number of motifs in the history of the AALL. In virtually all of the organization's legislative campaigns, its leaders faced serious questions about their standing in the policymaking process. They also provoked a good deal of concern about how they and their reform proposals might tip the industrial balance of power. Missing from the Industrial Commission fight, however, was another important motif—namely, dissension over the AALL reformers' philosophy of state action. As much as any other factor, their ideas on government caused them to alienate the very interest groups they hoped to lead and serve.

Throughout the later teens and into the twenties, the Association's economists engaged in a fierce debate with representatives of both capital and labor about the proper role of the state. The economists commonly articulated the belief that laissez faire was dead and that the modern state had a responsibility to regulate the labor market, particularly to protect the majority of American workers who were unorganized. On the other side, many of the nation's most prominent labor leaders and employers were jealous of their own prerogatives in the field of industrial relations. Union officials championed collective bargaining, while employers spoke about the sanctity of the private labor contract. Both preferred to see government excluded, as much as possible, from their affairs.[31]

Significantly, the dispute over state activism did not become a major issue during the drive for workers' compensation laws, which commenced in 1909. Leading employers and labor officials tolerated and even promoted this particular form of social insurance. They did not raise antistatist objections on a regular basis because the state was already involved in the problem of industrial accidents through employers' liability law, a common-law remedy. Though employers often could avoid or delay payment to injured employees through legal maneuvering, the state, at least in theory, held employers liable for all accidents deemed to be their fault. What worried employers was that the courts occasionally granted very large awards to accident victims. Workers, on the other side, generally were comfortable with the concept of employers' liability law but frustrated with the uncertainty and untimeliness of awards. Both sides, therefore, agreed that workers' compensation could be beneficial—assuring the injured worker of a certain award and protecting the employer from potentially unlimited liability. In 1918 John Commons suggested that the enactment of workers' compensation statutes had actually reduced governmental activity by removing most industrial accident cases from the courts.[32]

But there was no precedent for state action comparable to employers' liability law in the case of either unemployment or health insurance. As a result, when the AALL reformers launched campaigns for these newer forms of social insurance in the middle teens, they precipitated a bitter debate over the proper role of the state in industrial affairs. The rallying cry of their opponents was "statism."

Most employers resisted all forms of regular compensation for victims of unemployment or ill health, and they expressed particular aversion to the prospect of state provision for the victims of these hazards. Confronting demands for compulsory health insurance, a representative of the Associated Manufacturers and Merchants of New York State asked, "Shall our people be taught to lean upon the government to take care of themselves when they are sick, or shall they be taught to take care of themselves when they are well?"[33] Although a few employers (early welfare capitalists) and nearly all union leaders supported the principle of compensation, most favored only private, voluntary schemes. Employers who provided such benefit plans sought to increase worker loyalty, to tie workers to their jobs, and thus to reduce turnover.[34] Union officials, similarly, established union benefit funds to increase the attractiveness of union membership and to provide members with a vested interest in their unions. Public social insurance would serve only to undercut what the welfare capitalists and the trade unionists had to offer.

Of course, the AALL reformers were not satisfied with the voluntarist approach. They pointed out that the existing network of company and union plans was grossly inadequate. Benefit plans were unavailable to most workers, and what plans were available usually were poorly managed and actuarially unsound.[35] The only solution, they believed, was compulsory social insurance mandated by the state. "It does not mean that we turn over all of our affairs to the government," Commons explained before the Madison Civics Club in 1916. "It simply means that the government compels us to take care of our most important affairs . . ."[36]

The commencement of the Association's campaigns for unemployment and health insurance brought to the surface fundamental disagreements about the state's function, leading a number of previously loyal members to distance themselves from the organization. The most vocal dissenter was Frederick Hoffman, a statistician and executive with the Prudential Insurance Company. Hoffman had played an important role in many of the Association's early campaigns for sanitation regulations and workers' compensation, but he strongly objected to the campaign for health insurance and quickly became its most vocal and prolific opponent. Though Hoffman always denied the charge, AALL loyalists claimed that his position was motivated by the Prudential's interest in avoiding state competition with its industrial insurance plans. In 1917 Hoffman wrote a letter in his own defense to the president of the AALL, asserting that his "well-considered opposition to compulsory insurance is more disinterested and more patriotic than your own hearty approval of a form of legislation which is as unnecessary as it is un-American."[37] Another individual who previously had worked with the AALL reformers but found their support of health insurance intolerable was Ralph M. Easley, the chairman of the National Civic Federation's Executive Council. In a letter to the AALL, he dismissed the campaign for health insurance as "premature and ill-considered" and, even more fundamentally, as at odds with the demands of organized labor.[38]

Though perhaps disingenuous, Easley's expression of concern about the interests of organized labor was typical. Employers and representatives of the insurance industry regularly cited Samuel Gompers' staunch opposition to compulsory unemployment and health insurance as a justification for their own opposition. Indeed, Gompers' position was in many ways the most difficult obstacle for the AALL reformers to overcome.[39] Gompers lashed out in 1916 at the idea of compulsory health insurance in a sharply worded editorial entitled "Labor vs. Its Barnacles." He emphasized that labor preferred voluntary institutions to compulsory ones because the latter threatened the rights and liberties of workers. The superior alternative, in his view, was voluntary social insurance administered by the unions themselves rather than by the state.[40] Like many other labor leaders, Gompers became distrustful of state involvement in industrial affairs after facing the wrath of the American court system (overturned labor laws, injunctions against strikes, and so forth) in the late nineteenth century.[41]

Continuing his critique in "Labor vs. Its Barnacles," Gompers blasted the AALL reformers for pretending to know what was best for workers and for attempting to act as their guardians. With obvious bitterness, he announced:

> The so-called American Association for Labor Legislation has formulated the [health insurance] bill in question, had it introduced in several legislatures, and is pressing every energy for its enactment. And yet it has never asked or taken into consultation any official body of labor or its authoritative spokesmen and representatives. That association has, evidently, gone on the theory that the workers of America are still in the condition where they must be led by some "intellectual," that the workers have neither the judgment nor the will to protect and promote their own rights and interests, and that, therefore, this self-assumed guardianship must be exercised by would-be "uplifters."[42]

Gompers erred when he said that the Association reformers had made no attempts to consult labor leaders about their health insurance bill. In fact, they had consulted extensively with numerous labor officials, including the leaders of the New York State Federation of Labor. Gompers was correct, however, in his assessment of their operating theory. The AALL reformers did indeed believe that workers needed the help of intellectuals like themselves to secure essential reforms.[43]

As things turned out, the warning Gompers issued in his editorial, that organized labor would defeat the AALL in the battle over compulsory social insurance, proved accurate.[44] Not a single government, either state or federal, enacted health insurance or unemployment insurance during the progressive era. The opposition of influential capitalists and, especially, organized labor proved pivotal.

Yet Gompers overestimated the unity of his own movement. Individual workers and even labor leaders divided over the issue of social insurance. The AFL continued to reject all proposals for compulsory social insurance (except workers' compensation) until the Great Depression. Yet many labor leaders disagreed with the AFL's official position. The AALL managed to secure endorsements of state-mandated health and unemployment insurance from dozens of local unions and state federations of labor during the late teens.[45] Andrews felt confident enough as early as mid-1916 to write to a correspondent that he did not believe rank-and-file union members were in accordance with Gompers on the issue of social insurance. "My admiration for him as a leader of the trade union movement is very great indeed," Andrews insisted, "but I do think there is a new social order, the spirit of which Mr. Gompers has failed to comprehend."[46] Apparently, a small but growing contingent of the labor movement agreed with Andrews.[47]

The notion of a "new social order" was something about which the reformers of the American Association for Labor Legislation professed to have special knowledge and insight. They believed that industrial capitalism, for all its great promise, had some serious flaws. Intense competition drove employers to overwork their employees, to pay them inadequate wages, to expose them to unsafe working conditions, and to put them out of work whenever demand slackened. These failings could best be corrected, the reformers maintained, through legislation that placed protective floors under American labor. Their new social order would be one in which the state guarded all workers against the worst hazards of industrial life.

Many employers dismissed the reformers' vision as a mere pipe dream. Others believed that it could become reality, but only through the introduction of company-sponsored welfare and insurance programs. Many labor leaders agreed that private solutions were best, but insisted that the union (rather than the firm) was the most effective institution for assuring high standards of worker welfare and security. America's industrial leaders were therefore in agreement on at least one point—that state solutions and the reform organizations that promoted them often were injurious to social welfare.

It was into this inhospitable environment that the AALL reformers inserted themselves as scientific stewards. Whatever their shortcomings— and there were many—they were sincere in their belief that the Association served a vital social role. In early 1915 John Andrews wrote a letter to a concerned contributor, reassuring him about the value of the Association. A socialist had told the contributor that 3¢ sent to the textile workers' union would do more good than $100 for labor legislation. Andrews explained that although he firmly supported the trade union movement, he was confident "that the greatest *permanent social* gains have come and will continue to come from remedial legislation, slow and conservative as this movement sometimes appears and is."[48]

According to Andrews, history proved that unskilled workers generally were left out of the bargaining process and that even the strongest labor unions failed to stand up to determined and well-organized employers. Agitation and legislation, promoted by devoted reformers like himself, held the promise of "a social revolution" that would affect nearly every industrial worker. "It is for these reasons," Andrews explained, "that I personally have concluded that the legislative method is the one to which I want to devote my life."[49]

While in this letter Andrews highlighted how labor legislation would benefit workers, in many other cases AALL reformers emphasized the corresponding benefits for employers. In 1919 Commons wrote,

> Compulsory insurance . . . enlarges liberty by restraining it in other directions. And employers as a class get more liberty in the right direction than they lose in the wrong direction, for then the cut-throat competition of those who are indifferent or incompetent is eliminated at the point where they intensify class antagonism and prevent others from rising above their level.[50]

Leading members of the Association frequently suggested as well that employers would benefit from labor legislation because a secure workforce promised to be a more efficient workforce. Whatever argument they used, their point was almost always the same—that good labor legislation would not only serve the public interest but also benefit the vast majority of employers and workers, including those who initially opposed the legislation's enactment.

As has been suggested, the commitment of the AALL reformers to remedial legislation ultimately rested on their faith in social science. They assumed that rigorous investigation and careful reasoning were neutral vehicles in the pursuit of social betterment. Neutrality, however, proved more meaningful in theory than in practice. Because they were both intellectuals and policy advocates, set within a highly polarized political environment, the Association's leaders had difficulty defining their role in a coherent way. Subsequent chapters will suggest, moreover, that their conclusions about social policy were by no means the simple product of "scientific analysis." Of equal or greater importance were the reformers' personal biases and preconceptions about who the poor were, about how the economy worked, and about the nature of the obstacles they faced in their legislative campaigns. It should become clear as well that their political accomplishments depended in large measure upon the tolerance of the very industrial interests they claimed to stand above.

3

Security Floors and Opportunity Ceilings

The primary reason the American Association for Labor Legislation is of interest is that its leaders planted the seeds of the so-called American welfare state. Their campaigns for protective labor legislation and, especially, social insurance helped to shift the focus of social policy in the United States from pauperism to worker insecurity. Significantly, their long-term influence stemmed as much from their distinctive conception of poverty and social welfare as from their forays into legislative politics.

The historian Robert Bremner has argued that the progressive-era movement for more generous, worker-oriented welfare policies grew out of a new view of poverty, one that had begun to take root in the late nineteenth century. Whereas the old view held that the poor, in most cases, were the victims of their own vice and folly, the new view pointed to powerful environmental causes of poverty—such as industrial accidents and involuntary unemployment—over which victims had little or no control.[1] The AALL reformers probably would have agreed with Bremner's assessment. They prided themselves on having abandoned the old moralism and having adopted a more open-minded and objective approach to social welfare. It will be suggested here, however, that the reformers (and some of the historians who have studied them) overstated the conceptual break that became visible at the turn of the century.[2]

Since colonial times, two themes have pervaded the American discourse on poverty—the preference for prevention over relief and the distinction between the so-called worthy and unworthy poor. Even as attitudes about who the poor were and how to deal with them changed over time, these basic themes endured. They significantly influenced the development of

U.S. social welfare policy into the progressive era and, arguably, to the present day.[3]

During the seventeenth and eighteenth centuries, Americans generally believed that the social order was ordained from above. Poverty was thus regarded as inevitable and, to the extent that it provided the more comfortable classes with opportunities to demonstrate their benevolence, a positive good. The colonial attitude might be characterized as fatalistic do-goodism.

Significantly, the colonists differentiated sharply between impoverished community members and indigent strangers. In theory, the age-old dichotomy between worthy and unworthy poor was supposed to differentiate poor people who were victims of misfortune from those who were responsible for their own impoverishment. Because such clear-cut distinctions were often difficult to make in practice, however, more tangible characteristics frequently were relied upon as proxies. The characteristics considered relevant changed over time, but during the colonial period community membership was central. Destitute residents of a community generally were treated as worthy while transients almost always were regarded as unworthy.[4] Throughout the colonial period, the primary objective of poor relief was to provide assistance to needy community members while preventing outsiders from gaining access to the rolls. Indeed, one of the most regularly utilized policy instruments was warning-out, whereby strangers who seemed likely to become dependent on town support were threatened with punishment if they did not leave.[5]

By the nineteenth century, poverty no longer seemed a manifestation of divine intent. On the one hand, the perceived social stability of the colonial period apparently had given way to a more chaotic environment. The comfortable classes increasingly saw the destitute as a threat ("the dangerous classes") rather than as an opportunity to do good. On the other hand, the prospect of a wide-open frontier and unprecedented economic growth suggested that poverty was unnecessary. If only society, and particularly the poor themselves, could be reformed, poverty undoubtedly would disappear.[6]

Through the nineteenth century, the distinction between worthy and unworthy poor and the preference for prevention over relief remained, but the meaning of each of the operative terms underwent a dramatic transformation. As the relevance of discriminating on the basis of residency faded because of rising mobility, Americans increasingly focused on the character of the poor and, especially, the ways in which the poor supported themselves. The label "worthy" (or "deserving") came to be applied to poor persons who did not depend on relief. The "unworthy poor," on the other hand, were paupers—that is, those dependent on the good will of either generous individuals or the community. The primary goal of most social welfare reformers during this period was not to eliminate poverty but rather to eradicate dependency. Correspondingly, prevention in the nineteenth century meant preventing the worthy from becoming unworthy. Numerous cities had their Societies for the Prevention of Pauperism.[7] In 1818 the leaders of the New York Society attributed nine-tenths of poverty in New York City to the victims' lack of "correct moral principle."[8] Nineteenth-century campaigns for social welfare reform, therefore, focused almost exclusively on educating, reforming, and disciplining the poor—that is, instilling values of independence and encouraging and enforcing moral behavior.

As the century drew to a close, the moralism inherent in the nineteenth-century view struck many Americans as largely irrelevant and many others as mean-spirited. The logic of industrialism was transforming poverty from a social phenomenon into an economic one. How could one blame poverty on improvidence or intemperance when even entirely respectable workers fell into unemployment and distress during severe economic depressions? Surely the economic system, not the poor themselves, was primarily to blame. This environmentalist conception of poverty, what Robert Bremner calls the "new view," rapidly gained currency among social reformers during the late nineteenth and early twentieth centuries.[9]

In the case of the AALL, the environmentalist view offered direction, but it did not (and could not) determine the specific types of policies that the organization's leadership would champion. As has been suggested, the AALL reformers' novel ideas about poverty and social welfare were intermingled with deeply rooted American values. Just as important as their newfound environmentalist perspective was their commitment to the differentiation of the poor and their preference for prevention over relief, both of which they had inherited—apparently unknowingly—from generations of reformers before them. An understanding of the Association's peculiar combination of new ideas and old values is essential for explaining the nature and content of its policy agenda. The reformers' hidden penchant for discriminating between worthy and unworthy poor will be explored in the remainder of this chapter, while their very public preference for prevention over relief will be taken up in the next one.

Ostensibly, the AALL reformers' commitment to social welfare was as broad and inclusive as it was idealistic. The motto emblazoned on the back cover of the Association's 1915 *Review of Labor Legislation* announced, "To create a minimum standard of life below which no human being can fall is the most elementary duty of the democratic state."[10] This statement clearly articulated the public vision of the Association's leadership—a vision inspired by the complex process of industrialization still underway in the early years of the twentieth century. To leading figures at the AALL, the sword of industrialism was double-edged. It imposed upon American labor unprecedented new hazards and pressures that threatened individual workers and their families with financial ruin. Yet, simultaneously, it extended a promise of plenty that seemed, for the first time in history, to bring the age-old dream of abolishing poverty firmly within reach.[11]

The Association's fourth president, William F. Willoughby, declared at the annual meeting in 1913 that the worldwide movement for social insurance was a direct consequence of the industrial revolution. He explained that industrialization had left the individual worker alienated and insecure. The rise of large-scale industry, the bureaucratization of employer-employee relations, and the divorce of wage earners from the tools of production all contributed to depersonalizing employment and the production process, leaving individual workers with little control over their own condition.[12] Willoughby spoke poignantly of the workers' plight. "They have become almost literally but parts of a great impersonal mechanism," he said. "Their relation to this mechanism differs but little from that of the inanimate agencies employed. When disabled through old age or failing powers, and when not needed through a reduction in the scale of operations, they are discarded as other useless parts."[13]

The idea that workers could be "discarded"—that employers could and would decline all responsibility for the welfare of their employees—was deeply troubling to the reformers of the AALL. Especially within an age of unprecedented productivity and enormous new wealth, such treatment seemed inexcusable. The AALL reformers rejected the old moralistic notion that self-help was sufficient to protect working-class families from destitution. This objection to reform, Commons wrote in 1899, "falls, in the face of inadequate wages, unstable employment, and the failure of government to guarantee security for savings, and to educate in thrift."[14] Contemporary investigations of family budgets revealed that few workers could provide adequately for such contingencies as industrial accidents, unemployment, illness, old age, and premature death simply through saving a part of their wages. Even when regularly employed, many workers found their wages inadequate to support themselves and their families.[15] Progressive reformers occasionally suggested that self-insurance through personal saving might have been feasible when the economy was primarily agricultural—when common laborers, even in bad times, rarely went hungry. But in a highly monetized economy centered around the factory and the workshop rather than the farm, most workers could not save enough to provide adequately against even temporary losses of income.

Cognizant of the new threats industrialism posed to the worker and of the worker's weakened lines of defense, the reformers of the AALL searched for ways to bolster the American laborer's financial position. At the Association's first annual meeting in 1907, Henry Seager explained that the two goals of any program of social legislation must be (1) to protect workers and their families from falling below their current standards of living and (2) to assist them in reaching higher standards of living.[16] Over the following decade, the AALL reformers actively pursued the first objective but devoted little attention to the second, a choice Seager seemed to anticipate in his 1907 talk. Focusing his attention on the victims of industrial hazards, he said, "If the poverty from which they suffer could be remedied, a long step would be taken towards the elimination of poverty, and this might be done by providing in advance against the contingencies which drag them down."[17]

Seager's remarks revealed his commitment to an environmentalist conception of poverty. He attributed impoverishment mainly to contingencies (hazards) associated with employment and living conditions rather than to personal vices such as indolence and intemperance. All of the active participants in the AALL shared this environmentalist perspective. Like Seager, they surmised that poverty could be reduced, almost eliminated, by providing against hazards such as accidents, illness, and unemployment "in advance" of the suffering otherwise inflicted. This was one of their most crucial assumptions. On the basis of it, they began to equate social welfare almost exclusively with worker security. Willoughby claimed in his 1913 address that with the organization of a "just and workable" system of social insurance, "the problem of the economic security of labor, one of the greatest with which society now has to deal, would be solved."[18]

In championing the cause of worker security, the reformers of the AALL generally refused to acknowledge—either to others or to themselves— that their special focus had a narrowing effect on the scope of social welfare reform. They tended to ignore forms of poverty that were not the direct result of clearly identifiable hazards. Although they spoke vaguely about establishing a "minimum standard of life" for all, what they really meant was a minimum standard for all members of the working class. Individuals who failed, for whatever reason, to gain long-term membership in the labor force received little or no help from the American Association for Labor Legislation.

The leading members of the Association thus implicitly (and sometimes explicitly) discriminated against the most marginal classes of American society.[19] Their quest for worker security, itself partially a product of their environmentalist view of poverty, forced them to make certain choices.

Ironically, these choices mimicked old distinctions between worthy and unworthy poor—precisely the sort of moralistic divisions their environmentalist view of poverty was supposed to avoid. Like industrialism itself, the movement for social security to which it gave rise was double-edged.

R eformers of the progressive era inherited from the scientific charity movement of the late nineteenth century a penchant for classifying the poor, for differentiating them according to the reasons for their impoverishment.[20] Robert Hunter exhibited this inclination in his well-known 1904 treatise entitled *Poverty*. Early chapters examined "The Pauper" and "The Vagrant," while later chapters considered "The Sick," "The Child," and "The Immigrant." Those who say "The poor always ye have with you," Hunter asserted, "fail to distinguish between the poor, who are poor because of their own folly and vice, and the poor who are poor as a result of social wrongs." Pauperism and vagrancy, he acknowledged, would never disappear, but poverty stemming from environmental conditions could be prevented. The first step toward meaningful social reform was to distinguish between the two classes and to treat them separately.[21] Hunter's logic revived in a new context the old distinction between worthy and unworthy poor.

Although his self-identification as a socialist distinguished Hunter from nearly all of the leaders of the AALL, he corresponded with some of them, including Commons and Andrews, and likely became a dues-paying member of the Association in its early years. The AALL reformers shared many of his ideas about poverty and were probably influenced by his 1904 book. When they spoke of preventing poverty, they usually meant preventing poverty among the "upright" working classes. As Hunter had written, "Perhaps the most egregious error, is the belief, which exists in the minds of many, that the slum population and the working people are the same."[22] The reformers of the AALL made certain not to commit this error. Though they refrained as much as possible from uttering old moralistic terms like "worthy poor" and "unworthy poor," they managed to keep the dichotomy alive by employing new words to express it—"unemployed" and "unemployable" being the most common.

A few Association members occasionally voiced objections to the practice of classifying the poor. Mary Van Kleeck, an active reformer and researcher with the Russell Sage Foundation, once complained about a project involving personal interviews with poor people that aimed to identify the causes of their impoverishment and dependency. The interview, she wrote to Andrews, "throws far more light on the mental outlook of the interviewer than on the cause of poverty."[23] Such warnings, however, carried little weight at the AALL. Especially during the period of unusually high unemployment around 1914, Andrews and his colleagues focused much of their attention on differentiating among and classifying the great mass of jobless Americans.

In an issue of the *American Labor Legislation Review* devoted entirely to the problem of unemployment in 1914, there appeared a full-page box defining the terms "employable" and "unemployable." Whereas the former term covered all types of workers (both regular and casual), the latter referred to individuals "who have been ousted, or have willfully withdrawn themselves, from the ranks of the workers; e.g., the aged, the infirm, the criminal."[24] In theory, the distinction differentiated between those inside and those outside the labor force. In practice, however, few reformers worried about discerning the "employable" from the "unemployable." They were much more interested in separating the "unemployable" from the "unemployed". Of all the people without employment, some genuinely wanted to find new jobs (the unemployed) while others were either unfit or unwilling to work (the unemployable).[25] In 1915 Andrews wrote to Henry Bruere, the secretary of the New York City Mayor's Committee on Unemployment, "I believe it is generally agreed that in order to deal intelligently with the city's problem of unemployment a first step involves the separation of the unemployable from the unemployed."[26] Through the hard winter of 1914–15, AALL reformers encouraged municipalities to take this first step. They repeatedly warned that relief efforts that neglected to distinguish between the two classes would inevitably fail. An article entitled "Separation of Unemployable and Unemployed," which appeared in the Association's 1915 *Unemployment Survey*, explained:

> Where no attempts were made to separate unemployable and unemployed last winter, measures for the unemployed suffered and the public was given a false impression of the problem, which hindered the forwarding of constructive efforts. Where an effort was made to distinguish between the two classes, it was found that the machinery was usually lacking for dealing with the lazy and inefficient, who most often are confused with the genuine unemployed. Accordingly citizens are occasionally urging that prison farms be opened for the work-shy and that industrial or agricultural training be provided for the inefficient, but as yet only slight action has resulted from the winter's emergency. In order that work for the deserving need no longer be hindered on account of lazy and inefficient unemployables, measures of this sort should be actively pushed forward.[27]

As this passage suggests, the Association reformers advanced the practice of discrimination ostensibly as an administrative expedient. A work-relief program could not function effectively if it were flooded with individuals entirely unfit to work. But, as the passage also suggests, their interest in differentiation went deeper. If, in theory, the term "unemployable" referred to everyone outside of the labor force (including widows, orphans, and the like), in common usage it frequently was reduced to mean the "lazy and inefficient" or merely the "lazy." The word "unemployable" thus acquired a double meaning. Reformers could speak compassionately about unemployable invalids; but they could just as comfortably justify ignoring unemployables as a class on the grounds that most were shiftless and indolent. At the Association's 1911 annual meeting, Charles Henderson, a professor of sociology at the University of Chicago, presented his views this way:

> The "unemployable" cases in the labor market are often the "unhelpable" cases of charity organizations. It is impossible to give them any real and permanent relief by ordinary doles, whether of food or advice. They serve only to bid low against competent and self-supporting men who are trying to maintain or raise their standard of living; and they can do this just because they are irresponsible and partly parasitic.[28]

Until his death in early 1915, Henderson played a central role in the AALL's campaigns for labor legislation. He chaired the American Committee on Unemployment, sat on the Association's Committees on Women's Work and Social Insurance, and was a regular member of the AALL Executive Committee. His peers regarded him as a distinguished and sensitive student of the unemployment problem. When he depicted unemployables as "irresponsible and partly parasitic," it was not because he was a particularly callous man but rather because this was a familiar way to describe the class. Just as the terms "worthy" and "unworthy" had both formal and common meanings in the nineteenth century, so too did "unemployed" and "unemployable" in the progressive era.

The AALL reformers' first opportunity to look closely at the poor and to test their assumptions about who the poor were came in December 1914, when the New York City Commissioner of Public Charities appointed John Andrews chairman of a new Advisory Social Service Committee of the Municipal Lodging House. The Municipal Lodging House was one of New York's publicly funded shelters for the homeless. It opened its doors in February 1909 with regular accommodations for 1,064 residents, and in 1914 the city added an annex with 1,100 more beds and emergency spaces for almost 1,700. One dormitory was set aside for women and infants (78 beds and 18 cribs), but the vast majority of lodgers were men. Until April 14, 1915, the facility's superintendent was required by law to refuse individuals more than three days of lodging per month. After that, because of a change in the law, the superintendent enjoyed complete discretion over length of stay.

Applicants usually arrived in the evening and spent about 45 minutes going through the registration process. After first receiving soup, coffee, and bread, they were required to declare some basic facts about themselves—including name, age, and place of birth; the amount of time spent in the United States and in New York City; occupation, last employer, and marital status. They also were required to deposit whatever money or valuables they might be carrying. They then were sent to bathe, provided with clean nightshirts (their clothes were taken away and fumigated), examined by physicians, and finally assigned beds. They were awakened at 5:30 the next morning. After washing, dressing, and eating breakfast, most were expected to work on tasks inside the institution. Over the course of 1914, the Municipal Lodging House provided 364,511 accommodations for the homeless—that is, about a thousand per night.[29]

After reviewing the records of 1,500 homeless men who had applied to the city for shelter, Commissioner of Public Charities John A. Kingsbury determined that the Lodging House could do much more than simply provide a roof and beds for its clients. Contrary to the conventional wisdom, Kingsbury thought, the majority of applicants were not "without intelligence, without character, without courage, without hope." Confident that rehabilitation was possible, he sought to transform the Lodging House into "a great human repair shop, manned and equipped to rebuild the broken lives of those who enter its doors for help." He appointed the Advisory Social Service Committee, with Andrews at its head, to advise him on the best way to proceed.[30] Besides Andrews, twenty-three people served on the committee, including Bailey B. Burrit (general director of the Association for Improving the Condition of the Poor), Walter Lippmann (editor of the *New Republic*), and Mary Van Kleeck (secretary of the Russell Sage Foundation's Committee on Women's Work).[31]

In their final report, written by AALL special investigator Bertrand Brown, the committee analyzed the types of people who applied for lodging at the house, their problems, and their needs. "To the citizens of New York City," the report began, "the homeless man needs no introduction. According to a census made by the New York City Police Department for the United States Bureau of Labor Statistics on the night of January 30, 1915, he was here some 26,000 strong."[32] Though he needed no introduction, he did deserve more careful study, the report suggested, because the general public knew very little about the homeless. An investigation of 1,500 applicants to the Municipal Lodging House and medical examinations of 2,000 lodgers in March 1914 provided the empirical basis for just such a study.[33]

The committee found that "the men who frequent the Lodging House can be classified roughly into two distinct though constantly merging groups, namely the unemployed and the unemployable."[34] Most of the men seem to have belonged to the former class. As the report readily acknowledged, however, no method had yet been perfected "for the separation of unemployable individuals from the body of the unemployed, which would make possible any sharp classification."[35] About 90 percent of the men given physical examinations were judged physically able to do work, and only 21 percent of those surveyed admitted to begging either occasionally or regularly.

Of those who responded to questions about the length of their unemployment, fewer than one-half of 1 percent said they were currently working. About 10 percent had been out of work for less than a week, 65 percent for over a month, and only 6.7 percent for over six months.[36] Many of the applicants had only recently arrived in New York in search of work. Their stories, as well as letters from their past employers, seemed to convince the committee that a "substantial number of men who frequent the Municipal Lodging House" were victims of "honest unemployment."[37]

While the unemployed generally faced hard times during seasonal and cyclical downturns in business activity, the unemployables suffered from a variety of additional problems. The committee's report roughly classified the unemployables into six overlapping groups. Eleven percent of the men examined were physically handicapped (4 percent temporarily and 7 percent permanently) to the extent that they were unable to work. Ten percent of these cases of disability stemmed from old age. A significant proportion of the remainder were the victims of accidents and disease. According to the report, tuberculosis was the primary cause of physical incapacitation among the men.[38]

Another group of unemployables was the so-called mentally defective class. Although the report does not provide any statistics on their frequency at the Lodging House, the total number of mentally retarded residents probably was small. The untrained constituted another category for which no statistics were provided. All we are told is that the "records of this investigation show that a number of the men interviewed could have been self-supporting if they had been trained in some occupation which they were physically and mentally able to carry on."[39]

The two remaining categories of unemployables were "the inebriate" and "the habitually idle." The inebriate category must have overlapped with nearly all of the others. Of the men who responded to questions about their habits, 87 percent acknowledged that they drank alcohol, and 44 percent admitted that they drank excessively. The examining physicians diagnosed 39 percent of the 2,000 men in the sample as suffering from alcoholism and maintained that their figures probably underestimated the total number of alcoholics who passed through the Lodging House.[40]

Most significantly, the committee appears to have had a hard time identifying precisely which applicants were "habitually idle." The two proxy variables they chose were the subjects' duration of unemployment and tendency to beg. Of the 102 men out of work for more than six months, 50 (or 3.5 percent of the total sample) had been out of work for over a year. As noted above, 21 percent of the applicants interviewed admitted to having begged for money. The report did not indicate which of the two variables the committee regarded as the more accurate one, and it is likely that the committee members themselves did not know. Still the report offered a revealing paragraph describing the plight of the "habitually idle":

> Some of these men had degenerated through repeated periods of idleness into a voluntary state of unproductiveness and parasitism. Others were unemployed, apparently, because they had never disciplined themselves to obey orders. Others, moreover, were unable to keep their minds on their work, either because they were obsessed with an idea that they were more fit for something else, perhaps in a different city or state, or because some misfortune, such as the loss of a friend, had left them without the initiative and the purpose which had made their work worth while.[41]

The relatively few men who reasonably could be classified as habitually idle, perhaps somewhere between 3.5 and 21 percent of the pool of homeless applicants interviewed, were the ones who might have been called hard-core unemployables—the vagrants and tramps who made careers out of avoiding work. Considering how much energy some social reformers put into excoriating them, these so-called parasites proved remarkably difficult to identify in practice and surprisingly few in number.

Only after attempting to characterize and classify the Municipal Lodging House's residents did the committee finally address the commissioner's original charge to suggest ways of rehabilitating the homeless. Here the distinction between unemployed and unemployable supposedly became useful. The report recommended that every applicant receive a physical and a social examination. Those determined by the examiners to be employable—that is, both fit and willing to work—should be directed toward suitable jobs by the house's employment bureau (for which the committee urged new appropriations). The unemployables, of course, posed a bigger problem. "The unemployable man," the report reads, "needs either to be treated for the causes of his dependency, to be protected from the competition of the more fit, or to receive both such treatment and protection." The physically disabled who were not beyond help should receive medical and surgical care. The inebriate should be "restored to health and disciplined for rational living." The habitually idle should be "constrained (or compelled) to work." The aged should be placed in homes. The mentally defective should be "segregated, protected and trained." And the untrained should be found suitable employment and taught the necessary skills.[42]

The proposed remedies made sense but probably struck the contemporary reader much as they strike the modern one—as being somewhat simplistic and nearly impossible to implement. The report defined no formula for distinguishing the "habitually idle" from the "honest" unemployed. And it made no reference to where the employment bureau was supposed to find jobs for all of the men who truly wanted work. The authors seemed to imply that the homeless simply did not know where to look for available employment. Finally, the report was nearly silent on the issue of funding. It called for more money for the social service department (which included the employment bureau) and for salaries, but it never suggested a source of funding nor offered total cost estimates for the recommended programs (segregating the mentally defective, training the untrained, healing the disabled, disciplining the idle and inebriate, housing the aged).

Andrews and his fellow members of the committee were genuinely concerned about the city's homeless and genuinely interested in exploring the causes of their destitution. At a time when many references to the unemployable were disparaging, the committee's report stood out as a sensitive, if somewhat naive, document. Yet the city government, quite understandably, proved unable to follow up on most of the recommendations, and Andrews quickly turned his attention away from the needs of the dispossessed and back to the issue of worker security. When the problem of the unemployable or the economically marginal subsequently arose in AALL discussions, the usual remedy proposed was to segregate these groups from the labor market. If the dispossessed could not be saved, at least they could be prevented from dragging down "honest" and "efficient" workers.

One popular method for segregating unemployables from the general labor market was industrial colonization, whereby alleged tramps and vagrants were incarcerated in institutions and compelled to work. Historically rooted in the Elizabethan workhouse, the idea of the industrial colony rose to prominence in late-nineteenth-century England. English reformers such as William Beveridge and Charles Booth believed that in order to reduce the excessive reserve of unemployed labor, the most inefficient workers (who were, on average, the poorest as well) should be forced out of the labor market. Booth envisioned settling the very poor in industrial camps.[43] When New York State established America's first industrial colony in 1911, the AALL identified it as an important development: "It marks a belated tendency to recognize the presence of unemployment, which statistics show to be increasing."[44]

The New York law authorizing the construction and operation of an industrial colony became effective on July 28, 1911. It provided that any person deemed a tramp or a vagrant by a judge could be detained for a period not to exceed two years. The law stated explicitly, however, that "reputable workmen, temporarily out of work and seeking employment," were not to be committed. Its objectives were to punish the unworthy poor and, most important, to separate unemployables from the labor market.[45]

Many members of the AALL supported the idea of industrial colonies, and a number of them promoted it vigorously. Elizabeth S. Kite, of the New Jersey Department of Charities and Corrections, strongly stated the case for segregation during a general discussion at the AALL's Second National Conference on Unemployment in December 1914. "The habitually unemployed class," she said,

> is recognized to be the inefficient class. The scientific instruments to-day available enable us to penetrate the cause of this inefficiency and to learn that it lies primarily in a lack of intelligence . . .
>
> This class retained within competitive ranks has precisely the same effect upon wages as child labor . . .
>
> The remedy . . . seems to be segregation . . . Colonized upon waste land, this class can be made to contribute largely to its own support. Once recognized to be only children in mind, responsibilities beyond their power will no longer be placed upon these dependents or permitted to them. Being children they can easily be made happy and their comfort assured at a cost not exceeding what is at present so ineffectually expended upon them by charity organizations, while the benefit to society at large and to the labor problem in particular will be immeasurable.[46]

Kite was not the only one at the conference to voice such ideas. In a paper entitled "What the Awakened Employer is Thinking on Unemployment," another participant declared:

> First, the unemployable must be entirely separated from the unemployed. The unemployable must be taken care of by whatever methods shall prove wisest both for their greatest usefulness and happiness and for the greatest safety of the community, and this means that they must be taken out of the competitive market until they are able to return.[47]

A few months after the conference, Andrews noted in his correspondence that he had recently begun to recognize the urgency of developing industrial colonies for vagrants. Seager's correspondence also revealed strong support for the idea. In fact, at the Association's very first annual meeting in 1907, Seager had explained, "And as we make it easier for the self-respecting family to maintain its standard of living, we should at the same time make it more difficult for the shiftless, loafing type of man to get along at all outside of an industrial colony." By 1915 the AALL's list of Standard Recommendations to combat unemployment included one calling for the development of "penal farm colonies for shirks and vagrants, training colonies and classes for the inefficient, and special workshops for handicapped and sub-standard workers."[48]

Significantly, tramps and vagrants were not the only targets of the segregation strategy. Almost any group or class on the margin of the economy qualified for isolation. Irene Osgood Andrews, in a report on the relation between irregular employment and a living wage for women, singled out young girls as the class dragging down the broader labor market for women:

> It is this great throng of young, untrained, undisciplined workers which supplies the employer with help for the few busy months. At other times they drift in and out . . . cutting down the income of the steady responsible worker. Because this class of casuals is ever present the employer finds it easier to take them as they come and any question of regularizing his business is passed by. In this way they increase the discontinuous employment of the steady worker, and tend to make permanent a disorganized labor market.[49]

Osgood Andrews prepared her report in 1914 at the request of the New York State Factory Investigating Commission, which was then considering the merits of a minimum wage for women. Her central argument was that irregular employment was as significant as low wages in depressing the incomes of working women below an acceptable level. Women, she observed, were especially vulnerable to the scourge of unemployment. Employers continued to think of them as economic dependents, uninterested in permanent employment and after little more than spending money. "The right to a just and full compensation for one's labor regardless of questions of dependency is not yet universally accepted," she wrote.[50] Most "women's work" was in seasonal trades, such as the paper-box industry, the confection industry, and especially the clothing industry.[51] Combined with the fact that women workers tended to be relatively immobile, the seasonal nature of their employment opportunities meant that their incomes often were erratic. In response to variations in demand, employers found ways to save on labor costs—permanent layoffs, temporary layoffs, shorter hours, fewer days per week, and lower daily wages. Though the different methods affected individual workers differently, all of them meant lower total income for the labor force as a whole.

Osgood Andrews defined three broad categories of women workers: first, a small group that was permanently employed (what she called the "backbone of the labor force"); second, those workers who were employed through the busy season but laid off at its close; and third, the women who drifted in and out of industry, working only a few days or weeks at a time in any given place. Unfortunately, she insisted, a small part of the women's workforce (composed of members from the second and third categories) adversely affected the remainder. These were girls who, supposedly, were not dependent on their incomes and interested only in "pin money" and diversion. "Were it not for the tragic effect which the presence of this proportionally small group of workers has upon the mass of women employees we might pass them by unnoticed. But in this very group lies the key to not a little of the distress of the larger more responsible group." The presence of these girls, she claimed, depressed wage rates and displaced older and more responsible women workers.[52]

Osgood Andrews suggested that the best solution was to exclude all young girls from the labor market, beginning with girls under the age of sixteen and perhaps extending to girls under eighteen. The effect would be to draw off "a great mass of casual labor" and to "leave the field open" for others.[53] Her proposal is somewhat surprising given her appeal in the very same report for the "right to a just and full compensation for one's labor regardless of questions of dependency." Yet it is consistent with the Association's broader emphasis on worker security. As we have seen, one means of establishing a floor of security beneath a majority of workers was the erection of a ceiling on the opportunities of the economically marginal, which in this case involved excluding them from the labor market. There were other reasons for prohibiting young girls from working, of course, but in her report Osgood Andrews raised only the justification of greater job security for mature women workers.

When contemplating or promoting the concept of segregation, AALL reformers almost always focused on the positive side—that is, the greater security that "honest and efficient" working people would enjoy as a result. In rare instances, however, they addressed what might be called the underside of the theory, exposing (or at least considering) the consequences for those excluded. Two such instances involved Henry Seager speaking in support of a mandatory minimum wage, first before a joint session of the AALL and the American Economic Association (AEA) on

December 28, 1912, and next before the American Academy of Political and Social Science (AAPSS) just over three months later.

At the time of these addresses, the movement for minimum-wage laws for women was just beginning to bear fruit. Massachusetts enacted the first minimum-wage law in 1912. Like all such laws passed during the progressive era, it applied only to women. As the first, it failed to provide for any realistic enforcement mechanism and made the rates (to be set by wage boards) subject to judicial review. Nevertheless, as the Association's annual *Review of Labor Legislation* put it at the time, "the act is of great importance as the first step in the direction of legislative control of wages."[54] Eight states immediately followed Massachusetts' example and passed minimum-wage laws for women in 1913.[55]

Seager was an outspoken and influential proponent of the minimum wage, and he played an active role in the movement for a minimum-wage law in New York State during the teens. In his addresses of late 1912 and 1913, he argued that a legally mandated minimum (or living) wage would have two effects: it would eradicate those particularly exploitative types of employment that paid starvation wages to women and children; and it would expel from the workforce most women and children previously earning sub-living wages, marking them as unemployables. The latter consequence epitomizes the underside of the segregation theory. Seager did not describe it in this way, of course. In his view, the inefficient worker unable to earn a living wage belonged not in the labor market but rather on some kind of public assistance. She deserved either training or relief, or possibly both, depending on her condition. Seager suggested to his colleagues in the AALL and the AEA that they view the minimum wage as a social alarm system that would notify the public of citizens desperately in need of help:

> It is perhaps the most important service that may be expected from requiring employers to pay living wages, that under this system the individuals and families who are incapable of self-support must stand out sharply as unemployables, for whose relief society will be forced to bestir itself in providing, not soup-kitchen charities, but constructive measures, insurance benefits for widows with children to maintain and educate, and for old men and women, public employment exchanges to assist wage-earners to find remunerative employment, and industrial training for all classes, particularly young persons, to make them more efficient and consequently able to command higher wages.[56]

In his address before the AAPSS, Seager advanced a similar point but laid special emphasis on the definitional role of the minimum wage:

The operation of a minimum wage requirement would merely extend the definition of defectives to embrace all individuals, who even after having received special training, remain incapable of adequate self-support. Such persons are already social defendants [sic]. The plan merely compels them to stand out clearly in their true character, and enables them to receive that special consideration which their situation calls for.[57]

In both addresses Seager highlighted not only his hope for a more humane policy toward unemployables but also his faith that benefits would accrue to the majority of workers as a result of segregating the inefficient. A minimum wage, he predicted, would protect wage earners from "the wearing competition of the casual worker and the drifter" and make it easier for them to organize and demand better working conditions.[58] This particular assumption—that minimum-wage laws would yield security from substandard wages and excessive competition and that such security would become a new source of strength for the average worker—remained in dispute long after many states across the country had enacted minimum-wage statutes. It remains in dispute today. What is not in dispute is Seager's other basic assumption—that once minimum-wage laws marked the inefficient as unemployables, American society would then be "forced to bestir itself" and provide for them. This assumption proved false. After imposing minimum-wage laws, not a single state or the federal government ever enacted a comprehensive program designed to assist and train those economically marginal citizens who proved incapable of finding or keeping work at the minimum wage.[59]

Seager never considered the possibility that Americans would fail to deal generously with the unemployables and the inefficient once they became clearly visible. Some critics of the minimum wage, he had explained, objected on the grounds that such a law would force the state to provide employment at adequate wages or maintain in some other way those citizens adversely affected. He happily acknowledged that this was correct. "It is undoubtedly true," he said, "that a determination in favor of minimum wage regulations does commit organized society to a more responsible attitude toward the whole labor problem, than any American state has yet adopted. For one, I welcome this prospect."[60]

As with Andrews and the Municipal Lodging House report, Seager was full of good intentions. He supported industrial training for the inefficient and various forms of direct aid for widows and orphans, the elderly, the handicapped, and all other permanent unemployables. Still, he devoted most of his energy to the reform agenda of the AALL, which emphasized worker security rather than assistance for the dispossessed. Seager recognized the contradiction. He understood that security for the majority of the working class depended, at least in part, on the exclusion of the economically marginal from the labor market. He understood, too, that such exclusion would leave those on the margin even more helpless than before. He accepted the contradiction, perhaps, only because he overestimated the depth of the nation's commitment to public welfare. He failed to notice, for example, the absence of any organizations as powerful as the AALL that championed, not worker security, but rather extensive welfare and training programs for the long-term poor.

The great interest of many AALL reformers in separating the unemployables from the unemployed and in excluding the "inefficient and lazy" from the labor market exemplified the endurance of the distinction between the "worthy" and "unworthy" poor. In the nineteenth century, the goal of most social welfare reformers had been to prevent the worthy poor from becoming unworthy. They sought to encourage independence and to distinguish the independent laborer from the unworthy pauper by punishing all those who succumbed to the temptation of dependency.

By the early twentieth century, with the advance of industrialization and the emergence of an environmentalist view of poverty, the goal of many social welfare reformers had shifted. Like their nineteenth-century counterparts, they tended to believe in the inherent dignity of the independent laborer and the moral depravity of the able-bodied pauper. What was new was their recognition that industrialization had confused matters. While industrial wages held out the promise of adequate living standards for an ever enlarging subset of the working class, industrial hazards (such as accidents, disease, and unemployment) threatened individual workers and their families with impoverishment and descent into humiliating dependency. The nineteenth-century approach no longer seemed relevant. Instead of seeking to prevent the worthy poor from becoming unworthy, the progressive reformers hoped to prevent the worthy worker from becoming poor at all. Their goal was worker security. They sought to encourage independence and to distinguish the unemployed from the unemployables primarily by protecting members of the working class from financial deterioration.

As we have seen, however, punishment was not entirely absent from the new approach. One apparent prerequisite to a successful program of worker security, the AALL reformers discovered, was that the economically marginal had to be identified and segregated. Otherwise the "honest" worker would find living and working standards constantly eroded by desperate competitors. Equally important, policies designed to aid the worker in times of trouble could be overwhelmed by the unending demands of the unworthy and the unfit. Promoting worker security thus required the erection of walls between two classes of society—two classes that progressive reformers assumed were distinct but that industrialization rendered increasingly difficult to distinguish.

Though they never said so explicitly, the AALL reformers seemed to believe that contributory social insurance, like the minimum wage, would work almost automatically to separate regular workers, who would be covered, from those outside and those on the margins of the workforce, who would not. Presumably it would prevent poverty among members of the working class without extending aid to the unworthy. The reformers paid little attention to the possibility that some of those excluded from social insurance coverage might not in fact be unworthy. They were much more concerned that benefit payments might be misconstrued by critics as a form of demeaning public assistance, and they therefore took great pains to differentiate social insurance from poor relief. In his 1913 address, for example, Willoughby identified social insurance not only as the most efficient means of combatting poverty in the industrial age but as the most respectable as well. "Social justice, not public relief," he declared, "is its essential characteristic."[61]

The reformers argued that social insurance benefits did not constitute charity because the recipients (or their employers) contributed in advance to pay for them. Whatever the validity of this claim, the distinction between insurance and relief paralleled the division between worthy and unworthy poor. Even more important, it cast a shadow of suspicion over all noncontributory forms of welfare, and it helped to narrow the scope of politically acceptable social policy in the United States.[62]

There was, of course, no possibility that social insurance and other programs of worker security would protect all "worthy" persons. The AALL reformers recognized that some perfectly respectable individuals who were simply unfit to hold regular jobs would not be covered; but perhaps they assumed, like Seager, that society voluntarily would provide for these people. Equally troubling, they failed to recognize that members of some disadvantaged groups (African Americans, for example) had difficulty gaining regular access to the labor force even though they were highly motivated and fully capable of working. As long as such groups remained on the periphery of the labor market, contributory social insurance would tend to exclude them just as it excluded vagrants and tramps.[63]

The AALL reformers' promotion of worker security and their general preference for social insurance over noncontributory forms of welfare promised to benefit millions of regular workers and yet, simultaneously, threatened to handicap further many of the nation's most economically marginal citizens. The new, environmental view of poverty had produced this perverse result because the progressive reformers who adopted it had identified only some, but by no means all, of the environmental causes of poverty. They had failed, moreover, fully to come to terms with the underside of their segregation theory.

4

Internalizing
Industrial Externalities

I n addition to retaining the longstanding American distinction between
worthy and unworthy poor, the leaders of the AALL retained the associated preference for preventing poverty, rather than merely relieving
it. One does not have to search very hard to find expressions of this
preference in the organization's papers. A pamphlet outlining the aims of
the Association stated tersely, "Great emphasis is placed on PREVEN-
TION."[1] When a staff member preparing a report on British unemployment insurance ignored that dictum, John Andrews politely corrected her:

> On page 4, last paragraph, you say, "The supporters of unemployment in-
> surance do not advocate it as a remedy for unemployment, but as a dignified
> method of relief." My own belief is that advocates of unemployment insur-
> ance have very often emphasized it merely as a method of relief, but is it not
> true that the more far-seeing advocates of the insurance method in every
> branch of social insurance have in mind a second very important consider-
> ation . . . I know that Prof. Commons and I in all of the work we have done
> together have thought first of prevention and second of relief in dealing with
> each form of social insurance in this country.[2]

Andrews' remarks were quite sincere. Throughout the progressive period, he and his colleagues at the AALL exhibited a deep commitment to
the goal of prevention. They were mistaken, however, in heralding the
ideal as an innovation of their own making. What was innovative was
not the idea of prevention itself, which they had inherited from generations of reformers before them, but rather their notion about what ought
to be prevented. Their nineteenth-century predecessors had aimed to prevent the self-supporting poor from succumbing to the temptations of de-

pendency. The AALL reformers, by contrast, aimed to prevent poverty altogether by attacking the sources of economic insecurity.

Widespread worker insecurity, in their view, represented both an injustice to the individual and a threat to the continued existence of industrial capitalism. In order to overcome the injustice and remove the threat, they proposed reforms that they claimed would prevent not only poverty but also the industrial hazards that caused poverty and induced insecurity. They sought to redirect market forces in such a way as to make the prevention of industrial accidents, disease, and unemployment profitable for the employer; and they championed social insurance (and, especially, social insurance taxes) as the ideal means to this end.

A t the turn of the century, before any organized movement for social insurance existed in the United States, writers on the subject typically devoted their attention to the advantages of predictable compensation.[3] If covered by social insurance, victims of industrial hazards would not have to degrade themselves by pleading for private charity or public assistance. Instead they would receive payments automatically out of a fund to which they or their employers had contributed. The community would be spared the expense of relief, and the workers would retain their sense of dignity. Social insurance, or "workingmen's insurance" as it was called at the time, would prevent both poverty and pauperism. At the AALL's first annual meeting in 1907, one of its leaders suggested that adequate provision against the primary hazards of industrial life would "reduce very greatly the number of persons who sink to the position of social dependents."[4]

By the teens, however, progressive reformers were commonly ascribing another meaning to the term prevention. "Before all questions of indemnity for evil," Charles Henderson declared at a conference on social insurance in 1913, "is prevention of evil."[5] Reformers like Henderson saw social insurance as a means to prevent the industrial hazards that caused poverty. Workers' compensation would prevent accidents, unemployment insurance would prevent unemployment, and health insurance would prevent sickness. The issue of compensation in all three cases was of secondary importance. With regard to unemployment insurance, for example, Commons and Andrews wrote in their text on labor legislation: "The indications are that this branch of social insurance can be made to accomplish with respect to involuntary idleness a very considerable prevention of the evil itself, which from every point of view is much more important than the payment of benefits."[6]

Their logic was straightforward. An employer required to compensate all workers who were injured on the job, fell sick, or were laid off would take great pains to prevent the occurrence of such contingencies. Factory owners would invest in safety equipment and sanitation devices and would attempt to regularize employment, all in order to avoid paying compensation. Commons wrote in the 1920s, "It is amazing what business can accomplish when it has a sufficient inducement. If there is enough money in it, it can accomplish more than any other agency."[7]

Commons and his colleagues arrived at this position by focusing on what they perceived as the misplaced incidence of human costs in industry. When a machine breaks down in a factory, the reformers argued, the owner is responsible for fixing it. Indeed, industrialists take good care of their physical capital because regular maintenance is less costly than repair or replacement. The reformers suggested that one of the central problems of the new industrial order was that employers were not responsible for their human capital. When a worker fell sick, even with an occupational disease, the employer assumed no responsibility. He simply found another worker and shifted the cost of health care and lost wages onto the sick worker's family and onto the community. Nearly the same held true for accidents. A worker injured on the job occasionally could recover damages from his employer in court. But legal victories of this sort were more the exception than the rule, and, even when they did occur, they often involved interminable delays, small recoveries, and high litigation costs. The family of an accident victim could easily fall into destitution before a settlement was reached.[8] Unemployment was another hazard, the reformers claimed, that was mainly a problem of industry, not the fault of the average worker. Why then were the workers, their families, and the community (which had to dole out poor relief) forced to bear the heavy costs of unemployment?

In one of the early books on social insurance published in the United States, Charles Henderson posed a number of these questions. He acknowledged that the railroads had begun, without legal compulsion, to establish funds to compensate their injured workers. But although these schemes were advanced for their time, he observed, the public would soon find them intolerable:

> At a time when the narrow legal provisions of the employers' liability law were generally regarded as substantially equitable, when it was supposed that each employee individually assumed the ordinary risks of a hazardous occupation in the act of accepting employment and was expected to provide for himself out of wages and savings, it was an almost revolutionary step for an employing corporation to admit that this ethical and legal rule was not satisfactory, and to make at least partial provision for indemnities by associated action with the workmen and by making considerable contributions to the funds. But as the community comes to discover and accept the principle

of "professional risk," that a business which does not make good, as far as indemnity in money can do it, the losses of human energy as well as of broken and worn out machinery, is parasitic and socially bankrupt, the schemes of the railroad companies will no longer satisfy the reason and conscience of men.[9]

Henderson's notions of "professional risk" and of social parasitism were extremely important. In fact, Commons chose to quote the second half of the passage above in his review of Henderson's book for *The Economic Bulletin*.[10] AALL reformers agreed that the employer who shifted the costs of accidents, illness, and unemployment to the worker and to society was a social parasite. These were costs of doing business which, like all other costs of doing business, should be borne by the capitalist.[11]

What Henderson identified as a source of social parasitism during the progressive era, economists today call a market failure. According to orthodox economic theory, a properly functioning labor market should efficiently allocate costs associated with employment through the employer-employee wage contract. The AALL reformers understood this, but they denied that the wage contract worked fairly in most cases. They claimed that employers, because of vastly superior bargaining power, practically dictated the terms of employment to workers. Henry Seager wrote in 1915 that "the unequal bargaining power between employer and employe and the resulting absence of a free and voluntary contract between them in the determination of labor conditions is being more and more recognized."[12]

To support their view that meaningful wage contracts were often nonexistent, the AALL reformers pointed to the absence of wage premiums for hazardous work. Rational workers in competitive markets should, according to economic theory, exact higher wages for hazardous employment than for nonhazardous employment requiring a comparable level of skill. But the reform-minded economists of the AALL claimed that in reality workers often failed to secure such premiums. The theory of wage differentials, Seager explained at the Association's first annual meeting,

> is so plausible that it might still be accepted if it were not completely disproved by the facts. Wage statistics show, however, that wages in dangerous trades are little, if at all, higher than in comparatively safe employments. Knowing this to be the case, it is not difficult to perceive the defect in the reasoning of the older writers.

The defect, he continued, proceeded from two facts: first, that members of the working class were generally ignorant about the risks associated with particular jobs; second, that individual laborers tended to regard themselves as invincible to risks that they recognized affected others. The essential reason for the absence of compensating wage differentials, Seager asserted in another address, "is that each individual thinks of himself as having a charmed life."[13] Commons offered similar arguments about the irrationality of workers; and Adna F. Weber, the Association's first secretary, wrote in 1902 that the idea of compensating differentials was a "legal fiction" with "no basis in fact."[14]

Recent scholarship in economic history has called into question some of the AALL reformers' assumptions about the absence of compensating wage differentials.[15] The important point here, however, is not whether such differentials existed but whether pivotal Association reformers believed they did. And the evidence on this point is clear. Adherents of an institutionalist approach to economics, they generally dismissed wage premiums and even implicit wage contracts as fictions.

In their campaigns for legislation, many of the Association's leaders ignored the wage contract issue altogether. They assumed that severe inequalities between employers and employees—not only in bargaining power but also in information and even rationality—so perverted the institution as to place it largely beyond the reach of legislative remedies. They interpreted the adverse consequences of industrial hazards as social costs of industry that were not internalized in the wage contract; and they held that the state should force employers, consumers, or both to bear at least part of the expense. Seager insisted, "It is for the benefit of consumers that production is carried on and they should be made to pay—so far as this can be measured in money—what goods cost in maimed bodies and shortened lives as well as what they cost in hours of work and used-up raw materials."[16]

Although many modern economists would view the problem differently, the AALL reformers conceptualized the market failure in question as an externality problem. An externality is a cost of production for which a producer assumes no direct financial responsibility.[17] The classic example is pollution. A producer who pollutes the air imposes a cost on society: individuals who live in the vicinity of the polluting factory suffer lower air quality, unpleasant odors, and perhaps ill health. But none of these costs shows up on the producer's bottom line. In the case of an externality, then, Adam Smith's invisible hand—which mysteriously guides producers to advance social wealth even while their only intention is to advance their own personal wealth—is absent. The free market will never inhibit a producer from producing an externality, such as pollution, even though the externality adversely affects social well-being.

Industrial hazards, like pollution, are consequences of production. They differ from pollution in that the principal victims—the workers—are engaged in implicit contracts with producers at the time of injury. The

AALL reformers believed, however, that such a distinction was practically irrelevant. They argued, first, that the wage contract usually did not represent a true bargain and, second, that the costs of a given industrial hazard fell not only on the worker but also on two parties not present at the bargaining table—namely, the worker's family and the community that doled out poor relief. Employers had little interest in preventing accidents, illness, and unemployment because, quite simply, they did not have to pay for them. This was the reformers' argument. "Somebody must pay for the conservation of the nation's human resources," Commons declared in his book *Industrial Goodwill*. "If left to demand and supply, the most valuable resources are not conserved."[18] The AALL reformers did not use the term "externality" because it did not yet exist within the lexicon of economic theorists. But the term (and the formal economic problem it identifies) is useful in characterizing how the reformers interpreted the problem of industrial hazards and worker insecurity.

Across the Atlantic, the British political economist A. C. Pigou was defining the externality principle in theoretical terms at about the same time that the AALL reformers were employing it in rough form to justify social insurance.[19] Pigou was not the first economist to suggest the problem, but he treated it more extensively and more definitively than anyone had before.[20]

Without actually using the term "externality," Pigou characterized the phenomenon as a case in which the private net product of an investment exceeded its social net product—that is, when "uncharged disservices are rendered to the general public" as a result of private activity. He pointed out that this occurs whenever the use of an automobile wears down the surface of public roads or the erection of a tall building crowds neighborhoods and adversely affects the health and welfare of residents. To further illustrate his point, he quoted George Bernard Shaw, who suggested that the producers of intoxicants should "be debited with what it costs in disablement, inefficiency, illness, and crime, with all their depressing effects on industrial productivity, and with the direct costs in doctors, policemen, prisons, etc., etc., etc." Pigou himself argued that the most shocking illustration of the principle involved not the distillation of spirits but the employment of women in factories, especially just before and after childbirth. There can be no doubt, he wrote, "that such work often carries with it, besides the earnings of the women themselves, grave injury to the health of their children."[21]

According to Pigou, the one agency capable of correcting such divergences between social and private net product was the state, and the most obvious tools at its disposal were bounties and taxes. He cited a contemporary tax on gasoline, whose revenues were earmarked for service of the roads, as a good example of how the taxing power could be employed to mediate externalities.[22] Another example, which he deemed "ingenious," was the National Insurance Act of 1911, which provided for compulsory health insurance in Britain. "When the sickness rate in any district is specially high, provision is made for throwing the consequent abnormal expenses upon employers, local authorities or water companies, if the high rate can be shown to be due to neglect or carelessness on the part of any of these bodies."[23] Presumably, this procedure would discourage neglect and carelessness by making such behavior costly to the perpetrator.

Although Commons made no explicit mention of Pigou in his work on the subject of social insurance, the idea of utilizing taxation to counteract—or prevent—social externalities encapsulated his approach to reform. He explained in a 1919 address to government labor officials that workers' compensation was effectively a tax on the employer. "We tax his accidents," proclaimed Commons, "and he puts his best abilities in to get rid of them."[24] Commons sought to internalize a specific category of externalities—namely, hazards such as accidents, disease, and unemployment—through social insurance. Indeed, internalization was the central objective of the AALL in all its campaigns for social insurance. If employers could be taxed for hazards that occurred within their workplaces, then the costs of these hazards would no longer be external to the employers' income statements. The internalization of these costs—what Commons conceived of as the harnessing of the profit motive—would transform previously careless or callous employers into models of conscientiousness and decency. Workers' compensation, he contended, was best "described as a kind of social pressure brought to bear upon all employers in order to make them devote as much attention to the prevention of accidents and to the speedy recovery from accidents as they do to the manufacture and sale of the products."[25] This was the special meaning that nearly all of the proponents of social insurance at the AALL ascribed to the term "prevention."

Though Commons was not alone in advancing the internalization principle, he deserves special attention. Not only did he develop the principle more precisely and more extensively than did any of his colleagues, he also applied it more broadly—to institutions as wide-ranging as slavery and the business cycle. During the teens, his fascination with the promise of internalization proved highly contagious among AALL reformers; and it significantly influenced the way in which they formulated and marketed their legislative program. Indeed, the Association's distinctive approach to prevention can hardly be understood apart from the irrepressible John R. Commons.

The economist Wesley Clair Mitchell once described Commons as "a bewildering person."[26] Few of Commons' friends would have disagreed, for he was as full of contradictions as he was full of energy. On break from Oberlin College in the mid-1880s, Commons learned of Herbert Spencer's supposedly scientific claim that it was physically impossible to pitch a curve ball. An incredulous John and his brother Alvin decided to test the theory. They began to use a wall of their log house as a backstop, and soon John learned to throw a variety of curves. Spencer apparently had overlooked two simple facts—that baseballs have stitched seams and that there is friction in the air. "Ever after," Commons wrote nearly fifty years later about the episode, "I looked for the omitted factors, or the ones taken for granted and therefore omitted, by the great leaders of the science of economics. That was how I became an economic skeptic."[27]

Commons was an anti-intellectual intellectual—an academic economist (a theorist, no less) who revered "practical men" and regularly derided the social role of intellectuals.[28] Throughout his life, he struggled to combine theory and practice, economic analysis and social reform. In 1888, as a graduate student in economics at Johns Hopkins, Commons received instructions from Professor Ely to investigate building and loan associations and to become a case worker for the Baltimore Charity Organization Society. Commons found both experiences thrilling. His letters to his mother from the period, as he himself recalled, were "flaming with enthusiasm over this 'new' political economy. It was my tribute to her longing that I should become a minister of the Gospel . . . I was a social worker as well as a graduate student in economics."[29]

A few years later, Commons became secretary of the new American Institute of Christian Sociology. Inspired by the Social Gospel movement, he earnestly called for the blending of scientific analysis, social activism, and Christian morality. In 1898 he declared:

> The Christianity of to-day is being tested. Is it to withdraw and give up, or is it to ground itself on solid facts and exhaustive knowledge, and then to build itself into the whole life of man, and into the social institutions which encompass man? Is it to abdicate, or is it to show the way to the kingdom of heaven?[30]

Remnants of this fervent idealism still remained when Commons composed his autobiography over thirty years later. Surveying his life's work as a reformer, he wrote simply, "I was trying to save Capitalism by making it good."[31]

Christian sociology and German historicism constituted the two most powerful influences on Commons' early intellectual development. Although he learned about both from Professor Ely, he inherited from his mother, Clara Rogers, the evangelical fervor necessary to link the two. Clara was an ardent Presbyterian—Commons called her "the strictest of Presbyterian Puritans"—and she had always hoped that John, her eldest son, would become a minister. Before the Civil War she participated in the underground railroad to help fugitive slaves get to Canada, and she remained a loyal Republican forever after. She also became a staunch prohibitionist, her zeal being so infectious that John gave his first vote for president to the Prohibitionist candidate in 1884, even though Clara herself refused to abandon the Republicans. Three years later mother and son launched a publication associated with the Anti-Saloon League. Through these activities, they formed a spiritual bond. Although John ultimately entered the university rather than the church, he remained a vital reformer for life.[32]

After leaving (but not completing) graduate school and accepting a teaching position at the University of Indiana, Commons began to consider real-world economic problems from both a theoretical and a historical perspective. Of particular importance was the problem of unemployment. In 1893, when he published his first theoretical text, *The Distribution of Wealth*, joblessness loomed large in the eyes of academics and social reformers alike. The economy was falling into another severe depression. Popular economists spoke nervously about the crisis of overproduction, while socialists spoke confidently about the crisis of capitalism.

Commons chose to look at the big picture. He observed in his *Distribution of Wealth* that job insecurity, if viewed from a broad historical perspective, was a relatively new phenomenon. Slaves had never had to worry about lack of work. Although they enjoyed no personal or political freedoms, they usually had food and shelter. The introduction of slavery had marked a big step forward in human civilization, according to Commons, because it "laid the foundation for the recognition of the right of life for the lowest of men." The institution of slavery made possible the production of enormous new wealth and, significantly, "made it the direct interest of the ruling classes to preserve the lives of their slaves, and to furnish them with a regular supply of their wants, equal, at least, to their minimum of subsistence."[33]

Commons' interpretation of slavery was an early application of the internalization principle. Slavery supposedly internalized the costs of individual welfare by giving the ruling classes a financial stake in the health and efficiency of the lower classes (that is, their slaves). The abolition of slavery and the advent of political freedoms for the lower classes re-externalized the welfare of those classes.[34] Of what use, Commons asked, were all the new freedoms if the modern worker "is denied the right to produce for himself the food, and clothing, and shelter that preserve life, and that make liberty worth having? The rights to life and liberty are practically denied to labourers in our day, by virtue of the denial of the right to employment."[35]

Commons' answer in 1893 was to re-internalize worker welfare. He proposed giving the politically free, but economically insecure, worker a common-law right to employment. He sought to make unemployment, like industrial accidents, actionable. "The new courts that shall enforce the right to employment," he wrote, "are courts of arbitration, created by the government, and empowered to compel employers to submit to investigation and to suffer punishment for violating the right of employés to work. No man is to be discharged for any cause except inefficiency and dishonesty. Wages, hours of labour, conditions of work, are to be adjudicated by the courts."[36] If fired without reasonable cause, the worker presumably would have the right to sue the employer for damages. This would provide the employer with special incentives—indeed it would virtually compel him—to regularize employment. Commons' common-law method of guaranteeing a right to work combined the internalization principle with simple coercion. It was his answer to the pervasive problem of arbitrary discharge.[37]

In the aftermath of the politically charged 1890s, Commons abruptly abandoned his concept of a common-law right to work and increasingly turned to social insurance as the best remedy for unemployment and other industrial hazards. He never fully accounted for this shift in either his personal or his professional writings. It is reasonable to assume, though, that a combination of factors—including intense pressure from the political right, an improved macroeconomic situation, and growing public concern about the plague of industrial accidents—contributed to his reorientation.

C ommons began his foray into the field of social insurance by exploring arguments for workers' compensation (accident insurance). It was a curious place to begin since a common-law remedy for industrial accidents, comparable to his earlier proposal for unemployment, already existed in the form of employers' liability law. Many nineteenth-century students of tort law regarded it as an effective deterrent to employer negligence. But at the dawn of the new century, Commons joined a growing number of critics who claimed that the common-law remedy was no longer effective—if it ever had been effective—in preventing accidents.[38]

Commons differentiated between legal hazards associated with accidents and the accidents themselves. The contemporary system of employers' liability law, he argued in 1909, created an employer interest in minimizing legal hazards but not in minimizing accidents. The distinction meant that an employer might invest in expensive legal services in order to avoid payment, rather than in safety devices to prevent accidents. He suggested that under a system of workers' compensation, which assured automatic payments to accident victims and which superseded negligence law, expensive lawyers would be of little help. The employer's only means of lowering costs would be to lower the number and severity of accidents and related medical costs.[39]

It was during his involvement in the Pittsburgh survey of industrial conditions in 1907 that Commons first began to consider social insurance as a vehicle for preventing accidents. He found the work of the safety experts at United States Steel fascinating and began to contemplate how other firms could be encouraged to follow U.S. Steel's example. "I decided then," he wrote in his autobiography, "that a workman's accident compensation law, if properly drawn, would cost nobody anything . . . It was amazing to me how greatly accidents could be prevented by safety experts if employers could be furnished an inducement to hire them for the purpose. I wanted all employers to be compelled by law to pay accident compensation as an inducement to accident prevention."[40]

Commons began to translate these ideas into practice when he helped to draft Wisconsin's Industrial Commission statute a few years later. His first objective in writing the 1911 law was to unify accident insurance and accident prevention. Earlier policymakers, he claimed, wrongly maintained a barrier between the two. He contended that industrial safety should no longer be enforced through criminal prosecution and that the employer should no longer be assumed innocent until proved guilty. Instead, the employer should be held responsible for all accidents, taxed when they occurred, and offered help in preventing them. "Why not shape up legislation and administration on this assumption?" he asked. "Let the state furnish him with the inducements by taxing him proportionate to his employees' loss of wages by accidents, and then employ safety experts, instead of crime detectives and prosecutors, to show him how to make a profit by preventing accidents."[41]

The Wisconsin Industrial Commission was charged with administering the state's new workers' compensation program. Commons served on this commission from 1911 to 1913, during which time he refined his ideas about the preventive value of workers' compensation. One case from his three-year tenure particularly impressed upon him the extent to which the internalization principle could be carried. The case involved a drunken truck driver who was killed when he fell off his truck. The driver's widow sought compensation through the state's workers' compensation law, and the Industrial Commission's three members were responsible for determining whether an award should be granted. Commons and fellow Commissioner James D. Beck initially wanted to deny compensation on the grounds that the truckdriver's death was the result of his own gross negligence. But the third commissioner, Charles H. Crownhart, disagreed, dismissing his colleagues' moralism as socially inefficient. He was a lawyer, who Commons described as "the most astute and far-seeing lawyer of all whom I have known." Crownhart argued that because employers had the power to prevent accidents like this one by refusing to employ drunkards, the employer in this case should be held responsible and forced to pay compensation. In essence, Crownhart advanced a standard of strict liability. The state, he thought, should impose the costs of various contingencies not on the parties most responsible for them but instead on the parties best able and most likely to prevent them. In the case of accidents, employers were best positioned to ensure prevention. Crownhart convinced Commons, and the commission awarded the widow $3,000.[42]

Crownhart's legal reasoning was not unique. During the early years of the progressive period, a number of legal scholars who wrote about workers' compensation touched on the ideas of strict liability and internalization. Ezra Ripley Thayer provided such an analysis in the 1916 *Harvard Law Review*:

> A community which accepts the principle of such an act cannot be expected to find anything intrinsically unreasonable in the doctrine which seeks to throw upon the undertaker the full responsibility for harm arising from his enterprise, on the theory that the business should bear its losses in the first instance regardless of fault or proximate cause, and that ultimately, like any other overhead charge, they would fall on the consumer.[43]

Clearly, Commons and his colleagues at the AALL had not invented the internalization concept. It was almost intuitive to Crownhart, and it was explicitly present in some legal scholarship of the period. What distinguished the economists at the AALL was that they refined the concept, adapted it for public consumption, and made it the basis of a political movement for social insurance.

Once workers' compensation laws began being enacted and enforced after 1910, the AALL reformers displayed great confidence that their earlier predictions about accident prevention actually were being realized. Commons claimed that after the Wisconsin law went into effect, the accident rate fell[44] and many accident victims got better faster. He illustrated the latter claim by citing a case in which a company voluntarily spent at least $300 for a surgical operation on one of its injured workers, an operation the worker would never have been able to afford on his own. The company paid for the procedure in order to speed the worker's recovery and thus prevent permanent incapacity, which might have cost the company as much as $2,000 or $3,000 in long-term compensation payments. In other words, the existence of a workers' compensation law induced the company to invest in the worker's physical well-being.[45]

Between 1911 and 1918, 38 states, the federal government, Puerto Rico, Alaska, and Hawaii enacted workers' compensation laws. The AALL played an important role in many of the campaigns, and its influence was decisive in Wisconsin and New York and at the federal level. Although most of the state laws did not meet the AALL's strict standards for what a model workers' compensation statute should look like, the AALL reformers were emboldened by their political triumphs. They regarded workers' compensation not as a final objective but as an opening wedge into campaigns for unemployment and health insurance.

Commons noted in his autobiography that he began to extend the principle of internalization from accidents to unemployment in 1921.[46] In fact, he had begun to do so considerably before that. He and John Andrews floated the idea that unemployment insurance would prevent unemployment as early as 1914.[47] Commons' confusion over dates is understandable, however, since it was Andrews who took the lead on the issue of unemployment during the teens. Andrews assumed responsibility for writing most of the Association's "Practical Program for the Prevention of Unemployment in America" and for drafting the chapter on unemployment in the text he jointly authored with Commons, *Principles of Labor Legislation*.[48] Andrews' enthusiasm for the internalization principle is readily apparent in his correspondence from the period. In 1915, for example, he wrote to the labor activist Margaret Dreier Robins, ". . . I do not believe that we can force employers to regularize their own business unless we use the device of insurance to bring about cooperative pressure of a financial nature."[49]

As in the case of accidents, the basic idea was that unemployment constituted an inappropriately externalized cost of production. The reformers of the AALL therefore believed that much joblessness would be prevented through the application of a suitable tax levied as part of an unemployment insurance program. They took it for granted that employers would either self-insure or pay unemployment insurance premiums that were experience-rated. In either case, employers would feel a financial penalty for every worker they laid off.[50]

Although unemployment insurance marked a sharp departure from Commons' earlier proposal for a common law right to work, it still resembled that earlier plan in one essential way. In a 1923 article called "Unemployment—Prevention and Insurance," Commons maintained that an unemployment insurance law would provide workers with "a right of action" against their employers which would compel the latter to "stabilize their work."[51] A right to compensation, he seemed to suggest, would have almost the same effect in reducing unemployment as would a common-law right to work.

AALL reformers introduced unemployment insurance bills into the Massachusetts legislature in 1916 and into the Wisconsin legislature throughout the 1920s. None of these attempts proved successful. Still, it is of interest that during the early Wisconsin campaigns, Commons carried the internalization principle to an entirely new level. He claimed that unemployment insurance would be effective not only in preventing joblessness but in smoothing out the business cycle as well. Believing that sharp downturns were consequences of overexpansion during booms, he thought that downturns could be eliminated or at least moderated if the preceding expansions could be controlled. During booms, he argued, employers expanded recklessly because there was too little cost associated with overexpansion. If employers were faced with a compensation liability for every worker laid off, they would have to be more careful about expanding in the first place; and their bankers would be more cautious about loaning them funds for rush projects. "The overexpansion of credit is the cause of unemployment," he wrote in 1923, "and to prevent the overexpansion of credit you place an insurance liability on the business man against the day when he lays off the workmen."[52]

Commons' fascination with unemployment insurance became most pronounced during the early 1920s. His dramatic (some might say fanciful) rhetoric about stabilizing business cycles suggests the depth of his commitment. During the teens, however, Commons and the other AALL reformers' greatest passion was for compulsory health insurance. It was a passion that emerged gradually and perhaps inexorably as they attempted, year after year, to grapple with the colossal issue of ill health in the American workforce.[53]

The AALL reformers first began to apply the internalization principle to health in 1913. Previously, they had promoted laws and regulations directed against specific industrial diseases, such as phosphorus and lead poisoning. But they ultimately saw the limits of this strategy. "Gradually we realized," Andrews wrote to a correspondent, "that the best way to protect health in industry was not to attempt to forbid a shifting catalog of specific acts, but in some way to bring pressure to bear upon the employers so as to make them personally keen to keep down sickness."[54] Since workers' compensation had been so effective in reducing the incidence of industrial accidents, they reasoned, the logical next step was to amend workers' compensation statutes to cover occupational diseases as well as accidents.[55] The AALL initiated a vigorous campaign for such amendments in many states, and they met with limited success in Massachusetts and California.[56]

It soon became clear, however, that this strategy too was flawed. Although many diseases were associated with industrial work, very few were traceable definitively in an individual case to a worker's employment. Such cases were so rare that insurance companies in Massachusetts did not raise their premiums for workers' compensation coverage after the state Supreme Court ruled that the term "personal injuries"—as used in the workers' compensation statute—included occupational diseases as well as accidents.[57]

The final step in the AALL's evolving approach to disease prevention was compulsory health insurance. In November 1915 Andrews commented to a friend at the Life Extension Institute that "varying insurance rates with the incidence of sickness will offer the same incentive toward prevention which has been offered by workmen's compensation in the field of accident prevention." On the very same day he informed the social reformer Lillian Wald of the "vigorous educational campaign" that the AALL was just then undertaking to promote health insurance. "We want every body interested in public health," he wrote, "to be keenly alive to the great possibilities for sickness prevention contained in such a measure as that we are proposing."[58]

Andrews assumed that industry was responsible for a large proportion of sickness in the United States—perhaps as much as 40 percent, if the employer's contribution as specified in the AALL's model health insurance bill is any indication—and he assumed that much of that sickness was preventable. His friend and mentor John Commons described health insurance as a "sickness-tax on industry."[59] Commons, of course, had used nearly identical language to describe workers' compensation and unemployment insurance. What differentiated the health insurance tax was that it would be levied not only on the employer (40 percent) but also on the worker (40 percent) and on the public (20 percent), according to the theory that each party had a role to play in reducing the incidence and severity of illness. Still, while acknowledging that disease prevention would require a joint effort, the AALL reformers directed most of their propaganda to highlighting the employer's special role. Henry Seager explained his support for health insurance by stating, "The best way to get the attention of our American employer is to reach for his pocketbook." For William Hard, a magazine editor and an active AALL member, health insurance was a "nice little automatic machine" for regulating employers.[60]

Despite their enthusiasm, the AALL reformers fared little better with their health insurance bills than they did with their unemployment insurance bills. They came close in California and even closer in New York, but victory remained beyond their grasp.

I n the case of illness, as in the cases of accidents and unemployment, the primary goal of the American Association for Labor Legislation was prevention, not relief. Commons once declared, "There is, of course, also a philanthropic purpose in [health insurance], but that philanthropic purpose is really secondary. The main purpose is the business purpose of making sickness-prevention profitable."[61] He noted as well that compensation was of secondary importance in the unemployment insurance plan he proposed for Wisconsin: the plan placed benefit levels so low that the unemployed worker could expect to receive no more than enough to pay his rent.[62]

A few of the Association's members expressed unease about Commons' strategy of elevating the goal of prevention above all others. During a general discussion at a 1913 AALL conference on social insurance, I. M. Rubinow, an expert on the topic, announced that if he were a worker he would have very mixed feelings about what was going on there. Everyone seemed concerned only about what form the insurance payments should take, he said, but the worker "is primarily interested not in how the payments will be made, but in how much they will amount to."[63]

By the early 1930s, this question of prevention versus relief divided the movement for social insurance into two conflicting schools. Commons and Andrews at the AALL stood their ground as advocates of prevention. Rubinow and Abraham Epstein, meanwhile, had broken away to form a rival group, the American Association for Old Age Security (AAOAS).[64] Rubinow and Epstein stressed compensation, not prevention, as the primary purpose of social insurance. In practice, the difference between the two groups translated into two different methods of funding social insurance. The AALL reformers and their allies endorsed experience-rated mutual insurance and company reserve funds (self-insurance), which they thought would maximize incentives for prevention. Rubinow and Epstein at the AAOAS supported pooled insurance funds without experience rating in order to assure the highest possible compensation levels for all victims of industrial hazards.

The historian Roy Lubove has characterized the debate between the AALL and the AAOAS in the 1930s as one centering on the issue of income redistribution. Whereas Commons and Andrews sought to provide economic security with as little redistribution as possible, Lubove argues, Rubinow and Epstein were deeply committed to the dual goals of income maintenance and redistribution.[65] Another way to characterize the debate would be to say that Rubinow and Epstein aimed to redistribute *income* while Commons and Andrews hoped to redistribute the *social costs of industry*. As a result, the former pair focused on the scale of benefits while the latter fixated on the method of financing and the proper assignment of liability.

Whatever the case, the question of redistribution simply was not central to the progressive-era debate. Only in the depths of the Great Depression did redistribution of income become a pivotal political issue. During the progressive era, when there was no mass constituency demanding generous social welfare programs, the AALL approach to social insurance was not so much a conservative alternative to income redistribution as it was a somewhat idealistic effort to perfect flawed capitalist institutions. This is not to deny that the AALL approach was inherently conservative. With only a few exceptions, the leading members of the AALL sought to save capitalism by reforming it. They were against redistribution to the extent that they hoped their social policies would preempt socialism and, presumably, the large-scale redistribution of income and wealth that socialism would entail. Within the general context of capitalism, however, the central issue for Commons and his allies at the AALL was not *more or less* redistribution of income (as it would be in the 1930s), but rather *better or worse* capitalist institutions.

Commons in particular had great faith in the efficacy of capitalists and the power of the profit motive. If only that power could be harnessed to solve the worst problems associated with capitalism—poverty and economic insecurity—society would flourish. As early as 1908, Commons asked an audience at the New York School of Philanthropy to imagine what would happen if charity were turned over to an anti-poverty syndicate that would earn half of all the savings that accrued to society from its work. A labor force saved from the grasping claws of poverty, he suggested, would be healthier, more secure, and far more efficient. Presumably, the syndicate would prosper on the economic security of the workers.[66] Throughout his professional life, Commons searched for ways to modify capitalist institutions so as to provide employers with a financial interest in the welfare of their employees.

Though he did not have the modern word to describe it, the concept of the externality was central to Commons' understanding of capitalism's flaws and of economic institutions as diverse as slavery and the business cycle. The most threatening externality of all, he thought, was the insecurity of the individual worker. "The seriousness of the problem of poverty today is not that there are greater numbers of poor, relative to the total population, than ever before," he wrote in 1894, "but that greater numbers are constantly on the verge of poverty."[67] By 1919, when capitalism appeared under siege by radical attacks, Commons declared at a convention of government officials that "unless the capitalistic system begins to take care of the security of the laborer, begins to make jobs us secure as investments, then there is a serious question, with the growing number of wage earners who have no capital of their own, whether that system can continue to exist."[68]

According to the AALL reformers, the central problem—the source not only of widespread insecurity but also of a profound distrust of capitalism—was that the labor market failed to internalize the costs of workers' social welfare. The reformers' solution was to assure worker security by internalizing those costs, and they identified compulsory social insurance as the ideal vehicle. They hoped to put in place a new legal framework that would, in Commons' words, "make capitalism protect itself at its weakest point."[69]

5

Kindling a Flame
under Federalism

T he leaders of the American Association for Labor Legislation confronted their most formidable challenges in attempting to translate
policy concepts into actual legislation. They faced not only a wide
array of influential, and often hostile, interest groups but also numerous
institutional and ideological barriers. In most cases, their legislative campaigns proved exceedingly complex, requiring careful planning, a delicate
political touch, and plenty of good luck.

Historians, too, have found progressive-era politics to be a daunting
subject and have faced formidable challenges of their own in attempting
to untangle the history of the period.[1] Of the many historiographical de-
bates focused on progressive reform, perhaps the most contentious concerns the question of agency: who, if anyone, constituted the driving force
behind the enactment of reform legislation? Of particular interest has
been that subset of legislation regulating the conduct of business, such as
antitrust prosecution, food and drug inspection, rate regulation, worker
rights, and workplace standards.

Although several schools of thought have emerged to address the
agency question, there is still surprisingly little consensus about the answer. Some historians, for example, highlight the reform work of middle-
class professionals, while others insist that corporate elites orchestrated
the campaigns. Still others maintain that reform legislation resulted from
the clash of competing interest groups.[2] One reason for the ongoing disagreement is that the various schools have tried to explain too much.
Because the politics of progressive-era reform were so complex, most
broad generalizations about agency have tended to prove unsatisfying.

An alternative approach is to consider the reform process in four relatively distinct phases. This reduces the risk of overgeneralization and, at the same time, helps to pinpoint the role of the AALL. The first phase of the reform process involves boundaries and boundary setting. Some reform proposals will never receive serious consideration because institutional or ideological boundaries render them unacceptable.[3] John Commons' concept of a common-law right to work, for example, never went anywhere because it was inconsistent with American political values at the time. Similarly, few reformers or legislators ever seriously contemplated a national workers' compensation system because most assumed that such a system would violate the constitutional doctrine of federalism.

The second phase of the process is policy initiation. Typically, it comprises a series of steps that precede legislative consideration of a reform: a problem is identified and perhaps publicized; then a solution is proposed that is both institutionally and ideologically viable; and, finally, draft legislation is written and offered up to official policymakers. Although one person or group rarely orchestrates all of the steps, very often one party, such as the AALL, takes a leading role.

The third phase of the reform process commences when a legislature begins considering a proposal or when such consideration is assumed to be imminent. In this legislative phase, competing interest groups typically become visible, alternative bills appear, and the original bill is replaced altogether or at least subjected to revision.

Assuming that the reform is enacted, the final phase of the process is implementation. Somewhat surprisingly, the politics associated with implementation may be very different from those associated with initiation and passage. In some cases, the same business people who strenuously oppose a regulation during the legislative phase may become deeply involved in trying to shape the regulatory environment after enactment.[4]

As this chapter and the three after it demonstrate, the American Association for Labor Legislation played a pivotal role in policy initiation.[5] The organization's leaders sometimes exerted decisive or near-decisive influence in the legislative phase of a campaign, and once or twice they seem to have extended the phase-one boundaries of acceptable reform. In a few cases, the AALL reformers became involved in implementation.[6] Their greatest contributions and influence, however, consistently appeared in phase two. At root, the AALL reformers were agenda setters. They eagerly identified social problems, crafted plausible solutions, and drafted model legislation. Although they ultimately lost many more political battles than they won, they proved remarkably successful at raising and defining vital issues of public concern.

T he Association's first major reform initiative, which targeted a grue-some occupational disease, turned out to be one of its most exciting. The campaign was already in full swing when, on November 16, 1910, John Andrews penned an urgent letter to the organization's president, Henry Farnam. The letter concerned President William Howard Taft's support for the AALL's phosphorus-match bill." I am not sure that I told you in a previous letter," Andrews wrote,

> that I think we ought to keep the fact that President Taft strongly endorses our bill entirely confidential for the present. Of course, we make no secret of the fact that the purpose of our bill is to prohibit and not to tax, but it might not be advantageous to have it known so far in advance that the President of the United States definitely states that he favors the use of the taxing power for a non-revenue purpose.[7]

Farnam, one of Taft's personal friends, had been corresponding with the president about the proposed legislation since May. He and his colleagues at the AALL sought to eliminate the use of phosphorus in the match industry because it constituted a terrible hazard to match workers, pro-ducing a disfiguring and sometimes fatal condition called phosphorus ne-crosis, or "phossy jaw." After a thorough consideration of the legal op-tions, the leaders of the Association concluded that the best way to accomplish their objective was to tax phosphorus matches out of exis-tence from the federal level. President Taft privately endorsed the tax method in early November 1910 and, despite Andrews' warning about public statements, announced his support for the measure in his annual message on December 6.[8]

Behind Andrews' concern about President Taft publicly acknowledging that the tax was intended for non-revenue purposes lurked the question of constitutionality. The most obvious and conventional way to abolish the use of phosphorus in the match industry would have been to employ the states' police powers. Andrews and his colleagues were skeptical of this approach because they understood that nearly all the states would have to participate if the prohibition were to be effective and because they doubted that such uniformity was possible. No state wanted to be the first to enact such legislation. The prime substitute for phosphorus in the production of matches was sesquisulphide, a compound which both cost a bit more than phosphorus and was slightly inferior in quality. State legislators feared that if they prohibited phosphorus without the coop-eration of their neighbors, match producers in their states would choose to leave rather than begin to produce nonpoisonous sesquisulphide matches.

Many match manufacturers, including executives at the Diamond Match Company, shared the politicians' concerns. They regarded the prospect of uneven state regulation as highly unfavorable. When, in January 1911, Diamond and seven other match manufacturers urged match distributors across the nation to support the AALL's federal bill, they warned of "the undoubted demoralization to the wholesale and retail match trade of this country that would result from the serious consideration and enactment of [state bills]." A month earlier, several match manufacturers had explained in a letter to the House Ways and Means Committee that state legislation would "introduce chaotic conditions into the whole trade situation" and would put the match factory in a state that prohibited phosphorus "at a most serious disadvantage as compared with its competitors in other States having no such prohibition."[9]

On the basis of arguments like these, which evoked the problem of degenerative competition among the states, the AALL reformers deemed state legislation infeasible, and they looked to the federal government for a remedy. Though the Constitution denied the federal government police powers over state matters, it granted the federal government a very broad authority to tax. Miles Dawson, counsel to the AALL, reasoned that since a substitute for phosphorus existed, a federal tax on phosphorus in excess of the difference in cost would force manufacturers to abandon phosphorus in favor of the substitute. Because such a tax would not violate the letter of the Constitution and because it almost certainly would secure the desired result, the AALL championed it as the perfect policy instrument for removing phosphorus from the match industry.

The struggle for the match law served in many ways as a trial run for the Association. Soon its leaders would be pursuing larger objectives—minimum-wage and maximum-hours laws for women and children, workers' compensation, unemployment insurance, and health insurance. Through their phosphorus campaign, the AALL reformers tested the outer limits of federalism, a problem that would plague them repeatedly in their struggles for social welfare reform. They strengthened lines of communication with other reform organizations, with labor unions, with business leaders, and with state and federal government agencies; and they gained invaluable experience in lobbying Congress. The project provided them an opportunity to fine-tune their organizational apparatus and to attract the public's attention to their cause and its money to their coffers. When the battle finally ended, nearly three years after it began, the Association moved on confidently—perhaps overconfidently—to a much broader legislative agenda.

T he modern match industry dates back to 1827 when an Englishman, John Walker, invented the friction match. Alanzo D. Phillips secured the first U.S. patent for a friction match in 1836. The year before, the strike-anywhere match had attracted national attention with the advent of the Loco-Foco Party: when the lights went off unexpectedly at the conclusion of a New York Democratic nominating convention, insurgents against Tammany Hall dramatically lit their loco-foco matches, permitting them some illumination as they founded a renegade political party.

Within a generation, Americans had distinguished themselves in the art of match making. William Gates Jr. and W. J. Harwood patented the world's first continuous match machine in 1854. The new mechanized process provided for remarkable increases in output. By 1860, the Census identified 75 match factories, which collectively had $361,750 of invested capital and employed 648 women and 604 men. *Scientific American* estimated that these factories produced 35.7 million matches a day. After the Civil War, productivity continued to rise even as the structure of the industry underwent substantial changes. The combination of a federal tax imposed near the end of the war which favored large producers, a long period of depression and intense price competition, and, especially, continuing technological developments that offered substantial scale economies all contributed to a dramatic process of industrial consolidation. The total number of match factories in the country fell to 37 in 1880, the year that the Diamond Match Company was founded. By 1910, when AALL reformers first introduced their legislation to prohibit the use of phosphorus in the industry, there were 16 match factories left in America, producing a total of about 500 million matches a day.[10]

The one major blemish on this enormously productive industry was the plague of phosphorus necrosis. A physician in Vienna diagnosed the first case of the disease in 1838; but no cases were reported in America until 1855, when Dr. James B. Wood identified nine serious cases in New York City. From that point on, American newspapers reported periodically on the discovery of phossy-jaw cases and the plight of the victims.[11]

The disease attacked most violently at the mouth and jaw. When exposed to phosphorus, teeth rotted away (sometimes completely) and the jaw bone deteriorated, often in a honeycomb pattern.[12] To those who witnessed the disease first hand, what was most striking was probably the smell. Many victims suffered not only from the direct physiological effects of the disease but from the social alienation that usually resulted. "The odor from the suppurating bone," Andrews explained, "is something that can not be described in words, and is so nauseating that dentists and physicians alike prefer to avoid patients afflicted with advanced cases of 'phossy jaw.' " Surgical removal of one or both jaws, the only known treatment, left victims horribly disfigured. Andrews noted that most men who underwent the surgery immediately grew beards to cover up their mangled faces but that women possessed no comparable cosmetic option.[13]

Several American match manufacturers attempted to eradicate or at least to minimize the disease by refusing work to people with bad teeth, hiring dentists to examine their workers, and thoroughly ventilating their shops. Diamond Match's historian claimed that by aggressively implementing such preventive practices, the company completely eliminated phosphorus poisoning from its leading factories.[14] There is no corroborating evidence, however, that these procedures contributed in any way to controlling the disease.[15]

Real progress against phosphorus poisoning in the match industry originated in Europe. Swedish inventors were the first to produce a nonpoisonous "safety match." The only problem was that it had to be struck on a specially painted strip on the side of the box in order to ignite, whereas the phosphorus match could be struck anywhere. A more significant advance occurred in France, where the match industry was a state monopoly. Because the French government assumed responsibility for paying the health expenses of state workers, its treasury faced a disturbingly high health benefit bill for match workers who fell victim to phossy jaw. In the hope of cutting costs, state officials subsidized the search for a phosphorus substitute. A breakthrough came in 1897, when Henri Sévène and Emile David Cahen discovered sesquisulphide, a compound that could be used to produce nonpoisonous, strike-anywhere matches. Although sesquisulphide matches cost a bit more, the French were satisfied and immediately terminated production of phosphorus matches. Sévène and Cahen secured a U.S. patent on the new formula in 1898 and quickly sold it to Diamond Match for $100,000.[16]

Two countries, Finland and Denmark, had prohibited the use of phosphorus in the match industry over twenty years before the discovery of sesquisulphide. Switzerland, the Netherlands, and Germany imposed comparable prohibitions once a suitable substitute had been found. But Britain and several other industrial nations continued to resist such legislation for fear of damaging their match export trade. Unless almost all nations agreed simultaneously to prohibit phosphorus-match production and trade, those that refused would stand poised to dominate the remaining global market. Competition among nations thus posed a problem similar to what competition among the American states would later present to the AALL.[17] In fact it was this problem—degenerative competition—which motivated the establishment of the AALL's parent organization, the International Association for Labor Legislation (IALL).

As early as 1881, the Swiss had attempted to interest other European governments in the concept of cooperative international labor legislation.

Their pleas went unanswered until 1890, when the Kaiser suddenly embraced the idea and convened a conference in Berlin.[18] Though the Berlin conference produced no international agreements, subsequent meetings in Brussels (1897) and Paris (1900) gave birth to the IALL. The IALL had no official authority; yet, as Malcolm Delevingne has explained, it was a "matter of common knowledge . . . that the action of the Association had considerable official backing."[19]

In September 1903, two IALL commissions petitioned the Swiss government to convene an international conference dedicated to abolishing two evils—the employment of women at night and the use of poison phosphorus in the match industry. The Swiss gladly complied and invited sixteen governments to send representatives. The fourteen that accepted dispatched diplomats to Berne in 1906. All fourteen signed the convention against night work for women, but only seven consented to the phosphorus-match treaty.

The IALL reformers knew they had scored but a partial victory. Nearly all the nations that signed the match treaty risked nothing, having already prohibited or severely restricted phosphorus-match production within their own borders prior to 1906. All but one of the nations still producing poison matches refused to sign. Over the following decade, many of the governments that at first resisted the convention ultimately acquiesced. But, in the meantime, phosphorus matches continued to circulate widely in the global marketplace.[20]

Back in the United States, the AALL followed in the footsteps of its European parent organization and launched a national campaign for the prohibition of phosphorus matches.[21] John Andrews and his mentor, John Commons, recognized in early 1909 that an essential first step would involve a thorough investigation of the American match industry.[22] In a report for the *Bulletin of the Bureau of Labor,* Andrews compiled extensive material on fifteen of the sixteen American match factories,[23] and he uncovered 82 cases of phosphorus necrosis as a result of intensive investigation at three of the factories. Throughout his report Andrews emphasized one simple theme: so long as match producers relied on phosphorus, no amount of precaution or sanitation could eliminate the dread disease. The only remedy was the complete prohibition of phosphorus matches.[24]

Andrews' report succeeded in attracting considerable attention to the problem of phosphorus poisoning,[25] and the AALL reformers were quick to exploit their success. Henry Farnam wrote to President Taft urging action, and Andrews began working with Congressman John J. Esch of Wisconsin and Miles Dawson, a prominent New York attorney and actuary, to prepare a federal bill that would eradicate phossy jaw. In fact,

Andrews had contacted Dawson even before completing his investigation for the Bureau of Labor and asked him to report on the most effectual and constitutional means for prohibiting phosphorus matches.[26]

Dawson set to work at once to put together a comprehensive legal brief on the subject. After dismissing as unworkable the prospect of obtaining individual state prohibitions,[27] he focused on three possible ways to attack the problem at the federal level and outlined them in a six-page letter to Andrews on May 17, 1910. The three methods Dawson identified included (1) a direct prohibition of phosphorus-match production and sale; (2) a prohibitory tax on all phosphorus-match production; and (3) a broad application of the federal treaty-making power.

With regard to the possibility of direct prohibition, Dawson acknowledged that the federal government had no direct authority over intrastate production and sale. It is clear, he wrote, "that it cannot be extended under our constitution, to cover by act of congress the prohibition of the manufacture of such matches for sale within a state or of the sale of the same within a state." Only commerce between states, with foreign nations, and within the territories, the possessions, and the District of Columbia came under the regulatory jurisdiction of the federal government. "Accordingly, we are of the opinion that a direct prohibition would not be constitutional."[28]

The second option, that of levying a prohibitive federal tax, appeared far more promising. "This method of prohibition," Dawson counseled, "has been held to be constitutional in several cases, and it is now well settled that the intention of the government in levying a tax will not be questioned, even though the taxation results and is intended to result in the destruction of a business." The key precedent was *McCray v. United States* (1904), in which the Supreme Court upheld a prohibitive federal tax on artificially colored oleomargarine. Although the tax effectively destroyed an industry, including parts of it not in any way involved in interstate commerce, the court ruled that the tax itself was a constitutional application of federal power. As long as the tax was constitutionally exercised, it could not be invalidated on the basis of results stemming from its use, even if those results seemed to infringe on powers conferred exclusively to the states. In an earlier precedent, *Veazie Bank v. Fenno* (1869), the court ruled favorably on a federal law that taxed state banknotes out of existence, thus fostering the formation of a uniform national currency. Dawson concluded from these cases that the taxing power might be an extremely effective instrument for the AALL's purposes, and he recalled the words of Chief Justice Marshall in *McCulloch v. Maryland*, (1819) "that the power to tax involves the power to destroy."[29]

Dawson considered as a third possibility whether the AALL's objective could be accomplished through the federal government's treaty-making power. He explained that the Constitution placed no explicit limits on this power, which occasionally had been held to override state laws. The Court ruled in *De Geofroy v. Riggs* (1890) that as long as the treaty-making power was not used "to authorize what the constitution forbids," then "it is not perceived that there is any limit to the questions which can be adjusted touching any matter which is properly the subject of negotiation with a foreign country." On the basis of this decision, Dawson entertained the following idea: if the federal government entered into a treaty banning phosphorus-match exportation (which was certainly within its constitutional power), it might then argue before the court that it was necessary to prohibit all phosphorus-match production in order to terminate the export of poison matches. He acknowledged, however, that the argument probably would fail to impress the Supreme Court.[30]

While intrigued by the potential of the treaty-making power, Dawson found the tax method most compelling. Indeed, he and others who drafted the Association's phosphorus match bill adopted a prohibitory tax approach. They derived not only the means but also much of the language directly from the Oleomargarine Act of 1902.[31]

After several weeks of consultation with Andrews and Dawson, Representative Esch introduced the bill into the House of Representatives on June 3, 1910, and it was sent directly to the Ways and Means Committee.[32] The bill, H.R. 26540, would levy annual taxes on manufacturers, wholesale dealers, and retail dealers of phosphorus matches ($1,000, $500, and $50, respectively) as well as an additional (prohibitory) tax of one cent per hundred matches on manufacturers and importers.[33]

Andrews had hoped to secure hearings before the Ways and Means Committee as early as June 8, but this proved impossible. During the second week of June, while Andrews was away in Wisconsin, Esch notified Dawson that he had arranged with committee chairman Sereno E. Payne for hearings to be held around the 21st or 22nd, but he warned that the match bill was likely to encounter stiff resistance in the committee. Esch wrote:

Mr. Payne gave me no assurance that the Committee would act favorably thereon, although he recognized the necessity of legislation of some kind to diminish if not prevent the ravages of disease resulting from the manufacture of these matches. I think his attitude is a result of doubt as to the advisability of exercising the taxing power to destroy an industry. You know how bitterly Congress has been assailed for exercising the taxing power to practically putting oleomargarine out of business. This is the weak spot in the matter.

Opposition to the use of the taxing power as a regulatory device was a major obstacle to the AALL's campaign, but it was by no means the only one. The AALL staff learned a few days later that officials at the Diamond Match Company were working to postpone the hearings. When Andrews arrived back from his short trip to Wisconsin, all ready to attend the hearings in Washington, he discovered that Diamond's attorney had succeeded in postponing them until December.[34]

Top executives at Diamond Match were not hostile to federal legislation on the phosphorus issue. On the contrary, as early as March 1909, the president of the company had informed an agent at the Bureau of Labor that Diamond would gladly permit other American manufacturers to use its sesquisulphide patent on equal terms if the federal government prohibited the use of poison phosphorus in match production.[35] Diamond had several interests in eliminating phosphorus from the industry. A disease as terrible as phosphorus necrosis disturbed many reformers and some consumers; and since Diamond was by far the largest and most visible match manufacturer, it was the most susceptible to public pressure on this issue.[36] Diamond, moreover, owned the patent on sesquisulphide and had done more experimental work with the compound than had any other American company (with the possible exception of the East Jersey Match Company, which already was producing and selling a nonpoisonous match). Even if Diamond agreed to share the patent, as it promised, it would enjoy a significant experience-based advantage with the new compound over most of its competitors. Having closely followed developments in Europe, high-level Diamond officials believed that some sort of phosphorus legislation was inevitable. They knew that state legislation would be chaotic and thus detrimental to their interests, particularly because they catered to a national market. Federal legislation was therefore the best alternative for them, and their goal quickly became to secure the most favorable conditions possible. Delaying the Ways and Means hearings for six months simply gave them more time to prepare their case.[37]

Though Diamond's highest priority was to head off state legislation, the company was also interested in securing a return on its $100,000 investment in the sesquisulphide patent. Its leaders probably came to regard the AALL as a useful lever for both objectives. Andrews, for his part, was concerned about playing into Diamond's hands and expressed reservations to his friends about advancing its interests. But he sorely wanted the legislation and knew that the industry leader's support was crucial. Thus when Diamond offered other match manufacturers the opportunity to purchase rights to its sesquisulphide patent, Andrews helped to close the sale by convincing the independent producers that some sort of legislation was inevitable and that federal legislation was preferable to state legislation.[38]

With Andrews' assistance, Diamond persuaded most of the major independents to submit to its terms for sharing the sesquisulphide patent by mid-October. Collectively, Diamond plus the eight independents that agreed to purchase licenses produced 188.823 billion matches in the year ending June 30, 1910. Since Diamond originally paid $100,000 for the patent, it required each licensee to pay a part of that amount proportional to its share of the total collective match output. Manufacturers that produced in excess of their allotment would have to pay Diamond four-tenths of a cent for every additional thousand matches. Diamond's strategy of levying a substantial tax on any firm whose output grew at a rate faster than that of the nine firms collectively would, in effect, help to enforce maintenance of the existing market status quo.[39]

The eight independents that consented to Diamond's terms did so because they feared that a federal prohibition on phosphorus matches was imminent. In the absence of a licensing agreement, such legislation would give Diamond a monopoly on match production for the duration of its patent (for about five more years).[40] Diamond executives drove a hard bargain, but they chose not to push their competitors to the wall because they realized that passage of the Esch bill would be far less likely if Diamond appeared to be exercising monopoly powers.

To the surprise of top Diamond executives, the licensing agreement they regarded as so reasonable struck outside observers as too tough. The new president of Diamond, Edward Stettinius, tried to preempt public attacks by sending a conciliatory letter to the independents on December 11, just five days before the first Ways and Means hearing was scheduled to occur. He indicated his concern that passage of the federal bill might be delayed because of persisting fears about monopoly, and he offered unilaterally to improve the terms of the licensing agreements. He eliminated the four-tenths-of-a-cent excess-production levy as well as a clause specifying acceptable packaging procedures. He promised, moreover, that Diamond would grant licenses to other manufacturers on equally favorable terms in the future.[41] AALL reformers were pleased with Diamond's concessions. Although they hoped to exact still more concessions in the future, they felt confident that the new agreements would help to remove the monopoly issue from the debate in Congress.

A t the start of the hearings on December 16, Congressman Esch introduced a revised version of the bill, H.R. 29469.[42] Every witness represented either the AALL or the match industry. Only one, an independent match manufacturer who had refused to sign the agreement with Diamond, opposed the bill. Yet the committee's membership remained skeptical. Many members expressed either uncertainty or downright hostility toward the proposed legislation. They doubted that industrial regulation beyond the bounds of interstate commerce was an appropriate function for the federal government, and they were uneasy about using the taxing power for this purpose. Representative John Dalzell, a Pennsylvania Republican, insisted that the bill would "use the taxing power of the Federal Government for a purpose for which it was never intended, to destroy an industry or to regulate sanitary measures that belong entirely to a State."[43] Other committee members remained suspicious about what Diamond Match stood to gain from such legislation and whether Congress would be handing Diamond a monopoly on a silver platter.

Miles Dawson undertook for the AALL the delicate task of explaining why he and his colleagues were seeking federal rather than state legislation and why they sought to utilize the taxing power rather than the interstate commerce power. As for the issue of jurisdiction, he suggested that state legislation would lack the uniformity essential to competitive fairness; that the prospect of having to secure laws in dozens of states and territories, all of which were in competition with the others, was a formidable and perhaps impossible task; and that the states enjoyed no authority to endorse or reject the international phosphorus treaty, a document that the AALL reformers believed the U.S. government should sign. In short, he characterized potential state legislation as impractical, infeasible, and ineffectual.

Exercise of the federal government's interstate-commerce power, Dawson further explained, would prove inadequate. He suggested that because match production did not offer increasing returns to scale (a dubious economic assumption on his part), most producers of poison matches would find it profitable to sell their output within their own respective states, even if they were not allowed to send the matches across state borders. Only a prohibitive tax, targeting all phosphorus-match production, would solve the problem, he asserted.

The idea that a regulatory tax violated the spirit of the Constitution struck Dawson as ludicrous. Had not the founding fathers envisioned the tariff as a means to regulate imports? He reminded the committee that the Constitution defined the federal taxing power much more broadly than the other enumerated powers. The choice of using the taxing power in this case was not an extreme one, he asserted, but simply the right one:

> We are not before your committee or before Congress with any intention of asking that the power of the United States Government under the Constitution be stretched in an unusual manner, or that something be done that would

be even reasonably doubtful. We are not here as "progressives," or "insurgents," or "anti-insurgents," or in any capacity at all except as people who think they have found a perfectly constitutional means, already tried and thoroughly tested in the courts and passed upon, which will clearly accomplish the object for which we are here.[44]

Soon after Dawson completed his presentation, George Gordon Battle and William Fairburn of the Diamond Match Company offered their own testimony in favor of the bill. They said that the prospect of state legislation was potentially disastrous for the industry and that they had offered to share Diamond's patent on the use of sesquisulphide with their competitors. Battle, Diamond's counsel, noted as well that a group of nine American match companies, including Diamond, were petitioning the president for special tariff consideration should the federal legislation go through.[45]

The one witness who testified against the bill was John T. Huner, the owner of a small match factory in Evergreen, Long Island. Huner had refused to sign a licensing agreement with Diamond, and he proved to be a very colorful witness. He accused Andrews of doctoring his report for the Bureau of Labor and of lying about the condition of Huner's factory. He charged that the whole campaign against phosphorus matches was a scheme concocted by Diamond. "Well, I have been making matches for six years," he proclaimed, "and I have never had a case of necrosis in my factory. I have never had any sickness in my factory at all. In fact, we are all healthy there." Diamond, he maintained, had been trying to destroy him for a long time, and this was just the latest example of its machinations.[46]

Huner's fierce attack impressed several committee members and, indirectly, executives at Diamond. Over the following month and a half, the latter heeded suggestions from AALL reformers to give further ground on the patent issue. At a meeting in late December, Andrews convinced the president of Diamond to assign the company's patent rights over the sesquisulphide process to disinterested trustees. Ultimately, Diamond agreed to abandon the patent altogether. By this point, company officials presumably were more concerned about the prospect of losing the Esch bill than about recovering part of the cost of their patent from the independents.[47]

Even Diamond's cancellation of the patent, however, did not completely silence the bill's critics who feared monopoly. An AALL staff member in Washington noted that there existed a general impression that the Association was working to advance the interests of the match trust. Many critics charged that Diamond had a secret process—a nonpoisonous substitute for phosphorus that it had yet to unveil. Once Congress attached a prohibitive tax to phosphorus matches, they claimed, Diamond would spring this secret process and undercut all of its competitors. Members of the Ways and Means Committee were hardly immune to these fears. Payne told Farnam privately that he was sure Diamond was hiding such a process. AALL reformers tried to recruit independent match manufacturers to disabuse Ways and Means members of their suspicions, but without success.[48]

The phosphorus-match bill was effectively tabled in 1911 but received another hearing before the Ways and Means Committee in January 1912.[49] In the meantime, Andrews and his colleagues intensified an already strong lobbying campaign. They secured endorsements from major organizations (such as the American Federation of Labor and the National Association of Manufacturers); they provided copy on phosphorus poisoning to journals and newspapers; they sent circular letters directly to Ways and Means members; and, most important, they launched a direct-mail campaign to build grassroots support. AALL staff sent out many thousands of letters urging sympathetic citizens to communicate with their representatives in Washington (and with committee members in particular). The mailings paid off. Esch informed Andrews on several different occasions that Ways and Means members and other congressmen were being flooded with letters, telegrams, and petitions from constituents demanding favorable action on the match bill.[50]

In addition to overseeing the lobbying campaign, Andrews had worked hard throughout 1911 to bolster his case against phossy jaw and against Huner. At the 1912 hearing, he not only produced a living victim of the disease—thus graphically illustrating its grotesque effects—but also adduced hard evidence proving that Huner had lied when he described his factory as disease-free.[51] Complementing Andrews' performance, the new president of the AALL, Henry Seager, attempted to ease committee members' fears about employing the taxing power as a regulatory instrument. "I do not believe that your anxiety that this matter will serve as a precedent for other legislation of this sort is well grounded," Seager asserted, "because I can not conceive . . . of another situation like this that is likely to come up." It was an intriguing tactic—to sell the bill on the grounds that it would not establish a precedent. Although committee members gingerly sidestepped Seager's argument at the time, many would later adopt it as a primary justification for supporting the bill.[52]

Once again, John Huner was the only witness who aggressively testified against the proposed legislation. He renewed his attacks on Diamond Match and even accused Andrews of having used the phosphorus campaign as a personal moneymaking scheme.[53] But the balance of opinion on the committee turned against Huner. Two weeks after the hearing, Seager reported to Farnam that it had gone extremely well. "Certainly Huner made all kinds of an ass of himself," he explained, "and nothing is to be feared any longer from his opposition."[54]

While a number of Committee members continued to express concerns about abuse of the taxing power, the biggest obstacle standing between the bill and the House floor at this point was simple partisan pride. Esch, its sponsor, was a Republican in a now Democratically controlled House of Representatives. To assure Democratic support, Esch was forced to allow sponsorship of the proposed legislation to pass to a Democrat, Representative William Hughes of New Jersey. Hughes formally introduced the new match bill (H.R. 20842) on February 26, 1912. The only substantial differences from Esch's bill were the doubling of the tax rate per hundred phosphorus matches from 1¢ to 2¢, and the exclusion of a provision that would have assessed licensing fees on all match manufacturers—a provision that had been very unpopular with the committee. Esch gladly accepted the changes.[55]

By a vote of eleven to eight, the Ways and Means Committee agreed to report out the Hughes bill favorably on March 4; and on March 11 Hughes transmitted H.R. 20842 with an accompanying committee report to the House.[56] The report acknowledged the committee members' reluctance to use the taxing power, but it suggested that they chose to support the bill because they believed it represented a rare case. This was precisely the point Seager had raised at the January hearing. According to the report, the Committee believed "that their action in favorably recommending passage of H.R. 20842 will not serve as a precedent for the general employment of the taxing power to correct objectionable features of industries."[57] In addition to borrowing Seager's argument about precedent, the authors of the report relied heavily on contributions from the AALL. They quoted long passages from Andrews' testimony, cited the legal authority of Dawson and other AALL lawyers, and reprinted the memoranda of the Association's legislative committee, which alone occupied nearly five pages of the eleven-page report.[58]

The bill reached the House floor on March 28. Although fears of monopoly resurfaced, the debate focused on the propriety of employing the taxing power as a regulatory instrument. It divided along partisan and, especially, sectional lines. Representative Charles Bartlett, a Georgia Democrat, sounded the rallying cry for his contingent of the Democratic Party:

Mr. Chairman, Democratic doctrine, as I understand it, is that the power to tax can be used only for the purpose of raising revenue for the Government, economically administered. The Democratic Party has been in the past, ought to be in the present, and should be at all times opposed to pretexts and shams like this, which proposes, under the use of the great power of the Government, to tax, not because it needs revenue [but?] to accomplish some purpose which ought to be accomplished under an exercise of the police power of the State and not the taxing power of the Federal Government.

He added mockingly, "Are we to gather from all over this vast country, the men who become sick or diseased from labor, a vast list, not to protect them in their work, but to destroy the property which the people have the right to make and the business which they have the right to carry on?"[59]

Bartlett's comments betrayed one of the critical subtexts of the debate—the tariff controversy. Southern Democrats and their Jeffersonian predecessors had fought against tariffs, an early form of regulatory taxation, since the founding of the republic. They had done so mainly for reasons of economic self-interest, but they typically justified their position on the basis of high principle. True believers in the southern cause were hardly ready to give in on that principle now. Representative Thomas Upton Sisson of Mississippi exhorted, "I cannot conceive of any position that Democrats can take on this bill, if they vote for it, unless they at the selfsame time apologize to every Republican for the last hundred years for the position he has been taking." Sisson, a committed Democrat, must have winced as his words were greeted with applause from the Republican side of the chamber.[60]

Though sectional divisions were strong, they were not absolute. One of the bill's most determined defenders was Edward Saunders, a Democrat from Virginia. Saunders rejected the claim that it was inconsistent for a Democrat to support the bill. He was no less of a Democrat, he asserted, for giving the bill his vote. And what of those Democrats who feared the establishment of a precedent? Saunders was not sympathetic. "Precedents like these," he declared boldly, "will prove the salvation of the Republic."[61]

Hughes, the representative from New Jersey who sponsored the bill, also felt compelled to defend his status as a good Democrat. With an obvious sense of indignation, he exclaimed,

I know that human beings are suffering in this country today, and I say that the strongest indictment that ever was written against the Democratic Party is the indictment written against it by the gentleman from Georgia and the gentleman from Mississippi when they say that it is against the principles of the Democratic Party to reach down and pick up suffering humanity and stop disease and distress. [Applause.]

When they can convince me that the Democratic Party stands for that proposition, as they put it, when they thus rule me out of the party I will leave the Democratic Party willingly, and I will take everything with me in the Democratic Party that is worthy of taking. [Applause.]

Bartlett quipped, "You will leave some people who are much more worthy than you are."[62]

When the debate ended and the votes were counted, the bill passed overwhelmingly, 162 to 31 (with 8 answering "present" and 190 not voting). Its advocates at the AALL were both proud and pleased. While they knew that the bill still required Senate approval and a presidential signature to become law, they were confident that it would easily pass these remaining hurdles. Andrews explained to Esch on March 16 that he had spoken with Senator Henry Cabot Lodge (a prominent Massachusetts Republican), who assured him that he and John Sharp Williams (a Mississippi Democrat) were working diligently in support of the bill in the Senate Finance Committee. As expected, that committee reported the bill favorably and without amendment on April 2, and the proposed legislation arrived on the floor of the Senate the very next day.[63]

The debate in the Senate chamber proceeded much as it had in the House. The two main protagonists were Joseph Bailey, Democrat from Texas, and Henry Cabot Lodge. Once again, the immediate issue of poison matches faded into the background as these two men and their competing conceptions of the Constitution clashed at center stage.

Bailey bluntly attacked the bill as a sham and an assault on states' rights. "The whole purpose of it is, under the guise of a Federal tax, to invade the States and usurp their police powers." He reminded his southern colleagues that the same "false pretense" had been used a decade before to discriminate against southern oleomargarine in favor of the dairies. The Constitution, he pleaded, was not something to be interpreted and twisted in any way the legislators thought expedient. It was the law, the foundation of the republic, and it had to be respected. "Mr. President," he concluded, "it may seem a heartless thing to say, but I think it would be better to close up every match factory in the United States and go back to the time when our fathers struck fire from flint than it would be to practice this kind of fraud upon the Constitution of our country."[64]

Lodge, in response, did not blithely dismiss his opponent's constitutional concerns, but he insisted that extreme circumstances compelled action in this case. Phosphorus necrosis was a devastating disease, and uniform state legislation probably could not be secured to eradicate it. "Unless the United States Government acts," he warned,

we shall be put in a position that no other civilized nation on earth occupies; that, owing to technicalities under the Constitution, we can not put a stop to an industry which has the most hideous results on those engaged in it, and we are the only civilized nation that can not do it.

The Government has the power of taxation. I admit that it should be very rarely used for any such purpose as this; but it has been used. It was used in the case of oleomargarine.[65]

A fellow Republican, Senator Albert B. Cummins of Iowa, reinforced Lodge's position by observing that the Constitution had evolved significantly since 1789. Had the founding fathers been faced with the issue, he speculated, they probably would have agreed with Senator Bailey. "But now for more than 100 years the Constitution of our country has been otherwise interpreted and otherwise applied."[66]

The Senate passed the bill without a roll-call vote. Perhaps many senators felt the same way as Senator Weldon B. Heyburn, who reported that he had received an enormous volume of mail urging him not to oppose the bill. "I am not going to oppose legislation that will meet this difficulty," he said.[67] President Taft signed the phosphorus-match bill into law on April 9, 1912. He subsequently sent the pen he used on that occasion to the AALL as an acknowledgment of their crucial role in the bill's passage. Upon receiving the memento, Andrews joked to Seager, "There are only two tooth marks in the pen holder, which leads me to think that the bill was signed without very much anguish."[68]

The new statute, Public Law 118, imposed a tax of 2¢ per hundred matches made of poison phosphorus, to go into effect on July 1, 1913. It completely prohibited the import and the export of poison phosphorus matches as of January 1, 1913, and January 1, 1914, respectively. The tax law produced few surprises. It rendered the production of phosphorus matches unprofitable and effectively eliminated them from the American market. As a number of match manufacturers had anticipated, nonpoisonous foreign matches became comparatively more attractive to American consumers once phosphorus matches disappeared from store shelves, and, consequently, match imports increased substantially.[69]

One footnote to the story deserves mention: John Huner's match factory burned down during the summer of 1912. Although he had claimed in his testimony before the Ways and Means Committee that he would never accept any substitute for phosphorus, he apparently changed his mind once the match law was enacted. Huner blamed the fire in his factory on a new nonpoisonous formula that he was forced to resort to as a result of the law. A few years later, Farnam noted to a friend that Huner was again in business and marketing nonpoisonous matches under the trade name "Our Darling."[70]

The story of the phosphorus-match campaign yields a number of insights, two of which stand out as particularly important. The first concerns questions of motivation and agency. Several prominent proponents of the so-called corporate liberal thesis, especially James Weinstein, have characterized the movement for industrial regulation in the early twentieth century as a virtual conspiracy hatched by far-seeing corporate elites. Powerful business leaders, who regarded centralized regulation as a means toward market rationalization, "were able to harness to their own ends the desire of intellectuals and middle class reformers" for a changed society.[71]

Careful examination of the match campaign confirms that corporate executives at Diamond Match were eager to secure federal regulation of their industry in the hope of stabilizing and rationalizing the match market. But it cannot be said that corporate elites fully controlled the political process or that progressive reformers were the servants (witting or unwitting) of these elites. Leaders of the AALL initiated the reform process, and Diamond executives subsequently joined them in pursuing federal legislation against phosphorus matches. Both parties made significant concessions along the way. Most notably, Diamond ultimately yielded to pressure from the AALL and relinquished its patent on the sesquisulphide process.

The relationship between Diamond and the AALL was grounded on complementarity of influence. Without the Association reformers as partners, Diamond officials would likely have found it impossible to overcome pervasive fears about their motives—fears stemming from deeply ingrained American beliefs about the sanctity of the independent entrepreneur and the perniciousness of industrial giants.[72] The economists who ran the AALL lent to the campaign academic respectability and at least the semblance of disinterestedness. Without Diamond, however, the self-appointed experts at the AALL may well have been dismissed by policymakers (as was so often the case in other campaigns) as soft-headed do-gooders and intellectuals who knew little about the industry they sought to uplift. The rather uneasy alliance between corporate leaders at Diamond Match and reform-minded academics at the AALL was, contrary to the implications of Weinstein's analysis, a very real one—a successful adaptation to America's peculiar political environment.[73]

The second important insight that emerges out of this study concerns the impact of federalism on the development of industrial regulation and social welfare policy. In their campaign to eradicate phossy jaw, the AALL reformers sought federal legislation because they doubted that uniform state legislation was possible and because they believed that nonuniform state legislation, if it emerged at all, would create chaos in the marketplace. They urged employment of the taxing power because they recog-

nized it as the only available vehicle for bypassing constitutional constraints on federal regulatory power.

The match act thus represented an important crack in the wall of federalism. That crack remained small during the progressive era. AALL
reformers filed the tax method away and, in subsequent campaigns, pursued the idea of uniform state legislation as the best means of avoiding
the pitfalls of federalism. Their experience with Congress between 1910
and 1912 apparently had convinced them that use of the federal taxing
power as a regulatory device was simply too controversial to be applied
to anything more significant than margarine or matches.

Over the next generation, however, the crack widened substantially—
especially as reformers and policymakers discovered new ways of utilizing
the taxing power to circumvent federalism. The process culminated with
passage of the Social Security Act in 1935. Besides creating a national
system of old-age insurance, the act put in place a clever tax-offset scheme
that compelled the states to enact unemployment insurance laws. As in
the match campaign, constitutional considerations largely determined the
choice of policy instruments. When, in 1934, Secretary of Labor Frances
Perkins had asked for advice about how to satisfy the Court in structuring
a federal social insurance program, Justice Harlan Fiske Stone told her
knowingly: "The taxing power of the Federal Government, my dear; the
taxing power is sufficient for everything you want and need."[74]

6

The Gendered Politics of Protection

I n 1906, the same year that seven European nations signed a treaty prohibiting the sale and production of poison phosphorus matches, fourteen nations signed a convention prohibiting night work for women. These agreements emerged at a conference in Berne, Switzerland, and the agency instrumental in securing them was the International Association for Labor Legislation. Although the two prohibitions targeted different problems, both aimed to protect workers who, presumably, were unable to protect themselves.

The United States was not a party to either accord, but many progressive reformers followed the European developments closely and hoped to replicate them in America. The AALL's successful campaign for a federal law taxing phosphorus matches out of existence reflected its commitment to the need to protect workers, especially unskilled workers, against hazardous materials. Other leading reform groups, particularly the National Consumers' League (NCL) and the National Women's Trade Union League (WTUL), pressed hard for the regulation of hours and wages for women. While the AALL did not stand at the forefront of this movement, many of the Association's leading reformers—Andrews, Osgood Andrews, Seager, Freund, and Commons—conceived of restrictions on hours and wages as among the most important social reforms in need of enactment.[1]

As in the match campaign, proponents of hours and wages legislation faced formidable constitutional obstacles. State and federal courts frequently struck down protective laws as inappropriate uses of the police power on the grounds that they violated constitutional and quasi-constitutional principles—such as liberty of contract, prohibitions against class legislation, and due process. According to constitutional authorities, a state legitimately could employ its police powers in contravention of these principles only when a definite public purpose was involved. The state, for example, might impose a quarantine and even shut down businesses in order to protect the public against the spread of a contagious disease

Theorists at the AALL argued that virtually all labor contracts were imbued with a public purpose because every wage bargain affected the general welfare of the workforce. But the courts disagreed. Most judges maintained that the wage contract normally should stand free of state interference. Only in extraordinary circumstances, where the public safety was directly at risk or where workers faced especially dangerous conditions, was such interference legitimate. One major exception related to the protection of workers regarded as wards of the state—a category including not only children and the mentally disabled but also adult women. Numerous judges ruled that the protection of working women served a public purpose regardless of the nature of the employment involved. Women, they maintained, suffered distinctive frailties and served a unique maternal role in society, which justified special protection by the state.

The reality of this constitutional distinction between men and women created a dilemma for the AALL reformers. They agreed that women were weaker than men and that female workers required protection more urgently than did most male workers. Yet they also believed that all workers, men and women alike, deserved legal protection against overwork and underpay and that the protection of both sexes served a public purpose. While they were anxious not to miss the opportunity opened by the courts to enact laws protecting women, they remained painfully aware that to do so meant abandoning, at least temporarily, the larger fight for gender-neutral protective legislation.

This chapter examines the role of leading AALL reformers in the progressive-era movement for minimum-wage and maximum-hours laws. Nearly all of the wage and hour bills that were considered or enacted during the period were designed to protect women workers. The primary advocates were leaders of women's reform organizations, such as Florence Kelley and Josephine Goldmark of the NCL and Margaret Dreier Robins and Alice Henry of the WTUL. Much has been written about these women, their organizations, and their ideas on the purposes and merits of protective legislation for female workers.[2] The fundamental conflict between their philosophy of protective feminism and the competing philosophy of equal-rights feminism is another issue that has fascinated many historians.[3]

Little, however, has been written about organizations such as the AALL that were not exclusively women's organizations (or devoted exclusively to women's issues) but that nonetheless participated in the campaigns for protective legislation for women workers. The principal (primarily male) AALL reformers who took part in these campaigns did not identify completely with either the protective feminists or the equal-rights feminists. They espoused a distinctive, hybrid approach to protective legislation which emerged out of their traditional assumptions about innate gender differences, their conservationist views about the nation's labor force, their relatively advanced views about the role of married women in that labor force, and their predisposition to working within (rather than outside) the highly restrictive judicial environment of the period. Their approach by no means defined the progressive movement for protective legislation, but it marked an intriguing, if ultimately untenable, middle ground between the two dominant schools of feminism which did.

At the heart of the AALL reformers' dilemma over whether to support gender-neutral or gender-specific protective labor laws stood a complex constitutional debate concerning the states' police powers. Ernst Freund, a renowned legal scholar and active member of the AALL, defined the police power in a treatise on the subject as a form of government coercion that "restrains and regulates, for the promotion of the public welfare, the natural or common liberty of the citizen in the use of his personal faculties and of his property."[4] He explained that it was proper for a state to employ its police power to regulate dangerous activity that was beyond the control of potential victims, but improper to use it to protect individuals against themselves. "The right to choose one course of action even to the extent of incurring risks, where others are not concerned, is a part of individual liberty."[5]

Motivated by this aversion to protecting individuals against themselves, judges invented the liberty-of-contract doctrine in the latter part of the nineteenth century and used it to strike down numerous protective labor laws.[6] They assumed that workers engaged freely in labor contracts, which determined hours and wages and other working conditions, and that the state had no right to interfere. Yet the doctrine was not absolute. Some industries, such as the railroads, merited regulation because they were quasi-public in nature. An overworked and tired railroad worker might be a danger not only to himself but also to passengers, who were members of the general public and not parties to the contract between worker and employer. For this reason the courts validated legal limitations on hours for railroad workers.

Another twist in the liberty-of-contract principle was the legitimacy of protecting a class, rather than an individual, against its own acts. According to Freund, "if a portion of a class are willing to accept unsanitary conditions competition will force others to do the like, and . . . this portion must be restrained for the benefit of the class as a whole."[7] In the landmark *Holden v. Hardy* decision of 1898, the United States Supreme Court recognized the need to protect a class of workers from itself. It upheld a gender-neutral Utah eight-hour law covering miners and certain types of metalworkers (virtually all of whom were men) on the grounds that these workers were involved in extrahazardous employments and that they were the victims of inferior bargaining power.[8] Though many progressive reformers refused to acknowledge it, the majority in *Holden* stated plainly that the Utah law would not have been valid if it had applied to all workers. Only the extreme conditions of underground mines and metal works, the Court held, justified the limitation on hours in these employments.[9]

Seven years after *Holden,* in the landmark *Lochner* decision of 1905, the Court struck down a gender-neutral New York State statute limiting the working hours of bakers. The majority did not consider the baking of bread to be an unhealthful trade.[10] Frustrated reformers initially dismissed *Lochner* as an anomaly. According to Henry Seager, "it shows merely that the justices know more about the mining industry than they do about present-day city bakeshops."[11] With time, however, the AALL reformers recognized that *Lochner* was a critical precedent, not an anomaly.[12]

The *Lochner* decision affirmed the principle suggested in *Holden*—that states could employ their police powers to protect workers without regard to sex only in extraordinary circumstances, when public safety was at risk or when workers were subject to particularly dangerous conditions. To protect workers under less extreme conditions served no public purpose and thus constituted a violation of the employer and employee's so-called liberty of contract.[13] Like many of his colleagues, Seager bristled at the Court's rigid doctrinal formulation. "Such a view," he wrote in 1907, "seems to me to make 'liberty' not a reasonable object of desire but an irrational fetish."[14]

The most significant exception to the liberty-of-contract principle related to the special status of women workers. Freund wrote in his treatise on the police power, "It is clear that some special provisions regarding women's labor are justified by their greater physical weakness."[15] He explained that "reasonableness" was often an essential justification for exercise of the police power, and he identified the existence of a consensus of legal opinion about the reasonableness of a ten-hour maximum for women workers to ensure their physical welfare. This did not mean, he insisted, that an eight-hour maximum for women was equally justifiable or that the legislature could choose any limit it pleased. "This is one of the cases in which reasonableness is a matter of degree, to be determined in the last resort by the courts."[16]

Prior to the Supreme Court's landmark *Muller v. Oregon* decision of 1908, state court rulings on maximum-hour laws for women were mixed but basically consistent with Freund's characterization of the legal consensus. In 1876 the Massachusetts supreme court upheld a ten-hour law for women who worked in manufacturing plants; but the Illinois supreme court invalidated an eight-hour law for women nineteen years later. In 1900 the superior court of Pennsylvania introduced the so-called "mothers of the race" argument and used it to justify a twelve-hour law for women. State courts in Nebraska and Washington employed similar arguments in 1902.[17]

By 1908, when the U.S. Supreme Court ruled on the issue of maximum-hour laws for women for the first time in *Muller*, the "mothers of the race" argument and the "inherent weakness" argument were hardly novel. But Louis Brandeis and Josephine Goldmark endowed the arguments with new authority by submitting a detailed statistical brief to the Court which purported to prove them empirically. According to Felix Frankfurter, the Brandeis-Goldmark brief, for the first time, "breathed the air of reality" into American law. The Court majority found the brief compelling and upheld the Oregon ten-hour law for women as constitutional. The AALL reformers were also impressed: with the help of the Russell Sage Foundation and the National Consumers' League, they printed a thousand copies of the brief to distribute to members and friends.[18]

The *Muller* decision marked a turning point in the development of protective labor law. Subsequent state decisions universally upheld maximum-hour statutes for women, and the Supreme Court sustained these decisions. The Court, moreover, validated a broad eight-hour law for women for the first time in 1915.[19] A complementary step in many states was the prohibition of night work for women, which often was justified on moralistic grounds but which served practically as a means to prevent cheating on maximum-hour laws.[20] Without night-work laws, women could work day shifts in one factory and night shifts in another. New York lawmakers enacted both a ten-hour law and a night-work law for women in 1899.[21] Although the New York high court annulled the night-work law in 1907, it reversed itself and declared another such law valid in 1915. The Supreme Court ultimately confirmed the latter decision with a favorable ruling in 1924.[22] During the same period, numerous state courts, including those of Oregon, Washington, and Massachusetts, upheld minimum-wage laws for women. These decisions stood until 1923, when the U.S. Supreme Court finally struck down the District of Columbia's minimum-wage law for women, which Congress had enacted several years before.[23]

Leading AALL reformers reacted ambivalently to the rush of judicial rulings on protective legislation during the progressive era. On the one hand, they regarded protective laws for women as essential for conserving the vitality and the fertility of the female workforce. They believed in the essential frailty of women and the sanctity of women's special reproductive function.[24] On the other hand, most of the principal AALL reformers objected to the exclusion of men from the reach of protective labor laws. Though hours and wages regulation promised greater (and more urgent) benefits to women, they nonetheless promised definite benefits to men as well. Arguing in both social and constitutional terms, Commons and Seager, in particular, posited that hours and wages laws for men *were* legitimate applications of the police power, even if not for all the same reasons that justified laws for women.

In 1911 Commons proposed a minimum-wage bill for Wisconsin that covered both sexes. It was the first minimum-wage bill introduced in the United States. The clause that supported the bill's broad coverage held that all "employment property is hereby declared to be affected with a public interest to the extent that every employer shall pay to every employee in each oppressive employment at least a living wage."[25] Commons adapted this line of reasoning from the *Holden* decision. One of his colleagues wrote in defense of the bill: "The principle of classification is, therefore, not that of sex, or age, but of bargaining power in protecting themselves against conditions which it is the interest of the public that they should be protected against."[26]

Ever since reading the *Holden* decision, Commons had emphasized the significance of unequal power between employers and employees. He grounded his 1911 minimum-wage bill on a bargaining-power principle, and he subsequently argued that the mere existence of unequal bargaining positions was sufficient to justify application of the police power.[27] Significantly, this line of reasoning was gender-neutral since, according to the reformers, workers of both sexes bargained from inferior positions relative to employers. Commons also justified gender-neutral protective legislation on health grounds. He and Andrews wrote in their text on labor legislation:

whereas formerly, for the most part, the health of consumers, but not the health of producers, was a public benefit, now the health of the laborer as a producer is considered to be as much a public benefit as the health of the consumer of his product. If this be so, then the liberty of both the employer and the employee to make a labor contract may be restricted and regulated, if it is found that the contract is injurious to the laborer.[28]

Unlike the U.S. Supreme Court, Commons and Andrews assumed that long hours and inadequate wages were injurious to all workers (of both sexes) and, indeed, indicative of unequal bargaining power.[29]

In his 1904 treatise on the police power, Ernst Freund hinted at another possible justification for gender-neutral protective legislation. While explaining that women were weaker than men and that women reasonably deserved protection on health grounds that men did not, Freund suggested that the goal of "social advancement" might justify employment of the police power on behalf of both sexes. "If . . . the limitation of hours is merely a measure of social advancement," he wrote, "a separate rule for all women for all purposes hardly represents a reasonable classification, for in the effort to make a living men and women have a right to the greatest possible equality before the law." He observed that an eight-hour day, though not justifiable as a health requirement, might be "desired as a measure to raise the social and economic standard" of both male and female workers.[30] Within a decade, however, Freund had abandoned this position. Cognizant of the *Lochner* and *Muller* precedents, he insisted in an address to the AALL in late 1913 that the only way to secure general hour laws for men would be to argue the existence of a customary standard of ten hours a day. Other lines of reasoning, he now believed, would not stand judicial scrutiny.[31]

Henry Seager proved more resistant than either Commons or Freund to the legal reasoning that necessitated sex-based protective legislation. Speaking before the Association in 1915, he exclaimed:

> There is no sharp dividing line between women wage-earners and men wage-earners as regards their helplessness in the face of adverse industrial conditions. The Supreme Court of the United States has justified ten-hour laws for women on the ground that they are the potential mothers of the oncoming generation and that therefore the protection of their health and vitality is essential to the welfare of the nation. But is it reasonable to maintain that the health and vitality of the potential fathers of the oncoming generation are less essential to our national welfare? In arguing that protective laws for women are justified, while protective laws for men represent an unwarranted interference with their liberty, our judges appear to me to have been guided by a somewhat old fashioned attitude toward women rather than by sound reason.[32]

Seager not only alluded to the bargaining-power argument by stressing the equality of helplessness between men and women workers, he also challenged the near-sacred mothers-of-the-race argument by proposing what amounted to a fathers-of-the-race corollary. Seager's formulation was both novel and provocative. But it attracted little attention outside the AALL. Like the gender-neutral arguments of Commons, Andrews, and Freund, Seager's reasoning did nothing to alter the sex-based constitutional constraint confronting them.

Though uncomfortable with the prospect of protective legislation exclusively for women, AALL reformers nonetheless joined the political struggle for gender-specific laws. They regarded themselves as political pragmatists and, given the unyielding position of the courts, preferred legislation for women alone to no legislation at all. They also thought that laws for women might serve as an opening wedge into protective legislation for both sexes. At least through the end of the teens, however, the AALL reformers' discomfort at having to endorse gender-specific laws remained visible. This was most obvious in the case of the minimum-wage campaigns, in which several AALL leaders actively participated.

The first minimum-wage law in the United States was enacted in Massachusetts in 1912. Like all subsequent minimum-wage laws passed during the progressive period, the Massachusetts law covered only women and minors. It established a commission vested with the authority to appoint wage boards that would investigate conditions in particular industries and recommend minimum-wage scales for those industries. The recommended rates were supposed to represent minimum subsistence levels consistent with "the financial condition of the occupation." If approved by the commission, the rates would be obligatory but enforceable only through the publication of violators' names.[33] Through the teens, thirteen more states plus Puerto Rico and the District of Columbia secured minimum-wage laws. Most of them followed Massachusetts' example of establishing a commission and supplementary wage boards for individual industries, but most also included stricter enforcement mechanisms. Three of the thirteen states chose to set flat rates by statute for all covered industries rather than adopt the commission approach.[34] Interestingly, Massachusetts was the only industrial state to enact a minimum-wage law during this period. Writes historian James T. Patterson, "Business interests would seem to have been too strong in other industrial states for such legislation."[35]

One industrial state that considered but did not enact a minimum-wage law was New York, where AALL reformers were particularly active. A vigorous debate over workplace conditions and the value of state regulation had emerged from the ashes of the 1911 Triangle fire, which killed 145 (mostly women) shirtwaist workers. After a period of public mourning and a shocking discovery that the incinerated building had complied fully with city regulations, lawmakers in Albany created the New York State Factory Investigating Commission. The nine-member commission, led by state senator Robert Wagner and assemblyman Alfred E. Smith, was charged with identifying responsibility for the fire and recommending policies to protect factory workers in the future. Although the commission's first round of recommendations focused on safety (such as regulations requiring fire drills and automatic sprinklers in factories), the commission subsequently obtained from the legislature authorization to begin investigating wage rates and to report on the merits of a minimum-wage law.[36]

The commission's wage investigation commenced in 1913. It began as a close study of a few industries in New York City that employed disproportionately high numbers of women and minors. It ultimately expanded into a far-reaching inquiry exploring costs of living and wage rates across the entire state.[37] The directors of the statewide investigation, Howard B. Woolston and Albert H. N. Baron, oversaw the collection of wage data on nearly 110,000 employees; they also supervised over 2,000 personal interviews with employees. Based on the assumption that wage laws for men would not stand up in court, they chose to focus their analysis on industries dominated by female and child labor. According to the report:

> Many men are receiving low wages and the investigation shows that many men cannot properly support themselves nor support a family on what they receive. But in America, where the constitutionality of wage legislation is still undecided, even when it affects only women, and where legislation for the protection of men has been generally declared unconstitutional and has thus far received little public support, it has been deemed wiser to deal with this problem solely as it relates to women and minors. It is also clear that the number of women who receive a low wage exceeds greatly the number of men, and the need of remedial action in their behalf is immensely more urgent.[38]

Despite this self-imposed limitation on scope, the Commission's investigation proved highly provocative. The cost-of-living study determined that a wage of $8.20 per week was necessary for a working woman to "decently maintain herself" in a city like Buffalo and that $9.00 per week was necessary in New York City. Yet the survey of wages found that half of all workers in the four primary industries investigated (confectionery, paper-box making, shirt manufacturing, and mercantile establishments) earned less than $8.00 per week—that is, below a living wage.[39]

Critics of minimum-wage legislation argued that the discrepancy was not an indictment of the labor market but rather a consequence of the fact that most women workers lived with their families and thus did not have to support themselves. According to the Harvard economist F. W. Taussig, $6.00 per week might be inadequate for a woman who lived alone but not for one who lived with her family.[40] Many reformers, however, insisted that this was precisely why a minimum wage was necessary. They claimed that employers who paid sub-living wages were "parasites" since other parties effectively subsidized their budgets for labor (by making up the difference between what the employers paid in wages and what it cost to maintain the workers in reasonably good health). Some of the women who earned inadequate wages, the minimum-wage law supporters maintained, accepted either public or private charity to assist them in acquiring essentials like food and shelter. Even those who lived with their families implicitly received subsidies from their parents' and siblings' wages.

Henry Seager was a vocal proponent of the parasitism thesis, and he commented on the subject in his contribution to the Factory Investigating Commission's minimum-wage symposium. "These unfortunates," he explained, referring to workers who earned sub-living wages,

> are partly supported now at the expense of others. Other members of the family contribute something, charity contributes something, prostitution contributes something, and some are slowly losing vitality and such efficiency as they have left because they are constantly overworked and underpaid. The industries that employ them have been accurately characterized as parasitic industries. They do not pay their way, and consumers who get goods cheaper in consequence are living at the expense of the sweated workers or of those who supplement their earnings to save them from the disastrous consequences of earning less than suffices for decent living.[41]

Another economist who contributed to the symposium put the problem even more bluntly: "The inefficient employer, like the parasitic industry, has no right to economic existence."[42]

Reformers who complained of parasitism typically attributed such worker exploitation to the existence of gross inequality of bargaining power between employers and workers, especially unskilled workers. Their arguments were reminiscent of the reasoning that the Supreme Court had advanced in the *Holden* decision of 1898 and that Commons had developed in his writings on protective labor law.[43] Significantly, these arguments were gender-neutral since men could be the victims of unequal bargaining power just as easily as women. Yet not a single minimum-wage statute enacted during the progressive era included coverage for male workers.[44] It is impossible to know how many legislatures would have acted differently had gender-neutral laws appeared constitutionally feasible, but the final record is clear.

There is some evidence that in New York pressure developed within an advisory committee to the Factory Investigating Commission to propose a law covering both sexes. Henry Seager as well as a dozen other members of the AALL sat on the commission's Advisory Committee on Wages and Wage Legislation. One letter from Abram I. Elkus, the chief counsel for the commission, to John Andrews suggests that this advisory committee preferred a minimum-wage law covering all workers rather than one covering only women and minors. In the letter, Elkus quoted the advisory committee's recommendations as agreed on at a meeting on January 23, 1915. One sentence from those recommendations read, "The basis of fixing a living wage in any trade shall be the necessary cost of living to maintain the workers in health." Another tentative recommendation, which had yet to be approved by the full advisory committee, read, "Any worker who receives less than the wage fixed by the Commission shall be entitled to recover the full amount due . . ." The quoted recommendations did not suggest a law only for women. In fact, the passages Elkus cited included no mention of women at all, except for the proposal that one member of the proposed wage commission be a woman. Elkus went on to explain, however, that in response to these recommendations, the full Factory Investigating Commission drafted a resolution calling for the establishment of a wage commission and wage boards to determine living wages for women and minors. Without acknowledging any contradiction between the advisory committee's suggestions and the full commission's draft resolution, Elkus concluded the letter, "The Commission would also be very glad if you would submit a statement setting forth your views on the general subject of wage legislation for women and minors." Perhaps Andrews was confused about how and why the full commission transformed the advisory committee's gender-neutral proposal into a gender-specific one, because jotted in the margin next to Elkus' concluding paragraph stands a big question mark.[45]

The available evidence on the advisory committee's position is merely suggestive, not conclusive. Seager, one of the committee's members, testified to the Factory Investigating Commission in early January 1915 that while he supported a minimum-wage law for both sexes, he was well aware of the constitutional obstacle. "In my opinion," he told the commissioners, "there is no good economic reason why [the law] should not apply to men. So far as the economic argument is concerned it ought to apply to men. At the same time I am impressed with the great danger that if it did apply to men, as our Constitution is now interpreted, the measure might be declared unconstitutional." He suggested that the law adopted should apply initially only to women and children "with the expectation and hope that in time it will be extended to men."[46] Whether or not the individual commissioners shared Seager's hope of broader coverage in the future, they certainly felt obliged—or perhaps constitutionally constrained—to recommend a minimum-wage bill to the legislature that explicitly excluded male workers.

The New York Factory Investigating Commission modeled its bill after the original Massachusetts statute and submitted it in 1915.[47] The bill covered women and minors, established an administrative commission and supplementary wage boards to determine wage scales for the various industries, and limited enforcement to the publication of violators' names. It also included a clause allowing wage boards to "take into consideration the financial condition of the industry" when issuing minimum-wage determinations.[48] Seager, who had played an active role in the commission's work on wages from the outset, found the final product disappointing. "Our Factory Investigating Commission has shown the need of such legislation in New York," he wrote, "but it is so impressed by the probability that an obligatory minimum wage would be held unconstitutional that it recommends an optional minimum wage, which employers may or may not pay as they see fit."[49] Even more upsetting to reformers like Seager was the commission's failure to secure enactment of the bill, even in its weakened form.

In most states where minimum-wage bills were introduced, the resulting political debate proved highly divisive. During the phosphorus-match campaign, reformers enjoyed the unqualified endorsement of organized labor and substantial support from the business community. In the case of minimum-wage legislation, by contrast, both of these interest groups harbored powerful factions that opposed the proposed reforms. Labor leaders generally were suspicious of protective labor laws because they feared state encroachment in the arena of industrial bargaining. Some labor officials endorsed minimum-wage laws that would apply only to women; only a few supported wage laws for men as well.[50] Many others—including Samuel Gompers—opposed on principle wage legislation for either sex.[51]

Although employer support for minimum wage legislation was not unknown,[52] most employers opposed such regulation. Some lamented that a minimum wage would force them to dismiss all of their "girls" who were not worth the minimum.[53] Others claimed that a wage law would put their industries at a competitive disadvantage relative to comparable industries in other states, thus placing all of their workers' jobs at risk. A New York candy maker stated:

> We know that if there is a minimum wage law passed in this State the bulk of a certain class of goods that we make would be discontinued, and these

goods would be made in neighboring states where there are no laws to prevent the production of the same; in fact it would amount to driving not a
few manufacturers out of the State or out of business. We, for one, would
stay in the State, but we would produce only certain lines of goods and put
out of employment about fifty girls.[54]

A Massachusetts employer put the complaint more succinctly at a 1912
AALL conference, which was held just after the Bay State enacted the
nation's first minimum-wage law. "Massachusetts employers," he exclaimed, "are sick to death of being made the dog on which these schemes
are tried out."[55]

A number of reformers dismissed the interstate-competition argument
as invalid or irrelevant within the context of the minimum-wage debate.
One AALL member called it a "threadbare assertion," and another insisted that industries that did not pay living wages deserved to be driven
out of the state.[56] But most of the reformers probably saw it for what it
was—a plausible argument that threatened to convert already nervous
state lawmakers into reluctant opponents of protective labor legislation.[57]

Had political circumstances been different in New York, such arguments might have been very important. As it was, the commission's minimum-wage bill was squashed as a result of straightforward partisan politics. Democrats, who had created the Factory Investigating Commission,
lost control of the assembly after the 1913 election and lost the senate
and state house a year later.[58] Not surprisingly, the Republicans showed
little interest in the commission's minimum-wage bill. Viewing it as a
Democratic creation, they permitted it to die in the Labor and Industry
Committee.[59]

Although the New York legislature never passed the Factory Investigating Commission's minimum-wage bill for women, it did enact many
other of the commission's proposed bills, including a childbirth protection
law in 1912. The debate over childbirth protection, and particularly over
the related issue of maternity insurance, is of interest here because it re-
veals important differences and conflicts between the AALL reformers and
leading protective feminists—two groups that were allied politically but
not ideologically.

Childbirth protection was one of the few forms of labor legislation that
almost no one at the time considered applicable to men. In this case, at
least, the courts were not the limiting impediment to gender-neutral protection. The New York law prohibited the employment of women within
four weeks after childbirth. Massachusetts, which had passed such a law
the year before, prohibited an employer from knowingly employing a
woman in manufacturing, mechanical, or mercantile industries two weeks

before or four weeks after childbirth. Connecticut and Vermont enacted similar laws in 1913 and Missouri in 1919.[60]

Association reformers supported these laws but identified a critical flaw: the few states that had childbirth-protection statutes provided no compensation for the mothers who were prohibited from working. According to one AALL report on the subject, "These provisions, while they may save the mother from overstrain, serve merely to lower the already small family income and to increase the evil effects of poverty at this most critical time."[61] Irene Osgood Andrews began in 1913 to investigate this problem as well as the preferred remedy of European policymakers, maternity insurance. The AALL reformers doubted whether maternity insurance could be administered as an isolated program, but they thought it would fit well into a larger scheme of compulsory health insurance. They therefore wrote maternity provisions into their model health insurance bill in late 1915.[62] Such benefits, they insisted, would fill a pressing need: "The payment of the cash benefit will mitigate poverty during the period when the mother is obliged to be absent from remunerative work, and so will tend to reduce the infant mortality rate."[63]

The maternity benefits defined in the Association's model bill included all "necessary medical, surgical and obstetrical aid, materials and appliances, which shall be given insured women and the wives of insured men" as well as a weekly cash benefit for all insured working women equal to two-thirds of wages for eight weeks (at least six of which would be after childbirth). Recipients were required to abstain from gainful employment during the entire period of payment. In a detailed commentary on the bill, Association reformers justified the inclusion of maternity insurance in their health insurance bill on the grounds that "childbirth may be assimilated with sickness in its physical and economic effects, and since the interest of the public in better care of mothers is clear."[64]

Although maternity insurance was unfamiliar to most Americans when the AALL began to promote it in 1915 and 1916, a few companies had already begun to experiment with maternity as part of their emerging programs of welfare capitalism. B.F. Goodrich, for example, had such a benefit plan in place by 1915. When John Andrews inquired why the Goodrich plan covered only married women employees, a company official who knew him replied that the firm did not want "to do anything or hold out any apparent inducement or veiled approval which might serve as color of encouragement for young girls or unmarried women to expect assistance openly after breaking both the moral and the civil law." Disappointed by such blatant moralism, Andrews wrote back that sometimes social reformers had "to do things which are not entirely welcome— at least not at the time they are done," but that such things often appeared perfectly proper three or five years later. Maternity insurance, Andrews believed, was a coming issue.[65]

Ironically, what subverted the AALL reformers' plan to introduce public maternity insurance in 1916 was moralism of an entirely different sort—prejudice not against unmarried women and premarital sex but against husbands, especially immigrant husbands, who sent (or permitted) their wives to work. The AALL reformers were nearly ready to introduce their health insurance bill into the New York, Massachusetts, and New Jersey state legislatures when they suddenly fell under attack from a normally friendly quarter. Florence Kelley, the general secretary of the National Consumers' League and perhaps the nation's most prominent advocate of protective legislation for women, objected strenuously to maternity insurance and demanded that the Association reformers remove it from their health insurance bill. The controversy was short-lived. But it betrayed significant differences of opinion between Kelley and individuals like Seager, Andrews, and Osgood Andrews regarding the employment of women in industry and the ultimate purposes of protective legislation.[66]

Kelley charged that maternity insurance would encourage lazy immigrant husbands to send their pregnant wives to work in order to secure monetary and medical benefits at childbirth. She claimed, moreover, that a system of maternity insurance covering married working women and the wives of insured men placed an unfair burden on unmarried working women, whom Kelley seemed to regard as the only legitimate members of the female workforce.[67] "Offering a cash bonus," she declared mockingly in a memorandum on the subject, "amounts to saying to the wage-earning husband: 'Send your wife into a mill, factory, or sweatshop, and the public and the single women in her factory will send you a present for your next baby.'" In her view, a maternity benefit for "unskilled, unorganized aliens, particularly the non-English speaking ones," would serve as "an actual bribe to increased immigration of the kind of men who make their wives and children work."[68]

Association reformers who believed in maternity insurance were frustrated and bewildered by Kelley's charges. Andrews claimed to find her logic incomprehensible. He wrote to a sympathetic British reformer:

> Those who argue that a cash benefit given to the insured working women and not to the wives of insured men would draw women into industry, assume that married women work because their husbands are avaricious and require them to do so. From this assumption it is difficult to see why they consider that a cash bonus in the form of maternity benefit would be a still further inducement to the shiftless and lazy husbands who make their wives work.[69]

Seager, who initially suggested that Kelley's charge was not without foundation, later changed his mind, insisting to Andrews, "Mrs. Kelley is eventually going to be kept busy trying to defend her position even in her own special spheres of influence."[70]

Andrews and members of his staff relayed Kelley's charge to a number of reformers in Europe and inquired whether it was substantiated by their experience with maternity insurance. One correspondent in London replied that she had never heard any comparable criticism of Britain's maternity insurance program. Two others were familiar with the charge but denied its validity.[71] Such denials corroborated the AALL reformers' belief that maternity benefits would not play a significant role in enticing married women into the workforce.

Kelley's opposition nevertheless proved devastating. She first communicated her position on maternity insurance to the Association in December 1915. As early as January 5, an AALL staff member informed Kelley of the Association's capitulation: the social insurance committee had agreed to omit maternity insurance benefits from the New York bill. The revised bill would continue to cover medical care for insured women at childbirth, but it would provide no cash maternity benefits for insured women nor any maternity aid whatsoever to the wives of insured men. Andrews acknowledged to Alice Henry of the Boston Women's Trade Union League that he and his colleagues still believed in maternity benefits but that they felt obliged to omit the provision "in order to avoid disagreeable controversy at the beginning of the educational work for the bill in New York State."[72]

It is clear from AALL correspondence in late 1915 and early 1916 that many of the organization's key figures found Kelley's moralism both disagreeable and anachronistic. They prided themselves on being realists. "Legislation aimed to protect the working mother at the time of childbirth is in its infancy in this country," an AALL report explained, "due perhaps to a belief that 'married wage-earning women are not as yet an American tradition,'—a belief that overlooks the economic forces which are driving married women as well as young girls to seek gainful employment."[73] This constituted a clear response to Kelley, who had written in her memorandum to the AALL that the employment of married women in factories "is not an American tradition, and it is *not yet* an established institution."[74]

The AALL reformers contended that women were not entering the workforce in record numbers merely because their husbands (read: immigrant husbands) were lazy and made them go. Rather, the reformers attributed the shift to dramatically changing economic conditions. Between 1890 and 1900, the proportion of women workers who were married increased from 14 to 15.5 percent, and the total number increased from 515,124 to 775,924. Similarly, the percentage of married women at work rose from 4.6 percent in 1890 to 5.6 percent in 1900. The AALL report highlighted the role of "economic necessity in driving women into commercial employment," noting the significant share of family income that modern working mothers contributed in many families. Increasingly, Association reformers believed, the disruption associated with childbirth posed a dual threat—to the physical health of the infant and to the economic health of the family. While Kelley worried about the ethics of providing additional inducements to married women to enter industrial employment, leading figures at the AALL preferred a pragmatic approach. They were satisfied that maternity insurance addressed one of the detrimental consequences of a social transformation that they believed was already underway and bound to continue.[75]

The maternity-insurance controversy, though significant, was only a minor quarrel compared to the bitter struggle that arose in the mid-teens between protective and equal-rights feminists—a struggle that pressed many at the AALL to clarify and even justify their position. Unlike the Association reformers, who were suspicious of gender-based protective legislation but convinced that there was no practical political alternative, equal-rights feminists viewed the principle of equality as beyond compromise. Increasingly after 1915, insurgent women's groups lashed out at protective feminists by denying the supposed benefits of gender-based protection. Protective labor legislation for women, they argued, was inherently prejudicial against women and destructive to their employment opportunities.

In 1915 a group of women printers (the elite of the women's workforce) organized in New York the Women's League for Equal Opportunity. The founders believed that state laws setting maximum working hours for women and prohibiting women from working at night compromised the competitiveness of female workers and displaced many from their jobs. The first president of the league, Ella M. Sherwin, declared: "Welfare legislation, if persisted in, will protect women to the vanishing point." A similar group, the Equal Rights Association, emerged in New York in 1917. It too was led by women printers and lobbied aggressively against protective labor legislation in Albany.[76]

In the late teens and early twenties, equal-rights feminists enjoyed substantial gains in strength and number—especially after the experience of World War I and the ratification of the Nineteenth Amendment. Although some social reformers preferred not to take sides between the protective and equal-rights feminists, many of them found it increasingly difficult to remain neutral. The National Woman's Party (NWP) began to question the value of protective laws for women in 1919 after women hired during the war by the Brooklyn Rapid Transit Company were fired en masse, ostensibly because of a night work law that prohibited them from working between 10:00 p.m. and 7:00 a.m.[77] The leadership of the NWP soon faced the issue again as they began campaigning for equal rights at the state level and for an amendment to the federal constitution. The immediate question was whether such state laws and the federal amendment would nullify existing protective legislation for women.[78]

NWP officials initially hoped to circumvent the problem. In Wisconsin, where the legislature enacted an equal-rights bill in 1921, local reformers guarded existing protective laws by explicitly exempting "welfare legislation" from the purview of the statute.[79] Maud Younger, the NWP's national legislative chairman, wrote in December to numerous advocates of protective legislation about her organization's proposed constitutional amendment. She explained to a representative of the National Women's Trade Union League that "the Woman's Party did not desire to touch the industrial legislation in this amendment." She sent similar assurances to John Andrews the following month, although she admitted that some attorneys doubted whether an explicit clause exempting labor legislation for women would be adequate.[80]

There is no evidence in the Association's papers that Andrews ever responded to requests from representatives of the National Woman's Party for an opinion on their constitutional and legislative proposals. One of his legal advisers, however, reacted sharply against an equal-rights bill that the NWP introduced in New York—despite the fact that it explicitly exempted welfare legislation. "The bill," Joseph Chamberlain wrote, "is absolutely contrary to all my ideas of what legislation should be and would, I think, if enacted, be one of the greatest breeders of trouble that we have ever had, because of the difficulty of determining just what it means." He reminded Andrews "how strongly your association opposed the group that wanted equal rights for women in respect to the labor laws" and concluded with the recommendation that Andrews "should be very cautious in taking any position in favor of this bill, which has certainly not the support of all the women who are interested in women's rights."[81]

In late 1922 and 1923, the NWP finally chose between equality and protection: it resolved to remove the exemption for welfare legislation from its equal-rights amendment and thus shut the door on cooperation with protective feminists. The NWP continued to favor protective legislation covering both sexes rather than no legislation at all. But the practical political impact of its new position against gender-specific welfare laws was to polarize the women's movement further and to give new ammunition to longstanding opponents of protective legislation.[82]

Progressive reformers who endorsed the notion of protective feminism were accustomed to attacks from business associations and even from representatives of organized labor. But the new attacks, because they came directly from women workers and fellow reformers, were especially painful. Instead of moderating their position, the protective feminists intensified their fight. Even figures like Henry Seager, who originally supported protective legislation for women primarily as a constitutionally viable path toward protection for all, reacted with alarm to the threat posed by equal-rights feminists. Seager probably justified his compromise position as more flexible and more pragmatic than that of the NWP activists, but it would have been hypocritical had he criticized their ultimate goal of equal protection for both sexes.

When the Supreme Court declared the District of Columbia's minimum-wage law for women workers unconstitutional in the *Adkins v. Children's Hospital* decision of 1923, the full breadth of the split between the two schools of feminists became clear. On the subject of special protection for women, Justice George Sutherland wrote for the majority:

> In view of the great—not to say revolutionary—changes which have taken place since [the 1908 *Muller* decision], in the contractual, political and civil status of women, culminating in the Nineteenth Amendment, it is not unreasonable to say that these differences [between the sexes which were used to justify special protection] have now come almost, if not quite, to the vanishing point.[83]

The National Woman's Party found vindication and great encouragement in the decision. Certainly the idea of equality between the sexes was taking hold in the American mind, its leaders concluded, if so conservative an institution as the Supreme Court recognized the principle.[84] The advocates of protective legislation, on the other hand, were outraged. They repeated among themselves Justice Oliver Wendell Holmes's poignant dissent. "It will need more than the Nineteenth Amendment," Holmes wrote, "to convince me that there are no differences between men and women, or that legislation cannot take those differences into account."[85]

Following the decision, the *Survey* circulated a questionnaire to many of the most prominent figures in the minimum-wage debate in order to elicit their reactions to the *Adkins* ruling. Seager wrote the foreword for the resulting symposium, in which he characterized the court's decision as "the most severe blow which progressive American labor legislation has yet received at the hands of the Supreme Court." He wrote disdainfully of the legal process by which a few justices on the court could unilaterally overrule their fellow justices, Congress, and the president. Sounding an ominous note, he stated that unless the system were remedied a climate of revolution would develop. Angry and perhaps even fearful of public lawlessness, Seager endorsed a radical amendment to the constitution that would require a two-thirds majority of the Supreme Court to invalidate federal legislation. Many of the contributors to the symposium, including Commons and Andrews, agreed; Andrews even insisted on an amendment requiring a three-fourths majority.[86]

Thus, by 1923, the AALL reformers who were most concerned about protective legislation appear to have suppressed their principled objections and accepted the rhetoric of protective feminism. Their demand for a constitutional amendment to discipline the Supreme Court was a response not to a gender-biased decision but rather to a gender-neutral ruling that they found extremely disturbing.

Although the intensity of their reaction was perhaps more the product of a charged and transitory political environment than the consequence of a dramatic reversal of their position, their position had in fact changed over the preceding two decades. They continued to believe that the main purpose of hour and wage laws was to protect workers unable to protect themselves and not, as some protective feminists would have it, to protect women in their maternal and domestic role. Judicial invalidation of protective labor laws applying to men, however, had pushed these AALL reformers to forge a political alliance with protective feminists, since they regarded laws covering only women as better than no laws at all. Attacks by equal-rights feminists on the resulting gender-specific laws drove Association leaders to solidify that alliance still further. The *Adkins* affair, at the very least, exposed the tenuousness of their expressed commitment to equal protection of the sexes and the intuitiveness of their political association with reformers who championed protective feminism.[87]

7

Compensating for
Lost Time

Of all the Association's legislative proposals, social insurance was the most promising, the most controversial, and the most problematic. Promising because leading AALL reformers believed that social insurance, much more than protective regulation, would prevent industrial hazards and sharply diminish worker insecurity. Controversial because, in the minds of many critics, social insurance represented a longer step toward the socialization of production than did most other proposals for social welfare reform. And problematic because progressive-era campaigns for social insurance collided with all the usual constitutional and political obstacles as well as a few new ones.

At the Association's First American Conference on Social Insurance in 1913, the current president of the organization, William F. Willoughby, characterized social insurance as "the most effective device that has yet been discovered" for preventing want. At the same time, he pointed out that the United States had fallen nearly a generation behind the nations of Europe in enacting social insurance laws.[1] As of 1913, a number of states had workers' compensation programs, but most did not; and no state had even considered compulsory health, unemployment, or old-age insurance. By contrast, many European nations had begun enacting social insurance statutes in the late nineteenth and early twentieth centuries. Germany adopted health insurance, workers' compensation, and old-age and disability insurance between 1883 and 1889; Britain enacted workers' compensation in 1897, old-age pensions in 1908, and health and unemployment insurance in 1911.

Progressive-era reformers in the United States generally attributed the large and growing policy gap to "American distinctiveness." They took for granted that their country was different from its neighbors across the Atlantic—that Americans preferred to prevent poverty rather than merely to relieve it, that Americans found big government distasteful and threatening, and that American political institutions presented peculiar barriers to social reform. Writing in 1902, one of the Association's principal founders and its first secretary, Adna F. Weber, explained that the failure of the states to enact workers' compensation laws "may be in part ascribed to the prevalent individualistic philosophy."[2] Eleven years later, an employer from Illinois wrote to John Andrews that he anticipated U.S. employers would soon develop an interest in European-style reforms, provided the AALL modified foreign programs to accommodate distinctive American conditions.[3] Most reformers shared this view. Paul U. Kellogg, an AALL member and editor of the *Survey,* suggested in 1910 that while America could profit from European experience, an American system of workers' compensation "should nonetheless be grounded firmly in American conditions."[4]

If ideas about the purposes of social welfare policy and about the role of the state seemed to separate America from Europe, so too did American political institutions. Henry Farnam highlighted this point in his presidential address at the Association's second annual meeting. Acknowledging that the United States lagged far behind Europe in the field of labor legislation, he explained that "legal difficulties arise from the very framework of our government." The existence of over four dozen separate legislative bodies—the product of a federal system of government—was an enormous obstacle to reform. "Our country," Farnam declared, "presents a more complex legislative problem than all the states of Europe taken together."[5]

Nor was federalism the only institutional impediment. In 1915 Henry Seager described the right to due process—a right guaranteed in all forty-eight state constitutions as well as in the federal constitution—as the "constitutional rock" upon which most progressive social reforms foundered in the United States. Not only did judges often overturn legislators' handiwork, but reformers frequently censored themselves in response to the threat of constitutional invalidation. "If New York state and other American states are today behind progressive European countries in the field of social and labor legislation," Seager insisted, "it is chiefly because of this constitutional barrier."[6]

Despite the existence of such formidable challenges, progressive-era reformers, many of them associated with the AALL, launched legislative campaigns for social insurance with enormous confidence. They believed that they could modify European reforms to meet distinctive American conditions. Indeed, it was imperative that they succeed. A comprehensive system of social insurance, they claimed, would dramatically reduce worker insecurity and thereby remove one of the greatest threats to the stability of industrial capitalism in the United States.

Workers' compensation was the first item on the AALL's social insurance agenda. It seemed like the natural place to begin for at least two reasons. First, the nation's industrial-accident problem was widely recognized as deplorable. Although neither the states nor the federal government kept good statistics on work-related accidents in the first decade of the twentieth century, most students of the subject believed that the American accident rate was very high—especially as measured by European standards. In a 1915 report for the U.S. Bureau of Labor Statistics, Frederick Hoffman conservatively estimated that out of a total labor force of 38 million, 25,000 workers died (and 700,000 suffered injuries causing over four weeks of disability) as a result of industrial accidents in 1913. Although direct comparisons are difficult, the rate of fatal industrial accidents in the United States was probably about a third higher than in Britain. "That this rate is terrible is obvious," wrote Henry Farnam; "that it is greater than it should be, is seen by comparing our figures with those of European countries."[7]

The second major reason for beginning with workers' compensation—and the main reason why it proved less controversial than either health or unemployment insurance—was that a legal remedy for on-the-job injuries already existed in the form of employers' liability law.[8] Prior to the enactment of worker's compensation statutes, workers injured on the job could sue their employers for damages. Yet this employers' liability system was hardly optimal from the workers' standpoint. The existence of powerful employer defenses seemed to stack the legal deck against workers who sued; and even those workers who ultimately recovered damages often fell into poverty while awaiting judgments. Nor was this common-law system optimal for employers. They remained potentially liable for every employee injury and, in each case, faced the remote but real possibility that a sympathetic jury would grant a sizable award.

Like many progressive-era reformers, Seager believed that industrialization had rendered the employers' liability system obsolete. Indeed, in 1911 he described the system as "a complete failure."[9] Seager and his colleagues at the AALL contended that the introduction of workers' compensation would serve the interests of all parties by making compensation for industrial accidents automatic. Injured workers would be assured quick and certain awards; employers would no longer have to guess how much injuries were going to cost them or have to pay extravagant legal fees to protect themselves; and the public would be spared the costs of doling out poor relief to the victims of industrial accidents who fell into destitution. Workers' compensation, moreover, would internalize the costs of industrial accidents and thus induce employers to invest in preventive measures.

When the Association first injected itself into the emerging movement for workers' compensation in 1909, constitutional obstacles loomed large. Maryland had enacted a compensation statute in 1902 only to see it struck down by the state's own high court two years later. Still, many reformers remained hopeful. Adna Weber wrote in 1905, "It is not to be doubted . . . that a workmen's compensation act could be framed that would be entirely in harmony with the requirements of American constitutional law . . ."[10] The federal government established a rather primitive workers' compensation program for its employees in 1908,[11] and leaders of the AALL subsequently launched campaigns for universal workers' compensation laws in New York and Wisconsin in 1909 and 1910. Commons led a successful fight in his home state; and Henry Seager and Crystal Eastman played central roles in the New York campaign, which began in 1909 and continued through 1913.

For the historian, the five-year legislative and constitutional battle in New York serves as a grand illustration of more typical battles across the country. It lasted longer than most; and the commission proceedings, legislative hearings, court decisions, and even constitutional ratification documents that it generated serve as precious windows on its inner workings.[12] The movement began in New York, as it did in most states, with the appointment of a special commission to investigate the problem of industrial accidents and worker insecurity.[13] State lawmakers, strongly encouraged by AALL reformers, created the so-called Wainwright Commission in 1909 "to inquire into the question of employers' liability and other matters."[14] The commission consisted of three state senators, five members of the assembly, and six gubernatorial appointees. These fourteen members elected Senator J. Mayhew Wainwright as their chairman, Henry Seager as vice-chairman, and Crystal Eastman as secretary.[15] Seager and Eastman, both of whom were appointed by the governor, also served as president and secretary of the AALL's New York branch.

After many months of hearings and investigation, the Wainwright Commission reported to the state legislature on March 19, 1910. It attempted to explain the nature of the industrial-accident problem and the inadequacy of the existing common-law remedy. Prior to the introduction of machinery into the production process, the commissioners maintained, "industrial accidents were relatively few and unimportant." But mechanization induced a dramatic change. "The basic fact which has impressed this Commission in its investigation," the report continued, "is the astounding number of workers who are injured each year in the industries of the State and country." In 1909, for example, industrial accidents reported to the New York State Labor Department claimed the lives of 252 workers, seriously or permanently injured 3,739, and temporarily injured 12,839.[16]

The commission rejected the theory that workers were compensated in advance for hazardous work through wage differentials. "[T]hat theory does not work out," read the report. "Wages are not relatively higher in the most dangerous trades." According to the commission, workers received no meaningful wage compensation for the risks they assumed because there existed in reality no meaningful contracts between employers and employees regarding risk. "As a matter of fact, under modern industrial conditions the individual workman consents and assumes the risk only because in the ordinary case he has no option to do anything else." The commission documented, moreover, that in the majority of cases, workers in hazardous employments were unable to afford adequate private insurance against accidents.[17]

In spite of the fact that injured workers possessed the legal right to sue their employers for damages, the commission insisted that the employers' liability system was "fundamentally wrong and unwise" and in need of "radical change."[18] Perhaps the greatest problem was that workers had to prove employer negligence in order to win their suits. Under modern industrial conditions, fault was often difficult or impossible to determine. As a result, various employer defenses—originally intended to protect the employer who was not entirely at fault—became unreasonable hurdles to employee recovery.

The three most important employer defenses were contributory negligence, the fellow-servant rule, and assumption of risk. Under contributory negligence, an employer was immune to damages if the injured worker had been in any way negligent himself. Even if the court found that the employer were 90 percent negligent and the employee only 10 percent, the employee would lose his case and recover nothing. The fellow-servant rule blocked recovery if another worker, not the employer, had caused the accident.[19] Finally, if an employer could show that the injured employee had known the dangers associated with the job—that is, assumed the risk—when he accepted employment, then the employer was not liable.

In 1910 Crystal Eastman published a careful analysis of data from the Pittsburgh survey of industrial conditions, which had been conducted in 1907 and 1908. Her work, entitled *Work-Accidents and the Law*, revealed the complexity of the industrial-accident problem and highlighted the inadequacy of employers' liability law. First, Eastman refuted the common belief that virtually all industrial accidents were the result of worker carelessness. Out of 410 work-accident fatalities for which sufficient information was available, only 68 were due to the fault of the victim alone. (And even some of these cases arguably were ambiguous as to fault, since many of the supposedly "careless" victims were young boys.) Employers were partly or solely responsible for 147 of the fatal accidents, foremen for 19, fellow workers for 56, and the victims themselves for 132. Significantly, Eastman classified 117 accidents, or 28.5 percent of the total, as unavoidable because there existed no basis for assigning blame.[20]

Eastman's second major conclusion was that the existing system for distributing accident costs was inequitable. In at least 53 percent of the fatal cases in her sample, dependents (typically widows and children) recovered nothing and thus bore the full burden of the loss. Since victims were partly or solely to blame in only 32 percent of the cases, this distribution of costs seemed unfair. Eastman also insisted that the worker's loss did not redound to the employer's gain. "The always threatening possibility of having to pay heavy damages as the result of an accident," she explained, "puts [the employer] to the expense of maintaining a special claim department and hiring expert attorneys, although he rarely pays a verdict."[21] Seager echoed this point in his own writings; and Commons and Andrews observed years later that of every $100 employers paid in liability insurance premiums, only $28 ever reached the injured worker.[22]

The Wainwright Commission advanced essentially the same argument—that employers' liability law was wasteful and inadequate, benefitting neither employers nor employees. While the efficiency figures it presented differed slightly from those of Commons and Andrews, the point was the same. "[F]or every $100 paid out by employers for protection against liability to their injured workmen," the commission reported, "less than $37 is paid to those workmen; $63 goes to pay the salaries of attorneys and claim agents whose business it is to defeat the claims of the injured, to the costs of soliciting business, to the costs of administration, and to profit." On the plaintiffs' side, an average of 26.3 percent of settlement awards went to attorneys as contingency fees; recovery typically came only after long delays (often ranging between six months and six years); and in about 80 percent of cases involving fatal accidents, survivors received less than $500.[23]

The commission also made reference to the problem of externalized costs. Asserting that compensating wage differentials were not common in the real world, the commissioners challenged the idea put forward by laissez-faire economists that a free market for labor would maximize social welfare:

> We have been impressed by the fact that employers generally (there are many exceptions) pay less attention to prevention of accidents than the public in-

terest demands because the payment for the damages of accident bears very little direct relation under the present system of liability, to the number of accidents and we hope and believe that the changes in the liability laws which we recommend, because they tend to make the employer pay something for every accident, will have a real effect in making him put his mind constantly to the question of preventing accidents.[24]

Seager, the only academic economist on the commission, probably had helped to formulate this argument—the very same one that Commons was preaching with much success nearly a thousand miles away in Wisconsin.

The central conclusion of the Wainwright report was that the existing liability system for industrial accidents, which was based upon fault, was obsolete. The commission therefore recommended that New York State move away from this system and toward workers' compensation. It proposed a two-tiered strategy of reform. For especially dangerous industries, the commission urged the enactment of a compulsory workers' compensation statute. For nondangerous industries, the commission advocated (1) the restriction of employers' common-law defenses and (2) the creation of an elective system of workers' compensation for those employers and employees who chose jointly to utilize it.[25]

Although they would have preferred to propose a compulsory workers' compensation bill that covered all workers, the commissioners assumed that such a law would be struck down by the courts. They acknowledged that "any attempt to transplant and put in full operation in the State of New York any one of the foreign systems of workmen's insurance is not immediately possible."[26] Indeed, the compulsory bill they proposed focused on dangerous trades because the Supreme Court already had made clear in the *Holden* decision of 1898 that the application of state police powers to extrahazardous employments was constitutional.

The compulsory bill was based on the British model. It did not eliminate the common-law remedy but circumscribed it and created a legal right for workers injured on the job to collect compensation from their employers. The bill denied common-law defenses to employers who were even partially at fault, yet it also denied workers who accepted compensation the opportunity to sue for damages. The benefit levels defined in the bill, though modest, were still higher than typical awards through the courts. Survivors of a fatally injured worker who chose to take compensation would receive 1,200 times the daily wage up to a maximum of $3,000. Compensation levels for nonfatal accidents were indexed according to the severity of the injury.[27]

The commission's second proposal, the elective bill for nonhazardous employments, represented a distinctive American development. Fearful of violating due process and freedom of contract protections, the commissioners suggested a voluntary system of workers' compensation coupled with a substantial narrowing of employers' common-law defenses. The basic idea was that the state would create a workers' compensation system that employers and employees could mutually elect to participate in as a substitute for employers' liability suits. Workers who elected to do so would waive their right to sue for damages. Presumably, workers would be attracted by the prospect of certain compensation in the event of on-the-job injuries. Employers—whose traditional defenses (fellow-servant rule, assumption of risk, and contributory negligence) had been pared by the statute—would be goaded into participation by the threat of costly court judgments.[28]

New York lawmakers took up the commission's proposed bills quickly and enacted them with only slight modifications. The bills were by no means universally popular, however. Labor organizations in the state had been pushing for revisions of the employers' liability system since 1876 and began advocating the concept of workers' compensation in 1909. Of the 113 unions in the state surveyed by the Wainwright Commission, 77 supported workers' compensation and only 36 opposed it. Yet when the commission released its 1910 report, which included the proposed bills, several prominent labor organizations expressed dissatisfaction. They were frustrated that the compulsory compensation system would cover only a few hazardous employments and disturbed by what they regarded as an inadequate scale of compensation. On the other side, employers were deeply divided. Many representatives of large corporations, especially those associated with the National Civic Federation, strongly supported the principle of automatic compensation; but most smaller employers were more resistant. Of 207 employers that the commission surveyed on the issue of workers' compensation, 69 expressed support and 138 opposition. According to the commission report, many employers believed that the introduction of workers' compensation would increase production costs and place them at a disadvantage relative to competitors in other states. One employer complained that "if the State of New York places upon employers the heavy burden of compensating workmen for injuries they will be seriously handicapped in competition with employers in other states, who have no such burden." The same employer correctly observed that Britain's Workmen's Compensation Act faced no comparable constraint because it applied "equally throughout the entire kingdom and no such discrimination results."[29]

Like most successful reforms, the commission's proposed bills became law in part because they were carefully crafted compromises. They bowed to the worst fears of employers and to apparent constitutional constraints while still offering workers a more favorable system for recovering the costs of industrial accidents. Writes the historian Robert F. Wesser, "Still deemed 'conservative' by the social progressives and labor, the 1910 legislation nonetheless represented the most advanced in the nation."[30]

Precisely because it was so advanced, however, the 1910 legislation did not last very long. In the unanimous *Ives v. Buffalo Railway Company* decision delivered on March 24, 1911, the New York Court of Appeals struck down the compulsory workers' compensation law for hazardous employments. Earl Ives, a railroad switchman who sustained a severe on-the-job injury in September 1910, had demanded compensation from his employer under the terms of the new state law. Representatives of Buffalo Railway acknowledged the injury but claimed that the law requiring them to pay compensation was invalid because it amounted to a deprivation of liberty and property. The Court of Appeals agreed. Referring to the law as "plainly revolutionary" and of a "radical character," Judge William E. Werner, speaking for the court, rejected it as a violation of substantive due process. He praised the Wainwright Commission and its report, noting deferentially, "In arriving at this conclusion we do not overlook the cogent economic and sociological arguments which are urged in support of the statute." He nonetheless asserted that the constitutional law was clear and that those who supported the principle of workers' compensation should make their appeals to the people, who had the power to alter the constitution, rather than to the courts.[31]

Having worked so hard and compromised so much to secure the compulsory law, the AALL reformers were heartbroken. Seager recalled several years later:

> I still remember vividly, as a member of the Wainwright Commission, how much anxious thought we gave to trying to draft an act that the Court of Appeals would uphold. The result was doubly disappointing. Our act was maimed and twisted so that it might commend itself to the judges, and, notwithstanding our efforts, those judges unanimously condemned it as unconstitutional.[32]

The *Ives* decision marked a turning point in the movement for workers' compensation. Legislators in many states abandoned the idea of compulsory programs and began drafting elective compensation statutes based on the threat of reduced employer defenses. New Jersey lawmakers enacted an elective system in 1911 which abrogated all major common-law defenses for employers, but which AALL reformers criticized for having inadequate compensation scales and faulty administrative provisions. California established an elective system similar to New Jersey's the same year. Other states that enacted elective workers' compensation laws in

1911—including Illinois, Kansas, Massachusetts, New Hampshire, Ohio, and Wisconsin—put pressure on employees as well as employers: if the employer refused to elect compensation, he lost his common-law defenses; but if the employee refused, then the employer retained those defenses. Ernst Freund described this method as "double-edged coercion."[33]

In November 1911 Seager explained at a joint meeting of the Academy of Political Sciences and the New York Association for Labor Legislation that he opposed the elective approach. He questioned "whether the full advantages of a compensation system can be secured through free contract, that is, without making its acceptance obligatory on all employers and employees alike." More important, he insisted that instead of trying to circumvent the constitution, reformers and legislators should try to keep the constitution abreast of current ideas about justice. "We are thus confronted," Seager declared, "with the clear and manifest duty of amending the state constitution."[34] This, after all, was precisely what Judge Werner had suggested in *Ives*.

State labor leaders supported the idea of a constitutional amendment and soon proposed one that would not only empower the state legislature to enact a compulsory law but also exclude casualty companies from writing workers' compensation policies. Business interests reacted adversely to labor's proposal because they vehemently opposed the prospect of a state-controlled insurance fund. Functioning in their preferred role as mediators, AALL reformers helped to hammer out a compromise amendment that would permit the creation of a state fund without prohibiting private insurance coverage.[35]

Even more controversial than the details of the amendment were the provisions of the workers' compensation law which it would authorize. As the compromise amendment successfully proceeded through the state legislature in 1912 (the first step in a multi-step ratification process),[36] representatives of capital and labor battled over the form of the prospective law. Two leading compensation bills emerged in early 1913. Labor endorsed the Murtaugh-Jackson bill, which would mandate high compensation rates and an exclusive state insurance fund. Conservatives at the State Insurance Department drafted the Foley-Walker bill, which would set lower rates and permit employers to choose private or state insurance. Business figures at the National Civic Federation drafted yet another bill but ultimately supported a modified version of the Foley-Walker proposal.[37]

On the two divisive issues of compensation scales and insurance carriage, leading AALL reformers appear to have supported higher benefits for injured workers and at least some degree of choice for employers regarding form of coverage (state or private). Their position was not always clear. Displaying obvious embarrassment, President Willoughby wrote to Andrews in March explaining that he was confused about the two different bills (Murtaugh-Jackson and Foley-Walker) as well as about the AALL's position on them. One can hardly blame him. In a letter to a conservative correspondent the following day, Andrews explained that the Association supported the Foley-Walker bill, provided it were modified to include higher compensation scales, allowances for real competition between insurance carriers, and a clause making it compulsory upon ratification of the constitutional amendment. Only a week later, the secretary of the AALL's New York branch issued a circular endorsing an amended version of Murtaugh-Jackson, which would allow some private insurance coverage but not by casualty companies. Andrews subsequently indicated that the latter position—of allowing employers to choose between state insurance, self-insurance, and mutual insurance but not coverage by casualty companies—was in fact the position of the AALL.[38]

Through April and early May, AALL reformers lobbied hard for the revised Murtaugh-Jackson bill and for the compromise constitutional amendment, which faced a public referendum in November.[39] Though the state assembly passed Murtaugh-Jackson, both houses of the New York legislature passed an amended Foley-Walker bill, which enjoyed the support of the insurance companies, the National Civic Federation, and a wide range of employers throughout the state. The dashed hopes of the labor-progressive reform coalition were only revived when Democratic Governor William Sulzer vetoed the conservative bill.[40]

Sulzer delivered his veto message just as New York State was beginning to feel the early tremors of a political earthquake, whose epicenters were the governor's mansion and Tammany Hall. After an extended battle with Tammany politicians for control of the party, Governor Sulzer faced charges of fraudulent campaign accounting and was finally impeached and removed from office in October 1913. The following month, New York State voters ratified the workers' compensation amendment and humbled Tammany Hall, turning control of the legislature over to the Republicans.[41]

The former lieutenant-governor who replaced Sulzer in October, Martin Glynn, quickly called a special session of the legislature after the elections. He demanded passage of popular good-government reforms as well as a new workers' compensation bill. Henry Seager and Thomas Parkinson of the AALL played key roles in drafting the new bill. Even after it was modified by labor and business interests, it continued to meet the Association's specifications for high benefit levels (up to two-thirds of wages) and broad compulsory coverage. The Association compromised on only one of its earlier positions—the exclusion of casualty companies—a provision with which most AALL reformers had never felt entirely comfortable. Perhaps to compensate labor for this concession, the new bill would create a central workmen's compensation commission to administer the entire system.[42]

Highly optimistic, AALL reformers pressed forward with their lobbying efforts. Andrews met with political leaders in Albany, including Governor Glynn, and he supplied newspapers with statements about the bill. On December 9, he distributed to employers a letter from Henry Seager endorsing the pending legislation. "Although the plan is doubtless still susceptible of improvement in certain particulars," Seager wrote, "I have no hesitation in saying, after having given it careful study, that, if adopted, it will take its place as one of the best if not the best systems yet put into operation by an American state."[43]

Several days later, the bill became law. AALL reformers relished the victory, and Andrews sent a circular letter to members in New York reviewing the AALL's central role in making it possible. "The enactment of the Glynn Workmen's Compensation Act by the New York legislature on December 12th," he explained, "marks the culmination of a long struggle in which this Association has played an honorable part." He recalled the Association's influence throughout the campaign—from the creation of the Wainwright Commission to the ratification of the constitutional amendment to the final enactment of a broad, compulsory workers' compensation law, which he described as "the best and most carefully drawn compensation law that has yet been passed by any American state."[44]

Even before the bill's passage, Association leaders indicated their belief that the New York campaign was only a beginning. In a letter to New York employers, Seager connected the extension of workers' compensation with the crucial issue of degenerative competition, arguing that the best way to maintain a fair playing field was to support advanced legislation in other states rather than to oppose such legislation in New York. "It should be a source of pride to New York employers," Seager exclaimed, "to have their state again take the lead in compensation legislation, and if they will back up the efforts of organizations like the American Association for Labor Legislation to secure just and uniform labor laws in every state in the Union, they will not long be placed at a competitive disadvantage."[45] Employers across the state, even many who opposed the compensation legislation, probably found Seager's logic compelling once the bill became law. One employer, who supported the new law, wrote to Andrews in January 1914 expressing his concern that it might lead some manufacturers to favor New Jersey over New York as a place to build new factories. "We hear a great deal about the bug-a-boo of manufacturers moving away from New York or out of any state on account of severe labor laws," he wrote. "I do not take any stock in the argument when placed in this form, but it is a very real argument if we say that labor laws, like all other economic factors, play an important part in the selection of a location for a new factory." He added, "I sincerely hope that you will get through a stringent compensation law in New Jersey if for no other purpose than to offset the one which has been enacted in this state."[46]

In part to address the problem of degenerative competition, Association reformers launched campaigns to enact new laws in states that did not yet have workers' compensation and to raise standards in states like New Jersey that had laws which the reformers considered deficient. Though not always successful, the AALL scored many victories during the progressive era, including the enactment of an extremely liberal federal workers' compensation statute in 1916 covering nearly all federal employees.[47] Between 1911 and 1920, over forty states enacted workers' compensation laws. Most of these laws did not meet the Association's strict standards for adequacy and efficiency—standards that included a compensation scale set at two-thirds of wages for total disability, employer choice regarding form of insurance (but with stringent regulations applying to casualty companies), and a centralized accident board to administer the program. Over roughly the next forty years, however, state provisions tended to gravitate toward these standards, which the AALL reformers had first defined in 1914 in the aftermath of the New York campaign.[48]

H istorians have debated the reasons why workers' compensation spread as rapidly as it did during the teens, especially as compared to other forms of social insurance which failed to make much headway. Most agree that business approval was critical and that the preexistence of a system of employers' liability for industrial accidents made the idea of workers' compensation more palatable than that of any other form of social insurance. A related factor that so far has escaped much notice is the moderating influence that the existence of employers' liability law exerted on the problem of degenerative competition. As we have seen, employers typically opposed the enactment of new labor legislation in their own states on the grounds that it would place them at a competitive disadvantage relative to employers in other states who faced no comparable laws. The preexistence of employers' liability at common law in every state, however, meant that the introduction of workers' compensation in one state would not create enormous new costs from which employers in other states were exempt. One manufacturer, who complained bitterly that states enacting health or unemployment insurance would put their industries at a severe competitive disadvantage, admitted that workers' compensation was not subject to the same complaint. "Workmen's compensation," he wrote, "has never been considered as an entirely new expense, because it replaced the old employers' liability, the average cost of which was a large percentage of the present charges resulting from accident."[49] Of course some employers objected to the introduction of any new cost, but their arguments carried less weight when applied to proposed systems of workers' compensation than to most other forms of welfare legislation.[50]

Another issue, which has received a great deal more scholarly attention, concerns the nature and extent of business influence in the struggle for workers' compensation laws. Several historians have characterized the role and needs of business as decisive. "Business imperatives," writes Roy Lubove, "proved more influential in shaping the workmen's compensation system than considerations of equity and social expediency."[51] James Weinstein offers an even bolder interpretation. After describing the rush of workers' compensation legislation in the teens, he writes, "This sweeping achievement was made possible by the concerted activity of the National Civic Federation, with the strong support of its big business affiliates. It represented a growing maturity and sophistication on the part of many large corporation leaders who had come to understand, as Theodore Roosevelt often told them, that social reform was truly conservative."[52]

Business interests did indeed play an important role in helping to shape the workers' compensation law in New York, and they exerted varying amounts of influence elsewhere. Far-seeing business figures found workers' compensation attractive because they recognized that a system of automatic payments would rationalize the costs of industrial injuries and thus eliminate the disruption and uncertainty commonly associated with employers' liability suits.[53] It was mainly for this reason that both the National Civic Federation and the National Association of Manufacturers endorsed workers' compensation.

But there is little evidence to suggest that the influence of business was as overwhelming as Weinstein and even Lubove suggest. The New York case—which offers an unusually complete historical record and is also indicative of what occurred in many other states—is revealing on this point. The majority of employers polled by the Wainwright Commission in 1909–10 opposed compulsory workers' compensation outright. Though large employers, especially those associated with the National Civic Federation, were much more likely than small ones to support the principle of compensation, they were, in the end, far from successful in securing precisely the type of law they desired.[54]

In fact, the AALL reformers probably compromised less than anyone else in the extended struggle for workers' compensation in New York. It would be wrong to say that they secured everything they wanted or that their influence was preponderant. But it is fair to conclude that the leaders of the Association were pivotal in the process and that the bill finally enacted looked more like their original proposals than those of either the employers' groups or organized labor. From the beginning, the most important issues for the AALL were high compensation levels and provisions assuring effective administrative oversight—and they met with success on both.

One additional indication of the Association's independence and success relative to big business in the New York campaign was the great disappointment that prominent Civic Federation members expressed in the AALL throughout 1913. In June, P. Tecumseh Sherman, the lawyer who drafted the NCF's workers' compensation bill and a member of both the NCF and the AALL, wrote a detailed letter to John Andrews. He explained that he was embarrassed to hear Association reformers boasting about their defeat of the Foley-Walker bill and declaring that compensation should be fixed at nothing less than two-thirds of wages. "As you probably know," Sherman wrote, "I disagree with all of those propositions; and they are very important matters." He then distanced himself from the Association's activism on behalf of labor legislation, observing that he had no objection to an association committed to academic debate but that he could not support one actively campaigning for propositions he opposed. Six months later, Sherman again threatened to resign and again cited his intense opposition to the Association's position on workers' compensation and its political activity in New York. The following month, in January 1914, he finally made good on his threat and tendered his resignation.[55]

From that time on, the progressive reformers of the AALL and the representatives of big business and big labor who comprised the NCF found much about which to disagree. The Association reformers did their best to maintain constructive dialogue with their counterparts at the Civic Federation and occasionally joined forces with them. But the search for common ground became increasingly difficult as the decade progressed. Imagining in early 1916 what it would have been like to be secretary of the Civic Federation instead of the AALL, Andrews submitted to Irving Fisher, a strict prohibitionist, "It would, I feel sure, have driven me to drink long ago."[56]

8

Legislative Limits

As the New York workers' compensation campaign was drawing to a close in 1913, the leaders of the American Association for Labor Legislation began to devote serious thought to promoting two new forms of social insurance, covering sickness and joblessness. Only two years before, Britain had enacted health and unemployment insurance for its workers. The AALL reformers decided that the time was ripe to promote comparable legislation in the United States.

Progressive-era reformers generally regarded health insurance as more fundamental than unemployment insurance because sickness was thought to cause more poverty than joblessness or, indeed, any other factor. John Andrews wrote in a paper on social insurance, "America presents no exception to the finding of Sidney and Beatrice Webb, that 'In all countries, at all ages, it is sickness to which the greatest bulk of destitution is immediately due.' "[1] Since founding the AALL, the organization's leaders had conceived of worker insecurity primarily in terms of health and safety risks. The prohibition on poison phosphorus matches constituted the Association's first major victory and the enactment of workers' compensation laws its second. Andrews characterized compulsory health insurance as "the biggest next step in labor legislation."[2]

Though health insurance became the Association's top long-run objective, the problem of unemployment briefly diverted attention during the mid-teens as a result of a sharp economic downturn. Many economic historians do not recognize the recession of 1914–15 as having been particularly severe, but social reformers and wage laborers at the time certainly did. Labor unions across the country reported astonishingly high rates of joblessness among their members. In the six months ending April

1, 1915, 17.2 percent of union members in Massachusetts were unemployed, and the figure reached a startling 32.7 percent in New York State.[3] Local relief committees scrambled to aid the needy, but inevitably they found their small reserves exhausted prematurely.[4] Already in February 1914, at the AALL's First National Conference on Unemployment, the superintendent of the Rhode Island Free Employment Office declared that unemployment conditions in his state had not been worse since the panic of 1907. Numerous AALL reports echoed this observation—that in the "seven lean years" after 1907, the unemployed suffered most in 1914.[5]

The Association's legislative agenda was thus loosely tied to the business cycle. In 1914 and 1915, as the cycle approached its nadir, the leaders of the AALL chose to elongate the planning phase of their health insurance campaign and focus public attention on the problem of unemployment. Once the economy recovered, health insurance quickly regained its dominant position on the Association's legislative agenda, eclipsing all other issues and proposals for the remainder of the decade.

T he leading AALL reformers were both saddened and angered by the human consequences of rising unemployment, but still they recognized in the downturn of 1914–15 an important political opportunity. The crisis, they believed, had alerted the public to the scourge of involuntary unemployment and thereby made it more receptive to proposals for reform. In his annual statement to the International Association on Unemployment, Andrews reported:

> The past year [1914] is noteworthy on account of a change in the prevailing American attitude toward the question [of unemployment]. For the first time it is generally recognized that unemployment is a real and permanent problem in the United States, the result of industrial conditions, and that an appreciable number of wage-earners fall out of work not on account of faults of character or lack of ability, but because it is impossible for them to find places.[6]

Borrowing a phrase from his British friend William Beveridge, Andrews pronounced the following year that, as a result of the economic downturn of 1914–15, unemployment now "gripped and held the attention of leaders of thought and action as an AMERICAN problem and as a problem of INDUSTRY."[7]

Although AALL reformers had thought about the problem of unemployment before, it was only in the winter of 1913, with joblessness mounting, that they began to include remedies for unemployment as important components of their policy agenda. At the heart of their proposals was the belief that most joblessness stemmed from a disorganized and inefficient market for labor. "If we look more deeply into the problem of unemployment," the economist William Leiserson observed at the first national conference, "we shall find that it is entirely a problem of maladjustment. In the United States at least, there is no permanent surplus of labor in excess of demand."[8] Since maladjustment was the problem, the reformers proposed readjustment as the solution. Gradually, John Andrews crafted a four-point program—the AALL's "Practical Program for the Prevention of Unemployment"—which aimed to reduce unemployment by coordinating supply and demand in the labor market.[9]

The first recommendation in the "Practical Program" called for the creation of efficient employment exchanges, where civil servants would work to unite employers looking for workers with workers looking for jobs. The Association began pushing the idea in early 1914, and, in New York, the mayor of New York City and the governor of the state quickly complied, introducing employment-exchange bills in March 1914. Both bills were enacted into law that spring. Meanwhile, reformers at the AALL helped to draft a bill for Congress that would create an employment exchange bureau inside the federal Department of Labor; and, over the next year, five more state legislatures and a number of municipalities followed New York in passing employment exchange laws.[10]

The second recommendation in the "Practical Program" was for countercyclical spending on public works. Since seasonal unemployment tended to rise sharply during the winter months, it seemed reasonable that local governments should undertake a disproportionately large share of their public works projects during the winter. Governments at all levels, moreover, could conserve public work during prosperous times in order to permit the expansion of public employment during cyclical depressions. Well-timed public works, Andrews wrote, would "act as a sponge, absorbing the reserves of labor in bad years and slack seasons, and setting them free again when the demand for them increases in private business."[11]

In 1914 and 1915, Association staff launched investigations into the existence and efficacy of public works projects in the United States. The results confirmed not only the reformers' assumptions that concentrating public work during the winter could reduce unemployment, but also their suspicions that countercyclical public works remained an underutilized weapon in the American arsenal against unemployment. Andrews lamented to William Hard in 1916, "I am afraid three first-class illustrations of the use of public work to counteract hard times cannot be found in the United States. There has been lots of talk about the idea, but mighty little action."[12]

The AALL's third proposal, industrial regularization, was simply the private counterpart to countercyclical public works. Popular within the growing ranks of scientific managers, the notion of industrial regularization suggested that employers could reduce unemployment by stabilizing production patterns across seasons and across business cycles.[13] If toy makers, for example, produced steadily all year round rather than intensively just before Christmas, workers in their factories would have regular employment. In addition to reducing joblessness, the reformers argued, regularization would strengthen employer-employee relations and increase plant efficiency. Commons wrote several years later that employment regularization constituted "the first step in industrial goodwill."[14]

Although a small number of private firms claimed to practice regularization voluntarily and to find it profitable, the reformers recognized that most firms would not take up the practice until forced to do so. They regarded compulsory unemployment insurance, the fourth point in their "Practical Program," as the ideal means of coercing firms to regularize employment and thus as the most promising of their measures to combat joblessness.[15]

In 1915 leading AALL reformers began suggesting to a few friendly employers that it might be profitable for them to experiment with private unemployment-compensation schemes. At the same time, they commenced drafting a compulsory unemployment insurance bill for introduction into state legislatures. Though their proposals for private experimentation generated little enthusiasm,[16] their activities on behalf of compulsory unemployment insurance stimulated a great deal of public interest. Over the next two years, the organization's leaders pushed their nascent legislative campaign in a number of states, but most aggressively in Massachusetts.

In prosecuting their campaign there, the Association's Social Insurance Committee worked closely with the Massachusetts Committee on Unemployment (MCU).[17] Despite some conflict over which committee would take the lead in actually drafting the proposed legislation, the reformers in Massachusetts and New York made rapid progress and nearly completed a draft by the end of 1915. When they introduced the bill in the Massachusetts House of Representatives on January 14, 1916, it was the first time an unemployment insurance bill had been put before a legislative body in the United States.[18]

The bill's drafters had taken as their model the unemployment insurance section of Great Britain's 1911 National Insurance Act. Like the British act, the Massachusetts bill would have established a compulsory unemployment insurance scheme for specified trades and granted subsidies to trade associations that operated voluntary plans. Also like the

British system, the Massachusetts program would have rated contribution and benefit levels according to employee income. It would have denied benefits to any worker unable or unwilling to work. It would have mandated joint funding by employers, employees, and the state. And it would have targeted refunds—as inducements to the prevention of unemployment—to employers (annually) and to employees (in a lump sum at age sixty) who demonstrated especially good employment records.[19]

Notwithstanding a few minor changes, which tended to increase incentives for employers to prevent unemployment, the Massachusetts bill constituted little more than a replica of the British statute.[20] It certainly paled by comparison to the AALL's model health insurance bill, which was the product of several years of painstaking deliberation, drafting, and redrafting. The difference in care given to the two bills is telling. As economic conditions began to improve in the second half of 1915 and as public interest in the problem of joblessness waned, the AALL reformers focused less and less attention on unemployment insurance. Their bill died in the Massachusetts legislature in 1916. Although the leaders of the Association remained serious about unemployment insurance, they decided that public support simply was not strong enough to justify reintroducing their model bill in 1917. John Commons resurrected the campaign when unemployment rates surged again at the beginning of the next decade. But for the balance of the progressive era, the leaders of the AALL chose to focus their energies on their highest legislative priority, health insurance.[21]

T he Association's reformers conceived of their work on health insurance as a logical continuation of their struggle for workers' compensation.[22] Indeed, having seen workers' compensation laws spread quickly, they viewed the enactment of health insurance as virtually inevitable. At a general discussion during the Association's 1916 annual meeting, Andrews said of health insurance, "It is coming. It is inevitable, and you, I am sure, will help bring it about."[23]

Andrews and his colleagues had many good reasons to think they would be as successful with health insurance as they had been with workers' compensation. On the most fundamental level, they believed that the threat of ill health was an even greater cause of worker insecurity than was that of industrial accidents; and they believed that health insurance would do for sickness what workers' compensation had done for accidents. As the AALL's 1916 "Brief for Health Insurance" noted, "That in this country, as well as abroad, a decided improvement in factory hygiene may be looked for following the introduction of health insurance is shown by the American experience with workmen's compensation." Invoking the internalization argument, the "Brief" explained that money benefits "will set a cash value upon health, and will thereby stimulate the needed campaign for the prevention of illness."[24]

Equally important, the Association reformers maintained that health insurance would provide working-class families with vital financial security in the face of illness that could not be prevented. "As workmen's compensation has gone far toward eliminating industrial accident as a factor in poverty," an AALL publication read, "so health insurance will serve as a protection against the financial loss due to temporary illness."[25] Since workers' compensation covered both necessary medical care and lost wages resulting from industrial accidents, health insurance, the reformers argued, ought to cover both necessary medical care and lost wages resulting from sickness. In fact, most progressive-era proponents of compulsory health insurance believed that a cash benefit in time of sickness was as important as, if not more important than, free access to medical services. Miles Dawson explained to the Massachusetts Special Commission on Social Insurance in 1916 that "sickness insurance is primarily for the purpose of maintaining families when the bread winners are unable on account of sickness to maintain them." Another AALL member insisted that "social insurance is not merely a medical question, but . . . a question of the proper support of the family."[26]

Finally, the AALL reformers argued that health insurance, like workers' compensation, had to be made compulsory because most workers proved unable to save for periods of illness on their own and because the private insurance coverage actually available to workers was sorely inadequate. While the reformers acknowledged that physicians and hospitals often provided free services to the destitute, they emphasized that regular wage earners usually failed to qualify and, even when they did, typically resisted being classed as charity cases.[27] According to the Metropolitan Life Insurance Company's 1915 sickness survey of 7,638 families in Rochester, New York, only 45.3 percent of sick persons who were able to work and 63 percent of those fully incapacitated by illness were under the care of a physician or medical institution.[28]

While some private health insurance already existed in the 1910s and group insurance was just beginning to appear, policies available to workers were extremely limited.[29] Most wage-earning families earned either less or only marginally more than what contemporary economists defined as a minimally adequate income (about $800 per year), and these families thus found little room in their budgets for savings or insurance. Careful observers estimated that typical working families saved less than a single week's income per year. And although it was quite common during this period for workers to purchase various forms of insurance, they usually paid substantial premiums (about two weeks' income, on average) for very limited coverage. Under the most popular form of insurance, called "industrial insurance," workers contributed small weekly sums in return for death benefits, usually just enough to pay funeral expenses. According to Andrews' sources, 32 industrial insurance companies in the United States as of 1911 carried about 2.47 million policies, which grossed $183.5 million for the companies and paid out only a little over $50 million in benefits.[30] Reformers insisted that other forms of coverage to which workers subscribed—fraternal, trade union, and establishment (company) funds—were similarly inefficient. Seager asserted that compulsory health insurance was justified "on the ground that experience everywhere has shown that voluntary insurance will not reach the classes which need it most."[31]

The Association's Committee on Social Insurance had begun hammering out standards for a model American health insurance bill in late 1913, and the committee finally published its "Preliminary Standards for Sickness Insurance" about a year later. By November 1915, committee members had agreed on a tentative draft of an act, which the Association introduced in revised form in the New York, Massachusetts, and New Jersey legislatures the following January.[32]

In crafting their model bill, the AALL reformers attempted to address both economic and political problems. The system they proposed would have covered all manual laborers and all other workers who earned less than $100 a month. To pay for benefits and administration, it would assess employers 40 percent, employees 40 percent,[33] and the state 20 percent of total costs. Contributions, typically, would be paid into local mutual funds, which were to be administered equally by employers and employees. Labor union, fraternal, and company funds that met well-defined standards would be permitted to serve as substitutes for the local mutuals. In case of sickness, accident, or death not covered by workers' compensation, insured workers would be entitled to receive cash benefits of up to two-thirds of wages; medical, surgical, and nursing attendance; medical and surgical supplies; maternity benefits; and funeral benefits. Dependent family members of insured workers would be entitled to complete medical coverage including maternity care, and the maternity benefits of insured women would include both cash payments and medical care during an eight-week period surrounding childbirth.[34] It is worth repeating that the reformers viewed the cash benefit provisions as at least as important as the provisions assuring adequate medical services.

The insurance provisions of the AALL's model bill were patterned after the German system, which depended mainly on self-governing local mutual funds. The British, by contrast, had organized their system around existing friendly societies, which were not necessarily local in character and which were open to the involvement of large commercial carriers. With the notable exception of Frederick Hoffman, who worked for the Prudential Life Insurance Company of America, most of the members of the AALL's Social Insurance Committee favored the German plan. They believed that local mutual funds would ascertain risks more precisely, transmit prevention incentives more directly and effectively, present fewer opportunities for adverse selection problems, and cost less to administer than would dispersed voluntary societies that might be associated with commercial (for-profit) carriers.[35]

This marked a definite change from the wavering position of the AALL reformers regarding the proper form of insurance carriage during the workers' compensation campaign. By proposing to exclude commercial carriers, they had, almost unknowingly, guaranteed the development of a new political dynamic in the impending battle over health insurance. Between 1914 and 1917, Frederick Hoffman moved from being a strong supporter and active member of the AALL to being its most vociferous critic, regularly referring to the organization's compulsory health insurance proposals as "un-American."[36] In retrospect, his early resistance foreshadowed that of the insurance industry as a whole and might have served as an early warning to the AALL about the political minefield that lay ahead.

Before 1917, however, the Association's leaders spent little time worrying about either the arguments or the passions of their critics. Assuming that their campaign for health insurance was a logical extension of their campaign for workers' compensation, they patterned their new political strategy after their old one—repeating what had worked, while trying to correct in advance for what had not.[37] As in the case of workers' compensation, their first step was to begin building support among essential interest groups. They approached the usual parties, organized labor and employers, as well as one new one, physicians. While expecting disagreement and even opposition regarding the specifics of their model bill, the reformers nonetheless hoped that essential agreement could be reached on matters of principle, as had been true in the case of workers' compensation.

As early as August 1914, Andrews explained to a friend at Wellesley College that he was particularly interested in winning the support of physicians, for whom a social insurance campaign would be a new experience. "As you of course know," he wrote, "many of the physicians are not exactly what we would call social minded, but I have hoped that by interesting a few of the leaders in the principal industrial centers well in

advance of the introduction of bills it might head off much opposition."
Andrews then sent notes to an official at the American Medical Association (AMA) and to the editors of a variety of medical journals, informing them of the AALL's plans regarding health insurance and urging them to publish favorable editorials.[38]

Andrews' letters marked the beginning of a positive, but short-lived, relationship with leading representatives of the medical profession. The American Medical Association, so often characterized as an intensely conservative organization, was actually in the midst of a reformist phase during the early teens—a phase that dated back to the opening of the century.[39] AALL reformers were pleasantly surprised to find key figures at the AMA receptive to their proposals for health insurance. Frederick R. Green, the secretary of the AMA's Council on Health and Public Instruction, wrote to Andrews in November 1915 to express his full support for the AALL's public health agenda. He noted that Andrews' proposals were "so entirely in line with our own that I want to be of every possible assistance," and he suggested a definite plan of cooperation between the AMA and the AALL.[40]

Over the next four months, reformers from the two associations succeeded in establishing official links through which to cooperate and coordinate; and the *Journal of the American Medical Association,* as well as other medical publications, printed favorable pieces on health insurance. The apparent support of the AMA reassured Andrews, even though he knew that many doctors and medical societies openly opposed health insurance and that many more were likely ambivalent to it. Mindful of the resistance that British physicians had put up against the National Insurance Act, he boasted to an English correspondent in February that he did not "believe we are going to have the trouble with the doctors which you had in England. I hope they have learned from your experience."[41] No doubt Andrews also believed that his Association's consensus-building initiatives were superior to those practiced by his counterparts across the Atlantic.

In addition to forging ties with physicians, the AALL reformers sought to build support among workers and employers and to formalize relationships with representatives of organized labor and employers' associations. Yet they quickly discovered that representatives of big capital and big labor at the National Civic Federation unambiguously opposed this form of social insurance. There was little hope of converting men like Samuel Gompers and Ralph Easley, who had supported workers' compensation but characterized both health and unemployment insurance as irreconcilable with fundamental American liberties. The reformers were nonetheless optimistic about finding support at the grassroots and among smaller trade and labor organizations. In typical AALL style, the reformers tailored a different message to each audience. They advised employers to get involved quickly so as to avoid having health insurance passed without their input. At the same time, the reformers reassured workers that the AALL's health insurance bill strongly favored labor and would triumph "even though insurance companies and some employers' associations are out after us with an axe!"[42]

The vast majority of employers probably viewed the prospect of more social insurance with skepticism if not hostility. Yet officials of the National Association of Manufacturers and other employers' organizations seemed initially to accept the AALL's warning—that it was better for employers to take part in shaping new social insurance legislation than to have it enacted over their opposition.[43] AALL and NAM officials began communicating about health insurance in the middle of 1914 and continued to communicate amicably over the next year and a half. They disagreed about many details, such as whether or not commercial insurance carriers should be allowed to write compulsory health insurance policies. But they seemed to agree that legislation of some sort was necessary. In the eyes of the reformers, it must have appeared as if the NAM was moving in their direction, especially when its Committee on Industrial Betterment reported favorably on health insurance in May 1916.[44]

The AALL's early dealings with organized labor on the subject of health insurance were perhaps more contentious, but no less productive, than those with employers. Though Gompers and the AFL had changed sides, many state labor federations remained basically cooperative. Labor leaders in Massachusetts and New York, for example, differed with the AALL over details (especially regarding overinsurance[45] and occupational disease coverage) and often had negative words to say about the AALL, but they nonetheless endorsed the idea of compulsory health insurance. When the president of the New York State Federation of Labor spoke out against the AALL's bill at a legislative hearing in Albany, Andrews confidently dismissed his opposition as "half-hearted."[46]

The fact that most interest groups seemed to support health insurance in principle was crucial in sustaining the reformers' confidence in their campaign. In Andrews' testimony at a 1916 legislative hearing in New York, he appeared pleasantly surprised that there was not more vigorous opposition: "I think it is favorable, indeed, that the discussion has been almost uniformly in favor of the health insurance principle, and that objection has been merely to certain details of the bill."[47] Similarly, at a hearing before the Massachusetts Special Commission on Social Insurance, Carroll W. Doten of the AALL's social insurance committee observed "how mild and how weak" were the opponents' arguments compared to those presented years before by the critics of workers' compensation. "I can remember the assurance with which the employers and those who opposed such legislation came forward here and thundered their opposition," he said. "Today they mildly suggest that there are certain things that are not altogether satisfactory [with the health insurance bill], and that there are certain things which even this sort of legislation will not remedy."[48]

The leaders of the AALL also took comfort in the fact that their opponents' arguments were predictable—the same ones that had failed in previous years to block the enactment of workers' compensation.[49] The most formidable objections, which were advanced by employers, highlighted the threat of competitive disadvantage. The author of a July 1916 article in the trade journal *Iron Age,* for example, complained that new costs associated with both unemployment and health insurance "would not be uniform between the States. It is not difficult to conceive of such legislation increasing [labor costs] to the extent of compelling manufacturers to move their works out of State, or of causing the shutting down of plants the owners of which have factories in other States where manufacturing could be done more cheaply."[50]

Well prepared for the competitive disadvantage argument, AALL reformers counter-punched at every opportunity. At the March 1916 hearing in New York, Miles Dawson noted wryly that one of the employers who claimed health insurance would put him out of business had made exactly the same claim in reference to workers' compensation several years before. I. M. Rubinow reinforced this point: ". . . I want to see the industry in this State, at this time, that cannot bear a burden of one per cent. on its payroll, and that would have to move to New Jersey . . . Gentlemen, the same threat was made years ago, on the Workmen's Compensation, and I have still to hear of a single firm that had to move." The obvious implication of these remarks was that the opposition was old and tired and not to be trusted.[51]

At least through 1916, the AALL reformers believed—for all of these reasons—that their legislative campaigns were under control and proceeding according to plan. They had never assumed that they would secure enactment of their bills in the very first year they introduced them. What they wanted and expected was the establishment of investigatory commissions in the various states. Their quick introduction of health insurance bills was purely a tactical move. As Andrews informed Carroll Doten in late 1915, "Our experience has been that to work first for a legislative commission to study the subject is a mistake from the standpoint of tactics." A superior approach, he explained, involved introducing a live bill, lobbying hard for it, and then counting on the opposition to propose an investigatory commission as a diversion. And this is precisely what happened in both New York and Massachusetts in 1916.[52]

Although the proposal to create a commission died in the New York Assembly, investigatory commissions were created in California and Massachusetts.[53] Soon after Governors Hiram W. Johnson of California and Samuel W. McCall of Massachusetts publicly endorsed health insurance in January 1917, the two commissions followed suit by endorsing health insurance in official reports to their respective state legislatures. In addition, the California Social Insurance Commission recommended an amendment to the state's constitution that would remove all judicial obstacles to compulsory health insurance. To the surprise of Andrews and his colleagues, neither commission specifically endorsed the AALL's model bill.[54]

The dawn of 1917 marked the beginning of a new and much more dramatic phase of the battle over health insurance. Reformers exploited the momentum they had built in 1916 to expand the scope of their campaign, while opponents, freshly organized, began to identify their allies and to coordinate a powerful counteroffensive. In 1916 the AALL reformers had introduced their model health insurance bill in three state legislatures. In 1917 at least twelve legislatures considered similar bills,[55] and California lawmakers debated the merits of the constitutional amendment that their Social Insurance Commission had recommended for ratification. Andrews and his colleagues interpreted this expansion as confirmation of their belief that health insurance was inevitable. In retrospect, though, it is clear that they consistently underestimated the strength and resolve of their opponents.[56]

From the beginning, a formidable array of interests opposed compulsory health insurance: commercial insurance carriers, physicians, labor leaders, prominent capitalists, druggists, employers, fraternal societies, and Christian Scientists. Yet until 1917, most of these critics remained isolated and barely audible. What silenced or, at least, muted many of them in the early stages of the campaign was the aura of inevitability that surrounded health insurance. Why launch a public attack only to end up on the losing side?[57]

The resulting disorganization and ineffectiveness of much of the opposition instilled not only false confidence within reformers but also false fears within the opponents' own ranks. In many instances through 1916, opponents mistook their allies for enemies. Many employers insisted that doctors in search of guaranteed incomes were the driving force behind the health insurance bill, while some doctors charged that it was the big insurance companies that were "stirring up sentiment" for the proposed law.[58] No doubt, leaders of the AALL were misled by their opponents' internal bickering and finger-pointing. Reflecting on the campaign a generation later, Rubinow acknowledged that progressive-era reformers had been guilty of "over-enthusiasm, over-confidence . . . and last but not least failure to recognize the various class and group interests involved." After carefully reviewing a long list of opponents, he concluded that nearly everyone seemed to be against health insurance. "And who was for it?" he asked.

> An energetic, largely self-appointed group, which could compensate by its enthusiasm and literary ability what it lacked in numbers and which carried with it the profession of social work, to some extent the university teaching groups, the economic and social sciences, and even the political progressive organizations, but very little support beyond these narrow circles.

Of course, Rubinow himself had been one of the overenthusiastic and overconfident reformers who declared in December 1916 that it was "impossible to escape the conclusion that we are on the very eve of constructive [health insurance] legislation."[59]

By 1917, however, the thin threads of consensus that the AALL had attempted to weave together over the previous two years were beginning to unravel and fray. Reformers must have found the growing resistance among physicians especially disappointing after their apparent success in establishing links with the AMA. At the AALL's annual meeting in December 1916, physicians from Ohio estimated that at least eight in ten doctors from that state opposed health insurance. In February, Andrews began to receive the same message from doctors in New York.[60] Physicians worried about becoming "cog[s] in a great medical machine." They also feared loss of income that they expected would result from their diminished bargaining power relative to the big insurance funds. At a New York legislative hearing in 1918, Dr. Israel Strauss, who supported compulsory health insurance, explained that most doctors were wary of the bill "because of the experience they have had with the Workmen's Compensation Act . . . which puts the physician and patient at the mercy of the insurance company—the most unjust provision ever enacted."[61]

AALL reformers remained on good terms with a number of important figures at the AMA who continued to support their health insurance bill—especially Alexander Lambert, the chairman of the AMA's social insurance committee. Yet the Medical Association's leadership found it impossible to ignore the mounting opposition within both its own ranks and the general membership. Even Frederick Green, one of the earliest and most vocal proponents of health insurance in the AMA, radically altered his position sometime in 1917, now claiming that he had never supported health insurance.[62] Before long, the AMA stood as one of the pillars of the opposition to the AALL's health insurance campaign.

Less shocking than the AMA's gradual reversal, but no less disappointing, was the defection of the National Association of Manufacturers. The NAM's Committee on Industrial Betterment, which had reported favorably on health insurance in May 1916, downgraded its recommendation the following year—this time explicitly supporting only voluntary health insurance. A representative of the manufacturers' association, A. Parker Nevin, betrayed the significance of this change at the 1917 Judiciary Committee hearing in Albany. "I don't think there is a person in this room who opposes the principle of sickness insurance," he said, "but the principle of direct legislative mandatory compulsory insurance is a horse of a different color." Thereafter, NAM officials consistently and vigorously resisted proposals for compulsory health insurance.[63]

Like Nevin, many prominent opponents of social insurance expressed aversion to the prospect of state compulsion. To borrow a phrase from the historian Roy Lubove, they adhered to the American ethic of voluntarism.[64] One of the most passionate defenders of voluntarism was Samuel Gompers, the longstanding president of the American Federation of Labor. In his view, all forms of compulsory social insurance other than workers' compensation constituted state paternalism, which would compromise personal liberty, weaken the labor movement, and damage the individual worker's prospects for securing better wages and working conditions through voluntary collective bargaining. In 1916 the Executive Council of the AFL expressed its concern about "persistent agitation in favor of compulsory social insurance laws" and, like the NAM, strongly recommended consideration of voluntary but not compulsory legislation.[65]

Gompers' fierce opposition to health and unemployment insurance was frequently cited by other critics, especially by other members of the National Civic Federation. In a 1916 letter to an AALL staff member, Ralph Easley, the chairman of the NCF's Executive Council, highlighted Gompers' position and claimed that the American worker opposed health insurance because he "does not desire to be regulated in his personal affairs."[66] The Civic Federation was one of the only national organizations that openly opposed compulsory health and unemployment insurance—at both the state and federal levels—from virtually the moment reformers in the United States began their campaigns. By 1917, however, the uncompromising stance of men like Easley and Gompers had become commonplace.[67]

Of all the interest groups that ultimately aligned against compulsory health insurance, the best organized and most effective was the commercial insurance industry. Just three days after Senator Ogden Mills introduced the AALL's health insurance bill in the New York State Senate for the first time in January 1916, the president of the Great Eastern Casualty Company circulated a letter to his New York agents, urging them to join the New York Insurance Federation in opposing the bill. "This is only the opening wedge," the president warned:

> if once a foothold is obtained it will mean attempts to have such State Insurance of all kinds including Fire. It would mean the end of all Insurance Companies and Agents and to you personally the complete wrecking of the business and connections you have spent a lifetime in building and the loss of your bread and butter.

The only way to stop the onslaught, he counseled, was to organize, and this is why "insurance men" in a number of states had created insurance federations. Explaining that the New York Federation was "composed of thousands of earnest thinkers who realize that their living is at stake," he implored the agents "for your own sake to join this Federation and do all in your power in your own locality to combat this pernicious un-American idea of State Insurance with all its political evils and new burdens to be thrown on the public."[68]

As I. M. Rubinow later observed, the AALL reformers had anticipated a serious challenge from insurance interests but underestimated its strength because private health insurance comprised only a tiny fraction of the industry's business at the time. Two factors—one difficult to foresee and the other disturbingly plain—were, in Rubinow's view, responsible for the intensity of the industry's response. First, many insurance executives quickly recognized when confronted with the prospect of compulsory health insurance that they had failed to appreciate the potential of private sickness insurance, which constituted an enormously profitable field into which they could expand. Second, officials of the powerful industrial insurance companies viewed with alarm the death benefit provision that AALL reformers had written into their model bill. Industrial insurance, which typically covered the funeral expenses of insured workers, was very popular among working Americans who dreaded the prospect of pauper burials. The big firms that offered industrial insurance, such as the Prudential and the Metropolitan life insurance companies, earned huge profits on these policies. Since a compulsory health insurance bill that covered funeral costs would likely decimate the business of industrial insurance,[69] vigorous opposition from the affected carriers should have been expected. "By including the funeral benefit," Rubinow quipped, "the health insurance movement signed its own death warrant."[70]

Like nearly every other interest that opposed health insurance, the insurance companies initiated their counteroffensive quietly, hoping to extinguish the legislative threat while projecting a positive public image. Andrews noted in February 1916 that although various insurance carriers were privately advising their agents to join the Insurance Federation, "in public [they] are repudiating the hast[y] and ill-considered action of this body!"[71] No insurance representatives spoke at the New York hearing in March, and those who spoke at the Massachusetts hearing claimed not yet to have decided on their position.[72] As late as September 1917, Guy W. Cox of Metropolitan Life suggested diplomatically before the Massachusetts Special Commission on Social Insurance, "It is unthinkable that the Metropolitan Life Insurance Company as a corporate entity could have the slightest objection to the State embarking up any scheme of insurance, health or otherwise, provided the Commonwealth did not endow its scheme with special privileges and special opportunities under the law."[73] Of course Cox knew perfectly well that special privileges for the state (in the form of exclusive, nonprofit mutual funds) were precisely what the AALL reformers had in mind.

Without question, insurance carriers and their agents constituted the most effective opposition to health insurance in the country. Andrews estimated in 1917 that "nine-tenths of the opposition to social health insurance progress comes directly from men who are in the hire of private insurance companies."[74] While insurance representatives in a number of states organized statewide federations to lead fights against specific bills, others created a national organization, the Insurance Economics Society of America based in Detroit. Ronald Numbers has described the Economics Society as the carriers' "principal propaganda organization."[75] Its chief propagandist, William Gale Curtis (chairman of the society's Educational Committee), regularly red-baited reformers and their proposals for social insurance. "When Compulsory Health Insurance enters the United States," read one of the society's papers, "Socialism will have its foot upon the throat of the nation."[76]

Such inflammatory rhetoric pervaded the health insurance campaign and became especially conspicuous after America's entrance into World War I. As has been mentioned, the most prominent source of this type of rhetoric was an individual who had been an active member of the AALL for years, Frederick L. Hoffman. Hoffman worked for the Prudential Life Insurance Company and had played an important role in many of the Association's early campaigns, including those for the prohibition of phosphorus matches, the reporting of occupational diseases, and the enactment of the second federal workers' compensation statute.[77] After terminating his involvement with the Association at the end of 1916, Hoffman published *Facts and Fallacies of Compulsory Health Insurance,* a biting critique of both health insurance (which he characterized as un-American and socialistic) and its supporters (whom he described as "not only thoroughly untrustworthy but decidedly dangerous as self-constituted leaders of public opinion")[78] One hundred one pages long, *Facts and Fallacies* quickly became the bible of the opposition.

The proponents of health insurance continued to press their campaigns aggressively in numerous states and continued to speak of health insurance legislation as inevitable. Yet the opposition was becoming increasingly difficult to ignore. In 1917, *The Monitor* (the journal of a prominent trade association based in upstate New York) reprinted a New York legislative hearing on health insurance with the following subtitle: "Hearing before Judiciary Committee of Senate on the Mills' Health Insurance measure radically different from hearing of one year ago—Powerful speeches in opposition hurl incontrovertible facts at those who favor socialistic legislation."[79] Though the subtitle, like much of *The Monitor*'s editorial content, must be discounted for its obvious hyperbole and bias, it nonetheless announced an important shift in the political balance after 1916. The opposition, previously disorganized, muted, and insecure, was overcoming each of these deficiencies and expressing itself with ever greater vigor. Over the next three years, enemies of health insurance would proceed to defeat the AALL reformers decisively in battles all across the country.

Two heated political contests, at opposite ends of the continent, stand out as particularly important: the public referendum on the proposed health insurance enabling amendment in California and the ongoing legislative campaign in New York. In California, State Senator William Kehoe, who had inaugurated the legislation creating the California Social Insurance Commission in 1915, introduced the commission's proposed constitutional amendment into the legislature on January 25, 1917. The senate and assembly passed the bill in April, and the secretary of state signed it on May 4.[80] The final step in the ratification procedure involved a public referendum scheduled for November 6, 1918. In the interim, California became the center of the national debate over compulsory health insurance.

Leading AALL reformers had remarked on the special promise of California early on in their political campaign, at least a year before the California commission issued its report. Andrews wrote to a correspondent in January 1916 suggesting that although the AALL already had introduced a bill in Massachusetts and was about to introduce another in New York, he believed "that California should be the first state to adopt the compulsory bill . . ."[81] While Association leaders kept in close touch with activists there, the Golden State was one of the few in which reformers associated with the AALL did not run the campaign. Rubinow played an important role as a consultant to the Social Insurance Commission and an examiner during its hearings.[82] With this prominent exception, AALL reformers stayed out of California. For one thing, they were frustrated that the state's commission had not adopted their model bill, and they regularly wrote long letters touting their bill's superiority over the commission's proposal.[83] Even more important, the reputation of the AALL had become something of a liability in California's politically charged environment. When Andrews was considering a cross-country trip in June 1918, an active member of the California commission's staff counseled against it, noting that "the California public allows the opposition to social measures to make good capital of 'easterners coming out here to tell us what to do.'" Andrews, moreover, was not just any easterner. "I know you will take my question about the wisdom of your coming on the absolutely impersonal ground on which it is made," the staffer continued. "Mullen, the Editor of the Labor Clarion here, is going to fight us to a finish and goes out of his way to say that The American Association for Labor Legislation is The American Assassination for Labor Legislation."[84]

If nasty epithets had been the opposition's only weapon, reformers in California would have had little to worry about. But the opposition was also well funded and well organized. Physicians founded the League for the Conservation of Public Health, and an alliance of Christian Scientists and insurance interests chartered the California Research Society of Social Economics. Both were front organizations with the sole objective of defeating compulsory health insurance. Ernestine Black, the commission staffer who advised Andrews not to visit California, estimated that an "overwhelming majority" of doctors opposed the amendment and were willing to fight against it under the auspices of the league. The Research Society posed an even greater threat. According to a sworn statement subsequently filed by a member of its staff, the society was secretly supported by the Insurance Economics Society of America, whose secretary, Carleton D. Babcock, was also the secretary of the California affiliate. The California Research Society was thus well funded by the insurance industry. It was also able to tap into the seemingly limitless energy of the state's Christian Scientists. Said Black, "The Christian Scientists actually made it a religion to see that everyone had literature against the measure."[85]

Extensive and personalized distribution of pamphlets, letters, and fliers constituted the opposition's primary means of reaching the electorate.

"Every citizen received propaganda against the measure," Black explained to Andrews, "not coming as an anonymous communication, but signed by some friend, lists evidently having been made out and distributed to the proper people to get this personal touch everywhere." The opponents' literature usually appealed to wartime hatred of all things German as well as to fears of higher taxes and creeping socialism. One widely circulated pamphlet was emblazoned on the front with a picture of the Kaiser and the caption, "Born in Germany. Do you want it in California?" Another, put out by the League for the Conservation of Public Health, claimed that health insurance was an invention of the Kaiser and the plaything of a "handful of theorists." It would "engraft a monster political machine on California," serve as a magnet for the "semi-invalids" of the whole nation, and, of course, break the back of the California taxpayer.[86]

Proponents of the health insurance enabling amendment found themselves completely outclassed. About the only two organized bodies that actively supported the amendment were the Social Insurance Commission, which took charge of the campaign, and the state Federation of Labor. Unfortunately for the commissioners, Governor Hiram Johnson's successor, William D. Stephens, was not an advocate of social insurance. Stephens did his best to ignore the issue in public, but most of the amendment's champions believed that he worked behind the scenes to sabotage their efforts. Black claimed that a majority of Stephens' advisers were Christian Scientists, as were the chairman of the Board of Control and the state treasurer. When the commission put together a flier on the advantages of health insurance, the state Board of Control instructed that it not be distributed. And in the final weeks of the campaign, the state treasurer began withholding money appropriated for the commission because he maintained that it was being used to disseminate propaganda.[87]

By September 1918, even its strongest supporters recognized that the amendment was in deep trouble. One of the AALL's California correspondents wrote on the first of the month that she was not sure it would pass because "California is chafing somewhat under the large number of commissions at work." Six weeks later, Ansley K. Salz, an adviser to the Social Insurance Commission, sent a desperate telegram to Andrews. He insisted that the situation was "practically hopeless for our amendment" and offered the following assessment:

> Stevens Administration against us doing everything possible to hamper us. Opposition better organized and financed than any previous fight on any other measure. House to house canvass and real financed publicity campaign being made by Christian Scientists, insurance companies and most of the doctors spreading deliberate falsehood. Almost all press opposed. Situation getting worse all the time.

Salz pleaded for financial assistance from the east to prevent a terrible defeat, but it was no use. On election day the amendment was trounced, 358,324 to 133,858. It was the first and only public referendum on the issue of health insurance anywhere in the country, and, notwithstanding the reformers' suggestions to the contrary, the result was as bruising as it was decisive.[88]

In the aftermath of the California defeat, the progressive-era movement for health insurance enjoyed one last gasp in New York—which, for a brief period, seemed as if it might breathe new life into the campaign. Having failed to secure either a health insurance law or an investigatory commission in New York in 1916, the AALL reformers renewed their campaign in the Empire State in 1917, only to meet with precisely the same result.[89] By 1918, however, on their third attempt, the AALL reformers boasted a powerful new ally. They had begun in the previous year working with the Health Committee of the New York State Federation of Labor and succeeded in drafting a new health insurance bill that satisfied state labor officials. The most important changes included elimination of state contributions (other than for supervisory costs), exclusion of fraternal and trade union funds from the system, limitation on cash benefits to a maximum of $8 per week, explicit prohibitions on linking worker insurance to physical examinations, inclusion of family members, expansion of maternity benefits, and extension of coverage to all workers (that is, not only those who earned under $100 per month, as proposed in the original bill). For federation leaders, these modifications assured broader coverage and, most importantly, a minimum of interference with existing fraternal and union benefit funds. The federation's Health Committee described the new bill as "free from features objectionable to trade unionists and retaining the good points of the earlier proposals." On February 6, 1918, two hundred federation delegates gave it their unanimous approval.[90]

Senator Mills' successor, Courtlandt Nicoll, introduced the AALL-State Federation bill into the state senate in early 1918. Though Gompers and the AFL continued to oppose compulsory health insurance in all its forms, the new position of organized labor within New York significantly altered the political balance there. The new bill certainly frightened officials at the Associated Manufacturers and Merchants of New York. An article in *The Monitor* protested that if the State Federation secured passage of the bill, it "would absolutely have every manufacturer, merchant, or other employer in this State by the throat and could enforce any demand that any business agent desired to make." Mark Daly, the general secretary of the Associated Manufacturers, charged that the AALL "now has prostituted itself to the 'win-at-any-cost' faction of organized labor" and cautioned that "no chance should be overlooked to kill this insidious snake."[91] Sensing new momentum, Andrews explained to a friend two weeks before the March 26 hearing that the AALL was no longer interested in simply creating an investigatory commission. There had been plenty of time for study, he insisted; now it was time for action.[92]

Unfortunately for Andrews, the opposition held firm in 1918. Although he and the other drafters of the new bill had attempted to meet the AMA's leading demands, medical societies throughout New York State continued to contest even the revised version. As in the previous two years, doctors and employers comprised the bulk of the opposition at the hearing of the Senate Judiciary Committee. Some 115 representatives of the State Federation of Labor appeared in favor of the bill, but their presence was not enough to sway the committee. For the third year in a row, the Judiciary Committee refused to report the AALL's health insurance bill to the full senate.[93]

Despite this setback and the defeat of the health insurance enabling amendment in California just over seven months later, AALL reformers refused to become discouraged. In fact, they displayed surprising optimism. At the Association's annual meeting in December, the new president, Samuel McCune Lindsay, continued to speak of health insurance legislation as inevitable. He also suggested that, with the war over and reconstruction on the way, social insurance was more relevant than ever. "Social insurance," he declared, ". . . seems to me to lie at the heart of the most promising solution of the great task of social and industrial reorganization and reconstruction which the marvelous changes throughout the world . . . have forced upon us."[94]

As if to confirm the reformers' expectations, the late months of 1918 and the early months of 1919 brought several enormously positive developments in the New York campaign. The first was the solidification of an unprecedented alliance between the State Federation of Labor and five women's organizations (the Women's Trade Union League, the Consumers' League of New York City, the Consumers' League of New York State, the Woman Suffrage Party, and the Young Women's Christian Association) in support of six welfare bills. The State Federation had called for a conference of these organizations in early October, only eleven months after women had won the right to vote in New York. The women's groups authorized the creation of the Women's Joint Legislative Conference, and, together, the Federation of Labor and the Legislative Conference lobbied vigorously in 1919 for their package of welfare reforms. The package included not only a minimum wage and an eight-hour day for women but also health insurance for workers of both sexes.[95]

The second development was Governor Alfred E. Smith's ringing endorsement of the health insurance bill on New Year's Day. "Nothing is so devastating in the life of the worker's family as sickness," he announced before the state legislature. "The incapacitation of the wage earner because of illness is one of the underlying causes of poverty. Now the worker and his family bear this burden alone. The enactment of a health insurance law, which I strongly urge, will remedy this unfair condition."[96] Another major endorsement came on April 29, 1919, when the Reconstruction Commission of the State of New York, which had been charged with the task of investigating health insurance, issued its report to the governor. The report indicated the commissioners' complete agreement "with the principle that health insurance should be compulsory."[97]

AALL reformers welcomed these endorsements as well as numerous others that appeared on the editorial pages of many of the state's leading newspapers.[98] The true climax of the New York campaign, however, came on April 10, 1919, when the state senate finally voted on the Association's bill.[99] In an apparent appeal to bipartisanship, Senator Frederick M. Davenport, a Republican (and Progressive Party gubernatorial nominee in 1914), and Charles D. Donohue, the Democratic leader in the assembly, had reintroduced the health insurance bill early in the 1919 session.[100] The March 19 hearing proved so popular that it had to be moved from the senate chamber to the assembly chamber in order to accommodate the overflow crowd. Battle lines were drawn between representatives of the Associated Manufacturers and Merchants of New York State, physicians' organizations, and Christian Scientists, on one side, and state labor leaders, progressive social welfare reformers, and representatives of prominent women's groups on the other. After the hearing, Senator Davenport conferred with interested parties on both sides and agreed to amendments intended to win broader support. The amendments, many of which the AALL reformers found objectionable, would eliminate all non-maternity benefits to dependents of insured workers; offer greater recognition for existing company benefit funds; exempt firms with fewer than eight employees; eliminate doctors' panels and all forms of "contract practice"; provide county medical societies with greater control over fee setting; endow physicians generally with greater administrative and supervisory powers; and exempt Christian Scientists from the entire system through a conscientious-objection clause. With these substantial modifications, the bill was reported to the full senate and passed by a vote of 30 (21 Democrats and 9 insurgent Republicans) to 20 on the tenth of April. This marked the first time an American legislative body ever had voted favorably on a compulsory health insurance bill.[101]

The AALL reformers and their allies savored the victory, but their celebration was short-lived. The speaker of the assembly, Thaddeus C. Sweet, was himself an upstate manufacturer and closely allied with Daly's Associated Manufacturers and Merchants. Two days after the senate passed the health insurance bill, Sweet described the reformers who supported it and the senators who voted for it as Bolshevists, and he made it clear that the welfare package would never get past him. Citing a sudden flood of petitions (with as many as 12,000 signatures) opposed to the welfare bills, Sweet called a caucus of Republicans in order to kill the key components of the reform package. According to critics, he strong-armed his fellow Republicans and bound even those who previously had pledged to support the welfare bills to vote against the three he found most odious—the minimum wage for women, the eight-hour day for women, and compulsory health insurance. The caucus released a statement asserting that the action of the senate "makes it necessary for the Republican members of the Assembly to stand together in defense of those constitutional principles which protect the rights of property and the freedom of action of the individual." The statement concluded that the assembly Republicans "refused to be brow beaten or blackmailed into supporting a program which we believe to be a violation of the fundamental principles of Republicanism."

Sweet's maneuver was decisive. The key welfare bills, including the AALL's health insurance bill, never made it onto the assembly floor and officially died when the legislature adjourned. "Every employer in the state who followed the trend of events," observed *The Monitor*, "heaved a sigh of relief when the Legislature of 1919 adjourned, sine die, on the evening of April 19." For good measure, the editorial added, "The outstanding feature of the session was the courageous and determined stand of Speaker Thaddeus C. Sweet and the Republican majority of the Assembly against the avalanche of Socialistic and paternalistic legislation dumped in upon it from the Senate."[102]

The speaker's caucus trick struck many observers as entirely improper. Reformers were outraged, and they were not alone. The editors of the *New York Times* remarked, "Speaker SWEET's arrogation to himself of all the legislative powers and most of the executive powers of the State of New York went beyond any similar exhibition within memory of such contests at Albany." Similarly, the *New Republic* declared, "A modern Machiavelli would not have been able to arrange a better demonstration of the complete bankruptcy of the Republican party under its reactionary leadership." The leaders of the State Federation of Labor and the Women's Joint Legislative Conference were so incensed that they launched a campaign—ultimately unsuccessful—to unseat the Republicans who had betrayed them.[103]

By far the most powerful statement of contempt for the manner in which the welfare bills were defeated in 1919 was a report issued by the New York State League of Women Voters (LWV). The report not only attacked the "autocratic parliamentary methods used by Speaker Sweet" but exposed what the authors characterized as a full-blown conspiracy against the proposed welfare legislation. According to the LWV, the leaders of the conspiracy were Mark A. Daly of the Associated Manufacturers and Carleton D. Babcock of the New York League for Americanism, the latest secret offshoot of the Insurance Economics Society of America. The Associated Manufacturers, the report charged, had raised between $100,000 and $200,000 to support its "pseudo-patriotic ally, the so-called League for Americanism." Together, these two organizations spearheaded a publicity campaign against the welfare bills—and especially against health insurance—that was based fundamentally on deceptive appeals to patriotism. Daly and Babcock were in cahoots with Speaker Sweet, the report continued, and they had virtually manufactured the crucial petitions (having coerced and defrauded reluctant or ignorant employees into signing their names). In short, the LWV's report characterized the process by which the welfare bills were defeated as a travesty of the democratic process.[104]

The primary targets of the LWV probe—especially Daly—attempted to refute the report's charges and ridicule its authors. "The really pitiful part of the whole affair," read an editorial in *The Monitor,* "is the earnest sincerity of the women. They honestly believe, or at least most of them do, that the charges are true . . ." Daly acknowledged that the League for Americanism had garnered substantial support from members of the Associated Manufacturers and Merchants of New York State, but he emphatically denied any wrongdoing. And Frederick Hoffman, who also had been implicated in the report, wrote a letter to Governor Smith denying any formal connection with the California Research Society, the New York League for Americanism, or the Associated Manufacturers and Merchants of New York State.[105]

Daly and Hoffman's denials were hardly necessary. For one thing, their claims about participating in a fair, open, and patriotic campaign against health insurance could not have swayed many objective observers. Even more important, by 1920 they already had succeeded in vanquishing the reformers they so despised. Although the most ardent proponents of health insurance continued to insist on its inevitability, and the state's Reconstruction Commission endorsed health insurance for a second time on February 12, the AALL-State Federation bill had no real chance of enactment when Senator Davenport reintroduced it into the New York senate on March 11. Speaker Sweet, the most powerful man in the legislature, had made his position clear the year before, and the politics of reaction associated with that position showed no signs of abatement. In January, for example, the Buffalo Consumers' League announced that it could not continue to back the state league's position in favor of the health insurance bill because of "increasing difference of opinion as to the wisdom" of its provisions. Davenport's bill was routinely referred to the Labor and Industry Committee, where it was left to die.[106]

The AALL reformers chose not to reintroduce their model bill in 1921 or in any subsequent year. Health insurance remained in the public view because critics and proponents continued to trade personal and substantive attacks.[107] But, as the *Monitor*'s editorial writer observed in November 1920, it seemed "a little bit like trying to resurrect the dead to keep talking about compulsory health insurance."[108]

There is no simple explanation for why the health insurance movement failed in the progressive era. Bad timing was certainly one factor: the outbreak of World War I encouraged attacks on all things German, and the Russian revolution heightened fears of socialism. The entrance of the United States into the world war in April 1917, moreover, came just as the movement for health insurance seemed to be gaining momentum. Yet the movement's failure was not merely the consequence of global politics. The opposition was in fact gaining strength before any American troops crossed the Atlantic.[109]

Indeed, the American reformers who promoted health insurance legislation faced many obstacles more formidable than those arising out of conservative wartime attitudes. First, there was the question of constitutionality, an issue which critics regularly raised. On the floor of the New York senate in 1919, for example, the two primary arguments advanced against Davenport's bill were that it was unconstitutional and "ultra-socialistic."[110] Second, there was the issue of degenerative competition, which critics of health insurance alluded to at every opportunity.[111] Even as late as 1920, when the AALL's health insurance bill was clearly on its deathbed, Mark Daly continued to invoke the threat of competitive disadvantage. Concluding an address on the dangers of health insurance before the National Civic Federation, he said of the state's employers:

> They know the thing that thousands of other people, whose ears are not so close to the ground, do not know—that the economic limit is reached, and that we are facing the time when, if any more is added to production costs and is passed on to the consumer, the public won't buy, the employer cannot

manufacture goods to put in storage, and, consequently, the workman won't have a job.[112]

Third, there was the ethic of voluntarism. Representatives of big labor and big business resented intrusion into their affairs by either reformers or the state, and they feared that state insurance would weaken the attraction of their own private welfare programs. Fourth, there was the constant clamor of the red-baiters, which preceded the war but reached a fever pitch with America's entrance into the European conflict.

In addition to these standard obstacles, which impeded the paths of most new social welfare proposals in the United States, there were others—mainly of a political nature—that were distinctive to the movement for health insurance. Each was the consequence, either directly or indirectly, of the fact that this form of labor legislation threatened more special interests than did any other. The alliance of business and labor leaders, insurance interests, fraternal organizations, physicians, druggists, and Christian Scientists, which solidified in 1917 and 1918, simply overwhelmed the American Association for Labor Legislation and its occasional allies. The counteroffensive probably would have triumphed under any circumstances, but it proved especially devastating to a group of academic reformers who, at the outset, had expected little more than a repeat of their successful campaign for workers' compensation.

9

The Progressive Legacy,
1920–1940

hroughout this book, I have focused on the role of the American Association for Labor Legislation in promoting social welfare reform during the progressive era. The Association's leaders did not secure all, or even most, of the reforms they proposed in those years. But they nonetheless helped to set the trajectory of twentieth-century American welfare policy. They did so primarily through their conceptual equation of social welfare with worker security and their intensive political campaigning for protective labor legislation and social insurance. This final chapter traces the legacy of their work by surveying major worker security initiatives of the 1920s and 1930s against the backdrop of the Association's first fifteen years.

The sharp break between the progressive period and the 1920s, which many historians have characterized in retrospect, did not appear quite so sharp to leading AALL reformers at the time.[1] Particularly with regard to social insurance, the wartime experience seemed to suggest great promise. In early October 1917, exactly six months after declaring war on Germany, the U.S. Congress passed the Military and Naval Insurance Act as an amendment to the War Risk Insurance Act of 1914. The 1917 legislation guaranteed sailors and soldiers generous compensation, including both cash benefits and medical care, in the event of service-related injury or disease. It also offered all service men and women the option of purchasing life insurance at peacetime rates.[2] In a 1919 address entitled "Next Steps in Social Insurance in the United States," the president of the AALL, Samuel McCune Lindsay, described the Military and Naval Insurance Act as "the largest and most notable application of the principles of social insurance in the history of the world." This experiment, he continued,

> constitutes so striking a forward step in social insurance that it may almost be said to atone for our previous backwardness . . . Those who believe in social insurance will do well to see that our next step shall be to hold this gain.

Like Lindsay, many social welfare advocates—including those who derided the "reactionary" political environment of the war period—remained hopeful about prospects for reform at the dawn of the 1920s.[3]

A surge in the rate of joblessness in 1921 quickly revived the AALL reformers' interest in unemployment insurance.[4] Critics charged that Andrews and his colleagues were exploiting the misfortune of others to keep themselves in business. *The Monitor* observed cynically in January 1921 that "a business depression doesn't mean anything to Andrews except as it furnishes material for another 'cause.' This time it is unemployment insurance by compulsion."[5] Whether interpreted cynically or not, the severe postwar downturn riveted public attention on the problem of unemployment and thus provided the reformers with a second chance to sell their "Practical Program."

As the economic crisis took hold, John Commons formulated a new unemployment insurance bill, which Senator Henry A. Huber introduced into the Wisconsin legislature in 1921. The bill nearly received the approval of the state senate, but it was defeated after opponents attached an amendment that would have extended coverage to all employers, including farmers. Senator Huber reintroduced the bill at every subsequent legislative session throughout the decade (1923, 1925, 1927, and 1929). Similar bills came before the legislatures of Pennsylvania, Massachusetts, Connecticut, Minnesota, and New York—in most cases at the prompting of the AALL. None of these unemployment insurance bills was enacted during the 1920s, however. Employers and insurance interests put up strenuous opposition at the outset, and public pressure for solutions to the problem of joblessness began to ease with the return of prosperity in 1922. In fact, it was something of a miracle that the AALL reformers managed to sustain their campaign for unemployment insurance through over a dozen successive legislative failures in multiple states between 1921 and 1930.[6]

The same miracle did not revive compulsory health insurance as a serious legislative issue. While the defeat of the AALL's bill in the New York legislature in 1919 represented a staggering blow, the Association's failure to get the bill through in 1920 ended the fight. As Paul Starr has described, "the movement for health insurance slept through the 1920s." Association reformers supported a number of different public health campaigns during the decade, the most important of which involved maternity protection. When the federal government began moving in 1920–21 to enact the Sheppard-Towner bill, which provided federal matching funds to states that established maternity and infant hygiene programs, experts at the AALL drafted a companion bill for passage in the states. The subject of health insurance, however, almost disappeared from public view. Even more surprisingly, it nearly disappeared from the pages of the *American Labor Legislation Review*. Only toward the end of the decade did compulsory health insurance return as a moderately prominent issue, when the Committee on the Costs of Medical Care—a self-constituted investigatory body with no formal connections to the AALL—launched a high-profile study of social questions pertaining to medical care in the United States.[7]

Unlike health insurance, workers' compensation remained a live legislative issue through the 1920s. The movement for new state laws naturally slowed down, since much of the essential work had been completed during the progressive period. By 1920, 41 states, the territories of Alaska and Hawaii, Puerto Rico, and the federal government all had workers' compensation laws in effect. Only three new states and the District of Columbia joined the list in the 1920s.[8] Still, over the course of the decade, most states strengthened existing laws—either by including coverage of occupational diseases, shortening waiting periods, improving benefit scales, or assuring the provision of medical care. In addition, the AALL reformers succeeded in securing a long-sought federal law covering longshoremen and harbor workers in 1927. Although by the early 1930s the American workers' compensation patchwork remained stingy by European standards, its coverage was both broader and more generous than it had been a decade earlier.[9]

Probably the most important development affecting the social insurance movement during the 1920s was an organizational and conceptual split within the ranks of social insurance advocates. Ever since the early teens, these advocates had recognized a tension between the goals of prevention and compensation. The tension ultimately generated two competing models for social insurance financing. Those who championed prevention, such as Commons and Andrews, preferred methods of financing that created strong incentives for employers to prevent industrial hazards. The schemes they endorsed would calibrate individual employers' contributions (tax liabilities) to the frequency and severity of hazards in their plants. By contrast, champions of high compensation levels, such as Rubinow, favored financing schemes that would maximize the resources available for distribution to the victims of hazards. This generally meant pooled funds based on relatively strict insurance principles.

During the progressive period, the tension between prevention and compensation was barely visible. The movement for social insurance in the United States was so young and the potential for legislative success so great that progressive-era reformers worked to minimize their differences for purposes of mutual gain. After a series of legislative failures in the late teens and twenties, however, the earlier justification of suppressing ideological disagreements for reasons of political expediency was fast disappearing. The buried tension began to surface and, as it did, gradually broke the movement in two.

One of the main instigators of the rupture was Abraham Epstein, a leading proponent of old-age insurance who was determined to see the United States catch up to its counterparts across the Atlantic in the field of social welfare. Believing that the American movement for social insurance had begun to stagnate in the early 1920s, Epstein worked closely with Rubinow to outline a plan of action. Although both men were members of the AALL, they decided it was essential to found a new organization in order to inject new life into the movement. Epstein therefore established the American Association for Old Age Security (AAOAS) in 1927. (The organization changed its name to the American Association for Social Security six years later.) Andrews strongly objected to the creation of a new organization but was unable to stop Epstein and Rubinow who, over the late twenties and early thirties, increasingly diverged from AALL loyalists on matters of policy. The severity of the conflict between the Commons-Andrews school and the Epstein-Rubinow school became fully apparent once the Roosevelt administration began seeking advice on how to frame unemployment and old-age insurance programs during the New Deal.[10]

In many ways, the New Deal marked the climax of the progressive-era movement for social welfare reform. The most obvious connection between the two periods was social insurance. The campaigns for workers' compensation, unemployment insurance, and health insurance in the first two decades of the twentieth century served as vital forerunners to the enactment of Social Security in 1935. Yet this was by no means the only important connection between the two periods.

Well before the New Dealers gave any serious consideration to the issue of social insurance, they attempted to implement a program of work standards, including minimum-wage and maximum-hour regulations, for which progressive reformers had fought a generation earlier. Although the New Dealers viewed such standards more as components of an economic recovery plan than as devices for preventing the exploitation of labor, the two objectives were intertwined and the influence of the progressive campaigns for protective legislation was significant. Secretary of Labor Frances Perkins explained in 1934:

> To the thousands of people in this country who had always thought of the objectives of short hours and high wages as being part of a great moral aspiration for the welfare of the working people, there was both astonishment and satisfaction in the new realization that the moral law was also an economic law, and that out of the program which gave a living wage and shorter hours, there might flow economic stabilization and prosperity . . .[11]

The program to which Perkins referred was the National Industrial Recovery Act (NIRA), which created the National Recovery Administration (NRA). Signed into law in 1933, the NIRA was primarily a New Deal plan for stabilizing purchasing power. It authorized the establishment of industrial codes regulating not only prices but also hours and wages. Though states had begun enacting maximum-hour and minimum-wage laws during the late nineteenth and early twentieth centuries, the hour laws applied primarily and the wage laws exclusively to women and minors. Leading AALL reformers had hoped during the early progressive period to secure gender-neutral protective labor laws, but they quickly discovered that such laws were not constitutionally viable. By 1933, even minimum-wage laws applying only to women had become unenforceable as a result of adverse court decisions—particularly the *Adkins* ruling of 1923. Given these circumstances, the progressive reformers were overjoyed that the NRA codes set minimum wages and maximum hours for workers of both sexes. Commons and Andrews described the NIRA as a "far-reaching experiment in minimum wage regulation."[12]

The NIRA did not last long, however. The Supreme Court struck it down as unconstitutional in 1935, ruling that the code-making authority defined in the act amounted to an illegal delegation of legislative powers to the executive branch.[13] In the aftermath of this decision, concerned New Dealers worked diligently to reestablish minimum-wage and maximum-hour requirements through direct legislation. Their efforts reached fruition in 1938, when President Roosevelt placed his signature on the Fair Labor Standards Act (FLSA). The Supreme Court had cleared the constitutional path the year before by upholding a state minimum-wage statute, thereby reversing its earlier *Adkins* decision.[14] Though the FLSA was a weak law (and at least in part the product of northern industrialists who sought protection against cheap southern goods), it provided, in William Leuchtenburg's words, "a foundation on which later Congresses could build." Thomas Kerr has observed that the FLSA represented the crowning achievement of the minimum-wage movement and that it reflected the efforts of reformers, such as Frances Perkins and Robert Wagner, who served on the New York Factory Investigating Commission during the progressive era.[15]

Sandwiched between the NIRA and the FLSA was the Social Security Act of 1935. Franklin Roosevelt characterized this legislation as a "supreme achievement." Upon signing the bill into law on August 14, he declared, "If the Senate and the House of Representatives in this long and arduous session had done nothing more than pass this Bill, the session would be regarded as historic for all time."[16]

President Roosevelt formally launched the legislative process for Social Security on June 29, 1934, when he issued Executive Order No. 6757 creating the Committee on Economic Security (CES). The CES's charge was to formulate a comprehensive program of economic security for the nation's citizens based primarily on social insurance.[17] The progressive legacy was clear in the very name of the committee, which echoed the progressive reformers' bias for programs promoting security (as opposed to relief).

The members of the CES viewed general relief as something outside their purview and outside the responsibility of the federal government. "As for the genuine unemployables—or near unemployables," they wrote in their report to the president, "we believe the sound policy is to return the responsibility for their care and guidance to the States." Reinforcing and elaborating upon this point, Frances Perkins' assistant secretary of labor, Arthur J. Altmeyer, explained thirty years later that "those who had given particular thought to what came to be called 'social security' in the 1930's used the term to describe a specific government program to protect and promote the economic and social well-being of workers and their families. They did not use the term to connote a fundamental reconstruction of economic and social institutions."[18]

Because of the severity of the depression, unemployment insurance quickly became the centerpiece of the New Dealers' social insurance agenda. The irony for the AALL reformers was that this had been the weakest component of their program during the progressive era—the only serious legislative campaign for unemployment insurance having occurred in Massachusetts in 1916. They nonetheless felt prepared to address the issue because they had launched numerous campaigns for unemployment insurance during the 1920s. They also believed strongly that the internalization principle, which they had refined with regard to workers' compensation and health insurance during the progressive period, applied as much to unemployment as to accidents and ill health. While the principle ultimately did not influence the development of unemployment insurance in the United States as completely as the AALL reformers would have liked, it nevertheless imposed significantly upon the movement for state and federal laws throughout the twenties and thirties.

Wisconsin served as the political laboratory for the Commons-Andrews school of unemployment prevention. The model bill that Commons drafted for Senator Huber in 1921 relied exclusively on employer contributions and included provisions for experience rating by mutual insurance companies, meaning that employers with good employment records would pay lower premiums than employers with poor ones. A statement issued by the sponsors declared, "The fundamental assumption of this unemployment prevention bill is that industry can prevent unemployment."[19]

After five unsuccessful attempts to sell the Huber bill to the Wisconsin legislature, reformers crafted a new bill in 1930. The central objective remained prevention and the central principle internalization of costs; but the vehicle was new. The brainchild of Harold Groves and Paul Raushenbush, the revised bill would establish individual employer accounts without pooling. Employers would contribute up to a certain percentage of their payrolls and then make no more contributions until they laid off workers and benefits commenced, draining the fund below the specified percentage. This scheme was designed to maximize employer incentives for the prevention of unemployment. It also meant, however, that each employee was dependent on his or her employer's reserve fund since no formal insurance (i.e., pooling) system was authorized in the bill.

Assemblyman Groves introduced the unemployment-reserve bill into the Wisconsin legislature in 1931. Both houses approved it, and Governor Philip La Follette signed this first American unemployment insurance statute on January 28 of the following year. Several months later, John R. Commons, the proud policy grandfather, boasted over national radio that the Wisconsin model "appeals to the individualism of American capitalists, who do not want to be burdened with the inefficiencies or misfortunes of other capitalists, and it fits the public policy of a capitalistic nation which uses the profit motive to prevent unemployment."[20] Though Commons' language emphasized the power of capitalism more than it had during the progressive era, the legacy of his earlier ideas about internalization was nonetheless clear.

In the early 1930s, Andrews and the AALL backed away slightly from the Groves-Raushenbush reserves plan, promoting instead a modified version of the Huber bill known as the American Plan. While not as extreme an expression of the internalization principle as the reserves approach, the American Plan provided for mutual insurance funds and experience-rated premiums and was unquestionably a product of the Commons-Andrews school of prevention.[21]

As the depression deepened, both the Groves-Raushenbush reserves plan and the American Plan came under attack from an alternative school of reformers (many associated with the AAOAS) and from union leaders (once the AFL finally endorsed unemployment insurance in 1932). Both groups championed pooled funds and higher benefit levels. To them, prevention was nothing but a codeword for low premiums and low compensation awards. Their model program was the so-called Ohio Plan, based on bills drawn up in Ohio in 1931 and 1932 (which were never enacted). The Ohio Plan provided for a single statewide pooled insurance fund and joint employer-employee contributions. The goal was not so much prevention at the micro (employer) level but rather provision of maximum benefits for unemployed workers and economic stabilization at the macro level.[22]

Through the early thirties, the advocates of prevention and the advocates of high compensation battled, sometimes fiercely, for the soul of the unemployment insurance movement. The magnitude of the joblessness problem seemed to favor the latter, while the former gained an advantage from their experience and connections. The members and staff of the Committee on Economic Security, who were charged with drawing up unemployment insurance provisions for a federal statute, did their best to tiptoe around the edges of the battlefield. Maintaining the appearance of neutrality proved challenging, however, since two of the most important figures on the CES, Executive Director Edwin E. Witte and Assistant Secretary of Labor Arthur J. Altmeyer, were Wisconsinites and students of John R. Commons.

As enacted, the Social Security Act of 1935 offered strong incentives for states to establish unemployment insurance laws but left them almost entirely free with regard to standards. With the exception of Nebraska, no state followed Wisconsin's example of creating a system based on individual employer reserve funds. But nearly two dozen states enacted laws with provisions for experience rating, and all but a handful (each of which later joined the majority) based unemployment insurance financing exclusively on employer contributions.[23] The goal of prevention through internalization thus remained an important policy influence even in the 1930s.[24]

Of distinctly greater significance than the internalization principle in determining the structure of American unemployment insurance was the constitutional constraint of federalism. Indeed, the fear of constitutional invalidation was one of the most powerful forces guiding the Committee on Economic Security. In 1965 Altmeyer wrote:

> It is difficult to appreciate, after the passage of over a quarter of a century, the uncertainties and difficulties confronting the committee . . . If the committee had had the advantage of the experience acquired during this quarter of a century and had been able to pierce the veil of the future to ascertain the attitude of the United States Supreme Court, it undoubtedly would have made radically different recommendations in a number of respects.
>
> But in 1934 the previous decisions of the United States Supreme Court had created considerable doubt as to how far the Constitution of the United States permitted the federal government to go in enacting social legislation.[25]

Similarly, Frances Perkins observed a decade after the fact that in 1934 the "problems of constitutional law seemed almost insuperable." As was mentioned in an earlier chapter, Perkins was greatly relieved when Justice Stone whispered to her at a party that "the taxing power [of the federal government] is sufficient for everything you want and need."[26]

Ever since Congress had passed the Phosphorus Match Act in 1912, reformers had toyed with the idea of employing the taxing power to insert the federal government into the field of social welfare policy. Henry Seager announced in April 1912: "The situation presented by poisonous phosphorous matches was no doubt unique, and yet the same general conditions which made national legislation desirable in this case already present themselves in a number of other cases that will certainly be pressed upon the attention of Congress as time goes on."[27] Although social welfare reformers like Seager were reluctant to utilize the taxation trick again too quickly (because of the enormous difficulty they had faced in securing the match act), others latched onto the idea as a means of controlling narcotics. In January 1914, President Wilson signed a federal bill imposing a hefty tax of $300 per pound on smoking-opium, and the Supreme Court upheld the validity of the law five years later.[28]

The same year, in 1919, Congress enacted the Child Labor Tax Law, which levied a 10 percent federal excise tax on the net profits of all employers who employed children under age sixteen in mines or children under fourteen in any other industry. The Supreme Court had invalidated a similar federal child labor law based on the interstate-commerce power the previous year.[29] Sponsors of the new law apparently concluded that the weight of precedent would sustain use of the taxing power where appeals to the interstate commerce power had failed. They concluded wrong. On May 15, 1922, Chief Justice Taft—the man who as president had placed his signature on the Phosphorus Match Act of 1912—handed down a curious decision overturning the Child Labor Tax Act. Acknowledging that the Court had in previous cases allowed Congress extremely wide latitude in employing the taxing power, Taft argued that the Court would have to be "blind" not to recognize the true intentions of Congress in this case. He declared:

> Grant the validity of this law, and all that Congress would need to do, hereafter, in seeking to take over to its control any one of the great number of subjects of public interest, jurisdiction of which the States have never parted with, and which are reserved to them by the Tenth Amendment, would be to enact a detailed measure of complete regulation of the subject and enforce it by a so-called tax upon departures from it. To give such magic to the word "tax" would be to break down all constitutional limitation of the powers of Congress and completely wipe out the sovereignty of the States.

Reformers were frustrated and perplexed. Taft's reasoning made sense to them in isolation, but they could not understand how he could apply it to this case and not to the oleomargarine case (*McCray v. United States,* 1904) or to the Phosphorus Match Act. Thomas Parkinson, a legal consultant for the AALL, concluded that "the child labor tax seems to have been the straw that broke the camel's back."[30]

In the minds of many reformers, the Supreme Court's adverse decision in 1922 eliminated the taxing power as a possible means of circumventing the federalism obstacle. Association reformers were just then considering how to draft a federal law establishing minimum coal mine safety standards, and a legislative drafting expert explained at the Association's seventeenth annual meeting that the Court's recent decisions probably ruled out a safety law based on the taxing power.[31]

By 1926, however, policymakers in Washington had discovered a new way to utilize the federal taxing power to circumvent federalism, and they succeeded in securing the blessing of the Supreme Court. The problem was Florida's policy of attempting to attract rich elderly citizens from other states by advertising that Florida had no inheritance tax. By eliminating the tax on inheritance, Florida's legislators had managed to turn the dynamic of degenerative competition between the states to their advantage. Legislators in the other states were not at all pleased and looked to the federal government for help. In order to foil Florida's scheme, Congress enacted a special inheritance tax as part of the 1926 Revenue Act that included a tax-offset feature. The federal statute imposed an inheritance tax on all citizens but offered credits of up to 80 percent of the total (on a dollar-for-dollar matching basis) to citizens who paid state inheritance taxes. As intended, the federal tax nullified Florida's policy: wealthy senior citizens would no longer move to Florida with the expectation of dying tax-free.

Significantly, the Supreme Court upheld the federal tax as constitutional in a 1926 decision, *Florida v. Mellon*. "The act is a law of the United States made in pursuance of the Constitution and, therefore, the supreme law of the land, the constitution or laws of the states to the contrary notwithstanding," Justice George Sutherland wrote for the court. "Whenever the constitutional powers of the federal government and those of the state come into conflict, the latter must yield." [30]

The decision was largely forgotten until the summer of 1933, when Paul Raushenbush, one of the authors of Wisconsin's unemployment compensation law, was temporarily out of work. Raushenbush had been chosen to administer the new compensation system, but the severity of the depression provoked Wisconsin legislators to postpone the date when the law would go into effect. So Raushenbush decided to take a vacation with his wife Elizabeth and his father-in-law, Louis Brandeis. During the excursion Raushenbush complained to Justice Brandeis that other states were afraid to enact unemployment insurance laws for fear of putting their industries at a competitive disadvantage, and he inquired what could be done to solve the problem. The answer came in the form of a question. "Have you considered the case of *Florida vs. Mellon?*" Justice Brandeis asked, referring to the 1926 decision with which he had concurred. Brandeis' question alerted Raushenbush to the promise of the federal taxing power in enforcing uniformity among the states, and Raushenbush quickly set to work with Associate Solicitor Thomas H. Eliot in drafting a model federal statute.[33]

In late 1930 and early 1931, Senator Robert F. Wagner of New York had introduced, without success, two federal unemployment insurance bills. One, drafted by the AALL, offered federal subsidies to states that enacted unemployment insurance laws; the other offered tax exemptions to employers who established voluntary plans. The Raushenbush-Brandeis variation on these incentive schemes proved far more promising. On February 5, 1934, Senator Wagner and Representative David J. Lewis introduced into Congress the tax-offset bill that Raushenbush and Eliot had written. It provided for a 5 percent excise tax on all employers of ten or more workers as well as on most employers of fewer than ten. It also mandated, however, that employers who contributed into a satisfactory state unemployment insurance system would be allowed to deduct the full amount of their contributions from the federal tax. As Andrews observed at the time, "The Wagner-Lewis bill is an ingenious device to remove the 'interstate competition' obstacle to state legislation while giving a compelling economic incentive to state action [on unemployment insurance]." Though the Wagner-Lewis bill failed to pass Congress (largely because of inadequate support from President Roosevelt), the tax-offset method became the basis of the administration's approach to unemployment insurance in 1935.[34]

Most of the members of Roosevelt's Committee on Economic Security simply assumed that a purely federal system of unemployment insurance—like the one that reformers such as Rubinow and Epstein were calling for—would not be upheld as constitutional by the Supreme Court. Yet they also recognized that the states were not acting very quickly on their own. By the latter half of 1934, Wisconsin was still the only state that had enacted an unemployment insurance statute. The CES therefore considered two methods of encouraging more states to pass comparable laws. One would have offered federal subsidies and the other tax credits through the tax-offset method. The latter prevailed, in large part because of the Wagner-Lewis precedent. The CES recommended a 3 percent federal payroll tax with a 90 percent offset for employers who contributed to satisfactory state unemployment insurance systems. The plan ultimately became law when President Roosevelt signed the Social Security Act on August 14, 1935.[35]

At hearings on the bill before the Senate Committee on Finance earlier in the year, John Andrews had testified movingly, explaining that the unemployment insurance provisions provided a definitive solution to the greatest problem he had faced in his campaigns for labor legislation over the previous generation. ". . . I have been going to State capitols for many years with carefully worked-out constructive social legislation proposals," he said,

> and the most insistent objection raised is that this would drive business from the State, that the purpose is good and the plan is sound, and "We would enthusiastically support this local legislation if the cost were to fall equally upon all of the States." It gives me more genuine pleasure than you can perhaps imagine to have the opportunity now to support this measure, which wipes out that old "interstate competition" obstacle.[36]

As expected, the tax-offset scheme forced the states into compliance. Four states anticipated the federal action by passing unemployment insurance laws in the four months prior to August 14. Over the next two years, all the remaining states followed, with Illinois being the last to pass an unemployment insurance law on June 30, 1937.[37]

One final footnote to the federalism story deserves mention. The tax-offset method, though perhaps the most important, was not the only means that the drafters of the Social Security Act utilized to induce the states to enact social welfare legislation. Following the precedent set by the 1921 Sheppard-Towner maternity-protection law, the act established federal matching grants to states that provided assistance to the needy elderly, the blind, and dependent children as well as to states that established programs of maternal and child welfare. The first two programs for the elderly and the blind were later integrated into the Supplemental Security Income (SSI) program, while the third ultimately became Aid to Families with Dependent Children.[38] Together, the unemployment and old age insurance provisions and the categorical aid programs—all established in the Social Security Act—form the foundation of the so called American welfare state.[39]

So far, the focus of this chapter has been on connections between the progressive era and the New Deal in the field of social welfare policy. It is also necessary, however, to acknowledge disjunctions between the two periods. The two most obvious ones relate to old-age insurance (which was but a minor issue during the first period) and compulsory health insurance (which was nearly absent from the second).

In his 1907 address at the first annual meeting of the AALL, Henry Seager included "invalidity and old age" as one of the five leading contingencies that threatened the living standards of working families. Over the subsequent decade, AALL reformers occasionally considered the issue and generally endorsed the principle of public support for the aged outside of poorhouses. Yet they did not focus on the problems of the elderly until at least 1919, and even then they generally advocated noncontributory pensions rather than contributory, old age insurance.[40] In 1922 Association leaders worked closely with activists in the Fraternal Order of the Eagles to draft a model pension bill, which was considered in slightly modified forms in numerous state legislatures.[41] Over the next six years, six states enacted old-age pension bills that survived in the courts, and nineteen more states followed between 1929 and 1933.[42]

Like many other proponents of pension legislation, John Andrews insisted that pensions would serve a dual role: not only would they permit the "worthy" elderly to stay out of the dreaded poorhouse, but they would also offer vital security to American workers concerned about their later years. In public, Andrews claimed that pensions were superior to insurance because they would prove much simpler to administer, especially given the great mobility of American labor.[43] Privately, he probably also preferred pensions because he disliked the idea of applying the insurance model to old age. Aging, after all, was not a hazard like industrial accidents or disease, which could be internalized as a cost of production and thus prevented.

As enacted in 1935, the old-age provisions of social security included both pensions and insurance coverage. Title 1 authorized federal aid to the states to assure assistance (pensions) for the needy elderly; titles 2 and

8 created a contributory insurance system that levied taxes on both employers and employees and provided corresponding benefits to retired workers at age sixty-five.[44] Arguably, the conceptual roots of the old-age provisions can be traced back to the AALL reformers' special emphasis on worker security in the early progressive period.[45] Politically, however, these provisions had little to do with the AALL's progressive-era drive for social insurance. They were products of the state pension campaigns of the 1920s (in which the AALL played an important but not a dominant role) and the nascent movement for old-age insurance associated with Abraham Epstein's AAOAS in the late twenties and early thirties.

In sharp contrast to old-age insurance, compulsory health insurance had shown tremendous promise during the late teens but failed to revive during the New Deal. A number of important figures within the Roosevelt administration, including Harry Hopkins and Arthur Altmeyer, favored the development of public health insurance. Even the president described it as highly desirable. But political opposition from the medical profession was simply too strong. As Ronald Numbers has observed, physicians were able to employ the arguments they had refined during the progressive era to great effect in the thirties. Politically savvy New Dealers feared that the inclusion of health insurance within the Social Security bill might sink the whole project, and thus they left it out of the proposed legislation altogether. Reflecting on the heady days of 1935 thirty years after the fact, Altmeyer suggested, "The great gap in our present Social Security Act is its failure to include two forms of social insurance which are found in the social security systems of practically all other industrialized countries: insurance to cover wage loss resulting from nonoccupational temporary disability and insurance to cover the cost of medical care." Of course, both deficiencies would have been addressed by the progressive reformers' health insurance bill, which was designed to cover wage loss due to sickness as well as the costs of medical care.[46]

T he disjunctions relating to old-age insurance and health insurance serve to remind us that links between the progressive era and the New Deal were not complete. Yet they by no means negate the essential conclusion that the ideas and political activities of the AALL reformers during the progressive period helped to set the subsequent trajectory of U.S. social welfare policy. Speaking with a reporter in 1935, Commons remarked, "I call the New Deal the 'New Whirlwind.' That's how it shapes up in my mind. New Deal policies were really new, perhaps, two decades ago."[47]

Roosevelt's New Dealers benefitted enormously from the progressive movement for social welfare reform. In many ways, they were products of that movement. They inherited, for example, a nearly complete system of state workers' compensation laws, Commons' powerful internalization principle, a workable means for overcoming the federalism obstacle, and a detailed map of likely political land mines. Most important of all, they inherited the progressives' profound commitment to worker security, which guided the development of most social welfare legislation during the New Deal and beyond. Indeed, the AALL reformers' equation of social welfare with worker security stands as their most fundamental conceptual contribution and legacy.

Epilogue

The story of the progressive-era movement for protective labor legislation and social insurance affords many opportunities for comparison to our own time. Compulsory health insurance, for example, still looms on the public policy horizon. More generally, competition among the states continues to influence the development of American social welfare programs; and the progressive emphasis on prevention remains a staple of modern political rhetoric.[1] The most intriguing and important subject for comparison, however, is the progressive concept of security, which has become deeply embedded not only in the statute books but also in the public psyche.

The leaders of the American Association for Labor Legislation launched their movement for worker security in the wake of the second industrial revolution. They aimed above all to protect workers against sudden and catastrophic losses of income associated with industrial hazards such as accidents, illness, and unemployment. In their view, the risk of falling out of the workforce altogether posed a bigger threat to American workers—and one more readily remediable through enlightened public policy—than did inadequate wages. Although many American families lived at or below subsistence levels, wages in the United States were among the highest in the world. The AALL reformers chose, therefore, to devote their energies to the problem of deviations from a relatively high mean. More specifically, they sought to prevent dramatic deviations resulting from random or seemingly random events—ones that could not be attributed to the fault of the victim. In this way, they combined new ideas about environmental causes of poverty with old distinctions between "worthy" and "unworthy" poor.

Particularly since the onset of the Great Depression, public demand for government protection against seemingly random hazards has expanded dramatically—far beyond what the AALL reformers originally desired or envisioned. The protection is no longer even confined to the workplace. Take natural disasters, for example. When a massive flood struck the Mississippi Valley in 1927, wiping out the farms and residences of hundreds of thousands of citizens, the federal government responded with caution. Calvin Coolidge announced that he could do as much, or perhaps even more, for flood victims in his capacity as president of the American Red Cross as he could as president of the United States. Although Secretary of Commerce Herbert Hoover estimated total damage at $300 million, Congress ultimately appropriated only about $10 million for relief and reconstruction (or less than 3.5 percent of total costs).[2] Sixty-six years later, in response to another massive Mississippi flood, President Clinton easily garnered bipartisan support for a bailout of unprecedented proportions. This time, American public opinion expected nothing less. Congress authorized more than $6.4 billion in emergency aid, covering over 50 percent of estimated damages and representing a 64-fold real increase as compared to the 1927 federal appropriation.[3]

Beyond natural disasters, the states and especially the federal government now offer coverage against a broad array of seemingly random hazards, ranging from bank and pension-fund failures to crop losses and personal disability. The common-law tort system provides another vast arena for compensation of losses that can be blamed on parties other than the victims.[4] In short, personal security against seemingly random hazards has become a quasi-entitlement—not just for industrial workers, but for all citizens. In the introduction, I ventured to describe our public methods of risk socialization as constituting a "security state."

Given the great many extensions of the progressive concept of security, it is striking that the single most important item on the AALL's legislative agenda, compulsory health insurance, remains unenacted at the time of this writing. The politics of health insurance have continued to overwhelm the advocates of comprehensive reform. Regardless of whether universal health coverage is ever adopted in the United States, however, it seems clear that economic security will endure as a vital issue on the nation's policy agenda. What is less clear is whether the insurance-based approach to security that has been developed will remain sufficient to meet public needs.

When the AALL was founded in 1906, the American economy was bursting with energy. Between 1890 and 1905, the growth of real per capita GNP was quite strong, topping 2 percent per year. Average real wages grew at a healthy pace (1.3 percent per year), and labor productivity grew even faster (1.8 percent per year). Given this context of rapidly rising wages, output, and productivity, it is not surprising—at least not in retrospect—that the AALL reformers chose to focus on deviations from the mean rather than on the mean itself.[5]

With the exception of the 1930s, strong economic and wage growth continued through the early 1970s. And even during the Depression, those workers who retained their jobs experienced substantial increases in real wages.[6] An insurance-based approach to security—that is, one which targeted individual deviations from an upward wage trend—remained entirely consistent with economic conditions.

Since 1973, however, the real wages of production and nonsupervisory workers have exhibited a sustained decline.[7] Although real per capita GNP and labor productivity have continued to increase, wage earners have had to work longer hours to preserve their share of national income. Never before in American history has an entire generation of workers experienced such a deterioration of earning power. The wage trend could turn upward again, but there is no guarantee that it will do so anytime soon.[8]

Like industrial hazards in the progressive era, wage deterioration generates a great deal of anxiety. According to Ronald Brownstein, a national political correspondent for the *Los Angeles Times,* "it is clear that 1973 marked the pivot from the era of secure prosperity to a new era of economic anxiety."[9] Survey data suggest that insecurity about jobs and incomes has been rising independently of changes in the unemployment rate, leading Secretary of Labor Robert Reich to describe the bulk of the great American middle class as an "anxious class."[10]

The source of the new anxiety is well illustrated by the case of Craig and Susan Miller. Until the summer of 1992, Craig was employed as a union sheet-metal worker at Trans World Airlines in Kansas City, Missouri. Although he served as the primary breadwinner, his wife Susan supplemented the family income with earnings from a night job at Toys R Us. Together, they supported four children in a solidly middle-class style. Once Craig was laid off from TWA, however, he found that without an education he could not earn much more than $5 per hour (or about one-third of his former wage). In order to make ends meet, Craig worked both as a bus driver and as a server at McDonald's, and Susan retained her night job. Together, they earned about $18,000 a year, just below the poverty line for a family of six and less than half of what Craig had earned alone in his previous job. "For people like us," Susan told a reporter, "I'm afraid the good times are gone for good."[11]

The similarities and differences between the Millers and the Rogalases are instructive. As described in the introduction, the Rogalas family fell into poverty in 1906 after the primary breadwinner, Adam, was killed in an industrial accident. Like the Miller family, the Rogalas family suffered an economic decline that was both sudden and steep. But unlike the Millers, the Rogalases could blame a clearly identifiable and apparently random hazard, one that virtually no one would attribute to the fault of poor Adam. The AALL reformers championed social insurance as a means of protecting people like the Rogalases against random industrial hazards. Indeed, had Adam's accident occurred ten years later, after Pennsylvania adopted a workers' compensation law, his family would have been entitled to a small but stable income.

The Millers, however, found little comfort in the existence of social insurance programs because they were not the victims of an easily insurable hazard. Craig was not injured or sick or even unemployed for very long. He was definitely able to work; he simply earned much less than he and his family had come to expect. This is what is behind the new insecurity. It is particularly troubling because many of the nation's security institutions, originally designed to address sharp, seemingly random deviations from a rising wage trend, are incapable of relieving the pain associated with deterioration of the trend itself.

The juxtaposition of past and present thus suggests an intriguing and paradoxical story that continues to unfold. The progressive concept of security—widely attacked as socialistic and un-American during the progressive era—has developed into one of the bulwarks of American public policy. Over the course of the twentieth century, lawmakers have gradually built a security state of vastly greater scope and proportion than the AALL reformers ever imagined. Yet, in recent years, insecurity has grown as the economy has undergone what appears to be a profound transformation.

Many observers have characterized this new economic transformation as constituting a third industrial revolution. Its essential features—dramatic changes in technology and trade patterns—probably are of revolutionary proportions, and they certainly hold great promise for the future. At the same time, however, these new economic forces appear to be exerting sharp downward pressure on the earnings of low-skilled and less-educated workers, both in the United States and in most other industrialized nations.

It is too early to say whether the third industrial revolution, like the second, will provoke a fundamental reassessment of our social welfare institutions. Whether it does or not, there is no question that the unprecedented wage decline associated with it has radically altered the context in which our security institutions operate—an insight that becomes particularly clear against the backdrop of the progressive-era experience.

Notes

Introduction

1. Case described in Crystal Eastman, *Work Accidents and the Law* (New York: Arno, 1969 [1910]), pp. 3–4; Eastman used fictitious names in her case studies of accident victims. On historical wage estimates, see U.S. Department of Commerce, Bureau of the Census, *Historical Statistics of the United States: Colonial Times to 1970* (Washington: Government Printing Office, 1975), part 1, series D-766, D-802, D-804 (pp. 151–153, 168, 170). On comparison to Russia, see Angus Maddison, *Dynamic Forces in Capitalist Development: A Long-Run Comparative View* (New York: Oxford University Press, 1991), tables 1.1 (pp. 6–7) and 1.5 (pp. 24–25).
2. John B. Andrews to William F. Cochran, 5 January 1915, *Microfilm Edition of the Papers of the American Association for Labor Legislation, 1905–1945* (Glen Rock: Microfilming Corporation of America, 1973), reel 13. Hereafter cited AALL Papers.
3. The term "industrialization," though widely used in reference to the American economy of the late nineteenth century, requires some qualification. The first industrial revolution occurred in Britain in the late eighteenth and early nineteenth centuries. Its hallmark was a dramatic increase in manufacturing output associated with mechanization and the exploitation of new forms of power (especially steam). Within this context, industrialization was certainly not new to the United States in the late nineteenth and early twentieth centuries. Historians who use the term in reference to this later period generally have in mind the so-called second industrial revolution. The second revolution was distinguished from the first in that it involved heavy industry (such as steel) as opposed to light manufactures (such as textiles). The emergence of heavy industry required not only new forms of power but also revolutionary changes in industrial organization. In particular, the second revolution

involved the rapid development of an entirely new type of firm—hierarchical, vertically integrated, and legally incorporated. Like the first industrial revolution, the second generated dramatic increases in productivity and output and proved enormously disruptive to the social order. See Carl N. Degler, *The Age of the Economic Revolution, 1876–1900* (Glenview: Scott, Foresman, 1977); Alfred D. Chandler, *The Visible Hand: The Managerial Revolution in American Business* (Cambridge: Harvard University Press, 1977); Martin J. Sklar, *The Corporate Reconstruction of American Capitalism, 1890–1916* (Cambridge, Eng.: Cambridge University Press, 1988); Martin J. Sklar, *The United States as a Developing Country: Studies in U.S. History in the Progressive Era and 1920s* (Cambridge, Eng.: Cambridge University Press, 1992).

4. John Kenneth Galbraith, *Economics in Perspective: A Critical History* (Boston: Houghton Mifflin, 1987), p. 290. See also H. Roger Grant, *Insurance Reform: Consumer Action in the Progressive Era* (Ames: Iowa State University Press, 1979), pp. 5–6; Morton Keller, *The Life Insurance Enterprise, 1885–1910* (Cambridge: Harvard University Press, 1963), pp. 9–11.

5. See C. F. Trenerry, *The Origin and Early History of Insurance* (London: P. S. King, 1926); Keller, *Life Insurance Enterprise,* pp. 9–11; Barry Supple, "Insurance in British History," in Oliver M. Westall, ed., *The Historian and the Business of Insurance* (Manchester: Manchester University Press, 1984), esp. pp. 3–4; Lorraine J. Daston, "The Domestication of Risk: Mathematical Probability and Insurance, 1650–1830," in Lorenz Krüger et al., *The Probabilistic Revolution,* vol. 1 (Cambridge: MIT Press, 1987), pp. 237–260; *The Documentary History of Insurance, 1000 B.C.–1875 A.D.* (Newark: Prudential Press, 1915); Herman E. Kroos and Martin R. Blyn, *A History of Financial Intermediaries* (New York: Random House, 1971), pp. 35, 109–111, 165; *Historical Statistics of the United States,* part 2, series X-880, p. 1056. The number of life insurance policies in force does not equal the number of people holding policies because many individuals carried more than one life insurance policy at a time.

6. John B. Andrews, "Social Insurance" [1917?], AALL Papers, reel 62, p. 1. See also Henry W. Farnam, *The Economic Utilization of History and Other Economic Studies* (New Haven: Yale University Press, 1913), pp. 174–176; I. M. Rubinow, *Social Insurance* (New York: Holt, 1916 [1913]), esp. pp. 3–12.

7. Some employers carried accident insurance for their employees (typically deducting premiums out of wages), and some workers enjoyed coverage through special fraternal or union funds. Commercial insurance coverage against industrial accidents available to individual workers, if it existed at all, was extremely rare. See Eastman, *Work-Accidents and the Law,* pp. 190–206, 145; Rubinow, *Social Insurance,* pp. 136–139.

8. John B. Andrews to Harrington Emerson, 24 November 1915, AALL Papers, reel 15.

9. In fiscal year 1990, federal, state, and local spending (including mandated private spending) on old-age insurance, survivor and disability insurance, Medicare (health insurance for the elderly), workers' compensation, and unemployment insurance totaled $413 billion. (Spending on the various components of old-age security accounted for over three-fourths of the total, even without counting another $97 billion appropriated for public employee and railroad retirement programs.) By comparison, federal, state, and local spending on Medicaid (health care for the poor), Aid to Families with Dependent Children and other forms of cash assistance, food stamps, and Supplemental Security Income for the elderly totaled $146 billion. (Just over half of the welfare total is attributable to the cost of Medicaid.) See Ann Kallman Bixby, "Public Social Welfare Expenditures, Fiscal Year 1990," *Social Security Bulletin 56*, no. 2 (Summer 1993): 70–76, esp. table 1; *Social Security Bulletin 57*, no. 2 (Summer 1994), tables 1.A1 and 1.A2 (pp. 91, 92). See also Theodore R. Marmor, Jerry L. Mashaw, and Philip L. Harvey, *America's Misunderstood Welfare State: Persistent Myths, Enduring Realities* (New York: Basic Books, 1990), esp. chaps. 2 and 3.

10. John R. Commons, "Secretary's Report for 1908," in *Proceedings of the Second Annual Meeting. American Association for Labor Legislation* (Madison, 1909), pp. 14–22; [Commons?] to [Farnam], 19 August 1908, AALL Papers, reel 1; John B. Andrews, "Report of Work: 1909," *American Association for Labor Legislation. Third Annual Meeting. Proceedings, Reports, Addresses. Labor and the Courts* (New York, 1910), publication no. 9, pp. 9–36.

11. Commons to Farnam, 25 December 1909, Farnam to Andrews, 11 December 1909, Andrews to Farnam, 2 November 1909, Ely to Andrews, 29 August 1909, AALL Papers, reel 2; Minutes of Executive Committee Meeting, 30 December 1909, AALL Papers, reel 61. See also Andrews to Anne Morgan, 17 January 1910, Andrews to Berry, 14 January 1910, Andrews to Farnam, 8 February 1910, AALL Papers, reel 2.

12. "Constitution. American Association for Labor Legislation. Adopted Feb. 15, 1906. Amended Dec. 30, 1907," *Proceedings of the First Annual Meeting. American Association for Labor Legislation* (Madison, 1908), p. 6; "Constitution of the American Association for Labor Legislation," *American Labor Legislation Review* 1, no. 1 (January 1911): 121. Hereafter cited *ALLR*.

13. John B. Andrews, "Report of Work 1910," *ALLR* 1, no. 1 (January 1911): 115–120, 101; Farnam to Andrews, 30 January 1911, Andrews to Commons, 25 February 1911, AALL Papers, reel 4; Commons, "Secretary's Report for 1908," pp. 21–22; Irene Osgood to Farnam, 12 January 1909, AALL Papers, reel 1; Farnam to Andrews, 6 November 1909, AALL Papers, reel 2; Seager to Farnam, 23 January 1912, AALL Papers, reel 6; Farnam to Stephen Bauer, 9 August 1910, AALL papers, reel 4.

14. Ely's name appears in the correspondence of the AALL only sporadically after 1908.

15. The works of Lubove, Nelson, and Skocpol stand out as especially valuable. See Roy Lubove, *The Struggle for Social Security, 1900–1935* (Pittsburgh:

University of Pittsburgh Press, 1986 [1968]); Daniel Nelson, *Unemployment Insurance: The American Experience, 1915–1935* (Madison: University of Wisconsin Press, 1969); Theda Skocpol, *Protecting Soldiers and Mothers: The Political Origins of Social Policy in the United States* (Cambridge: Harvard University Press, 1992). Other important studies devoted wholly or in part to the AALL are Richard Martin Lyon, "The American Association for Labor Legislation and the Fight for Workmen's Compensation Laws, 1906–1942," M.S. thesis, Cornell University, 1952; Lloyd F. Pierce, "The Activities of the American Association for Labor Legislation in Behalf of Social Security and Protective Labor Legislation," Ph.D. diss., University of Wisconsin, 1953; Irwin Yellowitz, *Labor and the Progressive Movement in New York State* (Ithaca: Cornell University Press, 1965); Irwin Yellowitz, "The Origins of Unemployment Reform in the United States," *Labor History* 9, no. 3 (Fall 1968): 338–360; Hace Sorel Tishler, *Self-Reliance and Social Security, 1870–1917* (Port Washington: Kennikat Press, 1971); Ronald L. Numbers, *Almost Persuaded: American Physicians and Compulsory Health Insurance, 1912–1920* (Baltimore: Johns Hopkins University Press, 1978); Edward Berkowitz and Kim McQuaid, *Creating the Welfare State: The Political Economy of Twentieth-Century Reform* (New York: Praeger, 1988 [1980]); Uto Sautter, "North American Government Labor Agencies before World War One: A Cure for Unemployment?" *Labor History* 24, no. 3 (Summer 1983): 366–393; John Dennis Chasse, "The American Association for Labor Legislation: An Episode in Institutionalist Policy Analysis," *Journal of Economic Issues* 25, no. 3 (September 1991): 799–828. The historian Joseph Tripp noted in 1987 that, despite this literature, there existed "no published work fully exploring the AALL's intriguing make-up, its extensive operations, and its impact." See Tripp, "Law and Social Control: Historians' Views of Progressive-Era Labor Legislation," *Labor History* 28, no. 4 (Fall 1987): 476.

16. According to Skocpol, "Social scientists debating alternative theories of welfare state development have primarily examined U.S. social provision from 1935 onward." See *Protecting Soldiers and Mothers,* p. 6.

17. The literature on this subject can be divided roughly into five schools, which are similar but not identical to those suggested in Margaret Weir, Ann Shola Orloff, and Theda Skocpol, eds., *The Politics of Social Policy in the United States* (Princeton: Princeton University Press, 1988), pp. 10–27. One school points to the American liberal ethic as an important barrier to the development of modern social welfare policies. See especially Gaston Rimlinger, *Welfare Policy and Industrialization in Europe, America, and Russia* (New York: Wiley, 1971), p. 12; Lubove, *Struggle for Social Security,* p. 24; Kirsten Gronbjerg, David Street, and Gerald D. Suttles, *Poverty and Social Change* (Chicago: University of Chicago Press, 1978), p. 32. A second school highlights the notorious weakness of working-class movements in the United States. See e.g. Michael Shalev, "The Social Democratic Model and Beyond: Two 'Generations' of Comparative Research on the Welfare State," *Com-*

parative Social Research, 6 (1983): 316. A third school depicts a virtual conspiracy by corporate elites to control and contain the reform process. The best example of this is probably James Weinstein, *The Corporate Ideal in the Liberal State, 1900–1918* (Boston: Beacon Press, 1968). A fourth school emphasizes the inadequacy of public bureaucratic structures essential to welfare-state development. See Berkowitz and McQuaid, *Creating the Welfare State;* Ann Shola Orloff and Theda Skocpol, "Why Not Equal Protection? Explaining the Politics of Public Social Spending in Britain, 1900–1911, and the United States, 1880s–1920," *American Sociological Review* 49, no. 6 (December 1984): 731; Theda Skocpol and John Ikenberry, "The Political Formation of the American Welfare State in Historical and Comparative Perspective," *Comparative Social Research* 6 (1983): 87–148; Weir, Orloff, and Skocpol, eds., *The Politics of Social Policy in the United States.* Most recently, a fifth school has emerged (mainly from the work of Theda Skocpol) that points to progressive-era hostility against patronage politics and the consequent suspicion of all proposals for public spending. Subsequent chapters offer evidence pertaining more or less directly to the first four schools but only indirectly to the fifth. In *Protecting Soldiers and Mothers,* Skocpol argues that "broadsides against democratic patronage parties and the 'horrors' of social spending for the masses helped to ensure that Civil War benefits would become an obstacle rather than an entering wedge for more general old-age pensions and workingmen's insurance in the United States" (p. 532). My study does not examine the nascent movement for general old-age pensions because such pensions were never a critical item on the AALL's legislative agenda during the progressive period. In the case of social insurance, however, the papers and legislative records I have examined offer exceedingly little corroboration for Skocpol's argument. In fact, the bulk of the evidence she presents highlights the adverse effect of Civil War pensions on the demand for public pensions rather than on the demand for social insurance. As she correctly notes, AALL reformers occasionally cited the legacy of Civil War pensions as an obstacle—mainly to the extension of public old-age pensions. But such comments were few and far between. From my reading, it appears that the AALL reformers did not view public distaste for Civil War pensions as a significant obstacle to their campaigns for workers' compensation, unemployment insurance, and health insurance.

18. Skocpol, it should be noted, is a partial exception to this rule. In *Protecting Soldiers and Mothers* she devotes one section to explaining why the AALL reformers failed; but she devotes another section to exploring, in a positive way, the motivations and accomplishments of women's organizations dedicated to what she calls "maternalist" welfare policies (hour and wage laws for women workers, mothers' pensions, etc.). While hers is therefore not a "half-empty" approach, it highlights for constructive analysis very different types of policies from those considered here.

19. The economist Kenneth Boulding has suggested that "through his students Commons was the intellectual origin of the New Deal, of labor legislation,

of social security, of the whole movement in this country towards a welfare state." See Boulding, "Institutional Economics—A New Look at Institutionalism," *American Economic Review* 47, supp. 1 (May 1957): 7.

20. Weinstein, *Corporate Ideal in the Liberal State,* p. 48; Skocpol, *Protecting Soldiers and Mothers,* pp. 182, 205; Lubove, *Struggle for Social Security,* p. 29.

21. Robert H. Bremner, *From the Depths: The Discovery of Poverty in the United States* (New York: New York University Press, 1964 [1956]). "The chief point made in this book," Bremner writes in his introduction, "is that the humanitarian reform movements that swept the United States in the first two decades of the twentieth century proceeded in large measure from the new view of poverty" (p. xii).

22. John R. Commons, "Social Insurance," address to the Civics Club, Madison, 1 April 1916, *Microfilm Edition of the John R. Commons Papers,* reel 17, p. 5 (fr. 702). Hereafter cited Commons Papers.

23. In addition to the books and articles already cited with regard to the AALL, see Paul Starr's discussion of the progressive-era campaigns for compulsory health insurance in *The Social Transformation of American Medicine* (New York: Basic Books, 1982), book 2, chap. 1 ("The Mirage of Reform"), pp. 235–289.

24. See e.g. Clement E. Vose, "The National Consumers' League and the Brandeis Brief," *Midwest Journal of Political Science* 1, nos. 3–4 (November 1957): 267–290; Louis Lee Athey, "The Consumers' Leagues and Social Reform, 1890–1923," Ph.D. diss., University of Delaware, 1965; Diane Kirkby, " 'The Wage-Earning Woman and the State': The National Women's Trade Union League and Protective Labor Legislation, 1903–1923," *Labor History* 28, no. 1 (Winter 1987): 54–74.

25. *American Association for Labor Legislation,* pamphlet, reprinted from the New York Department of Labor *Bulletin,* March 1906, p. 1. The leaders of the Association understood that the ultimate solution was to be found in national legislation. Henry Seager wrote in 1912: "The thought I wish to emphasize is, that as our industries become more and more national, transcending state lines in their operations, and as our knowledge in regard to the regulations that ought to be imposed becomes better, national labor legislation . . . will be more and more a great national need." See "Labor Legislation: A National Social Need," remarks at the meeting of the Academy of Political Science on 19 April 1912, reprinted in Seager, *Labor and Other Economic Essays,* ed. Charles A. Gulick, Jr. (New York: Harper, 1931), p. 174. The dilemma of the Association reformers, however, was that virtually no one during the teens thought that federal social insurance programs would stand up as constitutional.

26. The uniformity strategy was emphasized as one of the AALL's objectives in its constitution (to "promote the uniformity of labor legislation in the United States"). See "Constitution," *Proceedings of the First Annual Meeting,* p. 6.

The strategy appeared consistent with the IALL strategy of encouraging competing industrial nations in Europe to enter into treaties defining common labor standards. But in the United States, nonparticipating governments (i.e., individual states) could not be punished through the imposition of tariffs or through other instruments of foreign policy.

27. William Graebner, "Federalism in the Progressive Era: A Structural Interpretation of Reform," *Journal of American History* 64, no. 2 (September 1977): 331–357; David Brian Robertson, "Policy Entrepreneurs and Policy Divergence: John R. Commons and William Beveridge," *Social Service Review* 62, no. 3 (September 1988): 504–531; David Brian Robertson, "The Bias of American Federalism: The Limits of Welfare-State Development in the Progressive Era," *Journal of Policy History* 1, no. 3 (1989): 261–291.

28. Although the phenomenon of degenerative competition between the states has received inadequate attention from historians of American social welfare policy, it has received considerable scholarly attention in a variety of other contexts, ranging from environmental law to banking regulation. In each case, as Harry Scheiber characterizes it, "federal effects have operated . . . to place practical upper limits upon a state's regulatory policies." Charles McCurdy, for example, has shown that intense competition between the states ended up destroying their ability to regulate the trusts in the late nineteenth century, thus necessitating the development of a strong federal role in antitrust law. According to the 1904 *Report of the Commissioner of Corporations* (cited by McCurdy), state legislation "gravitated with remarkable dispatch 'toward the lowest level of lax regulation.' " See Scheiber, "Federalism and the American Economic Order, 1789–1910," *Law and Society Review,* 10 (1975): 71; McCurdy, "The Knight Sugar Decision of 1895 and the Modernization of American Corporation Law, 1869–1903," *Business History Review* 53, no. 3 (Autumn 1979): 304–342. See also Raymond T. Zillner, "State Laws: Survival of the Unfit," *University of Pennsylvania Law Review* 62 (1914): 509–524. At present, there is no universally recognized, descriptive term for the phenomenon. Although economic game theorists might characterize it as a special case of the generic prisoner's dilemma, historians and public policy analysts require a more specialized term. A number of scholars have employed the phrase "race to the bottom," and a 1974 *Business Week* article on banking regulation cited the bankers' expression, "competition in laxity" ("Are the Banks Overextended?" *Business Week,* 21 September 1974, p. 54). The term offered here, "degenerative competition," is by no means perfect but enjoys the dual benefit of being more compact and more comprehensive than either of the others.

29. See e.g. William F. Willoughby, "The Philosophy of Labor Legislation," *ALLR* 4, no. 1 (March 1914): 44. Willoughby declared in late 1913: "It is part of the philosophy of our organization that, in striving for the welfare of the individual, we are at the same time striving for the increase in strength and power of the nation."

1. A Strategic Moment in History

1. John R. Commons, *Myself* (New York: Macmillan, 1934), p. 139.
2. There is no evidence that any of the Association's leaders voted for Eugene V. Debs, the socialist candidate for president who polled over 900,000 votes in 1912. But it is possible that some members who were socialists, such as I. M. Rubinow, supported Debs.
3. Commons, *Myself,* pp. 52–53.
4. John R. Commons, "Abstract Studies and the World," *Oberlin Review,* 7 February, 1888, Commons Papers, reel 15, fr. 10.
5. Henry W. Farnam, "Labor Legislation and Economic Progress," *American Association for Labor Legislation—Third Annual Meeting—Proceedings, Reports, Addresses—Labor and the Courts* (New York: AALL, 1910), p. 39.
6. William F. Willoughby, "The Philosophy of Labor Legislation," *ALLR* 4, no. 1 (March 1914): 41–42, 43–44.
7. Henry Farnam, "Practical Methods in Labor Legislation," *ALLR* 1, no. 1 (January 1911): 7–8.
8. *Historical Statistics of the United States: Colonial Times to 1970* (Washington: GPO, 1975), pp. 8, 231, 240, 138; Hace Sorel Tishler, *Self-Reliance and Social Security, 1870–1914* (Port Washington: Kennikat Press, 1971), chap. 1; Lance E. Davis et al., *American Economic Growth* (New York: Harper and Row, 1972), chap. 5; Carl N. Degler, *The Age of the Economic Revolution, 1876–1900* (Glenview: Scott, Foresman, 1967), chap. 2.
9. Joseph A. Schumpeter, *History of Economic Analysis* (New York: Oxford University Press, 1954), p. 812.
10. Richard T. Ely, *Ground Under Our Feet* (New York: Macmillan, 1938), pp. 126, 44.
11. Benjamin G. Rader, *The Academic Mind and Reform: The Influence of Richard T. Ely in American Life* (Lexington: University of Kentucky Press, 1966), pp. 28–53; Richard T. Ely, *The Past and the Present of Political Economy* (Baltimore: John Murphy, 1884), esp. pp. 45, 49; Ely, *Ground Under Our Feet,* pp. 121–164, 185–189; Richard T. Ely, *Studies in the Evolution of Industrial Society* (New York: The Macmillan Company, 1906), pp. 12–24; Commons, *Myself,* pp. 43–44; John R. Commons, *Social Reform and the Church* (New York: Crowell, 1894), pp. 46, 58–62. Ely attributed the economic maxim "look and see" to the English economist, Richard Jones. See Richard T. Ely, "Conservation and Economic Theory," in Ely et al., *The Foundations of National Prosperity: Studies in the Conservation of Permanent National Resources* (New York: Macmillan, 1923), esp. p. 12.
12. See John R. Commons, *The Distribution of Wealth* (New York: Macmillan, 1893); Commons, *Legal Foundations of Capitalism* (Madison: University of Wisconsin Press, 1957 [1924]); and Commons, *Institutional Economics: Its Place in Political Economy* (New Brunswick: Transaction, 1990 [1934]). See also Ben Seligman, *Main Currents in Modern Economics* (New Brunswick: Transaction, 1990), pp. 159–178.
13. Commons, *Distribution of Wealth,* p. 59.

14. Commons, *Social Reform and the Church*, p. 62. Similarly, Ely wrote in 1894, "This social theory of private property justifies a regulation of its use." See Richard T. Ely, *Socialism: An Examination of Its Nature, Its Strength and Its Weakness, with Suggestions for Social Reform* (New York: Crowell, 1894), p. 309.

15. Henry W. Farnam, *The Economic Utilization of History and Other Economic Studies* (New Haven: Yale University Press, 1913), pp. 28–29; Farnam, "Practical Methods in Labor Legislation," pp. 9–10.

16. Farnam, "Practical Methods in Labor Legislation," pp. 9–10. Similarly, Commons conceived of the AALL as a culminating achievement of social scientific work. In his typically arduous but insightful prose, he wrote in 1909 that the Association marked "the practical outcome towards which the [other social science associations] have been converging. First statistics, the means of measuring the amount and movement of social forces; next economics, the anaylsis and valuation of the more compelling forces; then sociology, the coordinating and balancing of all the forces; then legislation, the control of the forces for social ends." See John R. Commons, "The American Association for Labor Legislation," *Charities and Commons*, 9 January 1909, p. 1909, reprinted in Commons Papers, reel 16, fr. 862. Commons' description was also cited in an AALL circular letter of 1913, AALL draft circular letter to John Doe, 24 November 1913, AALL Papers, reel 10.

17. Rader, *Academic Mind*, p. 103. The title *Socialism and Social Reform* was (and still is) used to refer to Ely's *Socialism: An Examination . . .* already cited.

18. See Ely, *Socialism and Social Reform*, part 4. Ely borrowed much of his analysis of natural monopolies from Henry Carter Adams, who offered a careful examination of increasing returns in "Relation of the State to Industrial Action," *Publications of the American Economic Association* 1, no. 6 (January 1887): 465–549. Adams, however, never endorsed the socialization of monopolies as a solution. See Rader, *Academic Mind*, pp. 88–91.

19. Ely, *Socialism and Social Reform*, p. 253.

20. Henry W. Farnam, review of Ely's *The Labor Movement in America*, in *Political Science Quarterly* 1, no. 4 (December 1886): 686.

21. Ely, *Socialism and Social Reform*, pp. 254–255, 306–307, 255–256.

22. Lafayette G. Harter Jr., *John R. Commons: His Assault on Laissez-Faire* (Corvallis: Oregon State University Press, 1962).

23. Commons, *Distribution of Wealth*, pp. 109–111, 79–85; Commons, *Social Reform and the Church*, p. 128.

24. Harter, *John R. Commons*, p. 40; Commons, *Myself*, pp. 21–22; "Discussion of the President's Address," *Economic Studies* (American Economic Association) 4, no. 1 (February 1899): 111–113; Joseph Dorfman, *The Economic Mind in American Civilization, 1865–1918* (New York: Viking, 1949), vol. 3, p. 288. Commons' reply to Ely is cited in Dorfman, *Economic Mind*, p. 285; see Commons to Ely, 6 May [1895], *Microfilm Edition of the Richard T. Ely Papers*, reel 9 (hereafter cited Ely Papers). Although Commons wrote

in his autobiography that he voted for a Communist candidate for governor
of New York in the 1890s, he was mistaken about the name of the party
because the Communist Labor Party was not founded in the United States
until 1919. Commons probably cast his vote for the Socialist Labor Party
which fielded gubernatorial candidates in New York several times in the
1890s.

25. Dorothy Ross, *The Origins of American Social Science* (New York: Cambridge University Press, 1991), pp. 115–116. See also Dorothy Ross, "Socialism and American Liberalism: Academic Social Thought in the 1880's,"
Perspectives in American History 11 (1977–78): 5–79; Mary O. Furner, *Advocacy and Objectivity: A Crisis in the Professionalization of American Social
Science, 1865–1905* (Lexington: University Press of Kentucky, 1975),
chap. 6.

26. Ross, *Origins of American Social Science,* pp. 116–117; Ely, *Ground Under
Our Feet,* pp. 218–233; Rader, *Academic Mind,* pp. 131–157. In August
1895 Ely wrote to Hamilton W. Mabie, the associate editor of *Outlook:*
"Suppose if you should become known as a radical you would lose your
position on the 'Outlook', and on account of alleged radicalism you could
never secure any other position. Would you not under these circumstances
feel a little sensitive about the epithet 'radical'?" See Ely to Mabie, 24 August
1895, Ely Papers, reel 10, p. 13 (cited in Rader, *Academic Mind,* p. 153).

27. Commons, *Myself,* pp. 52–53, 58; Dorfman, *Economic Mind,* vol. 3, p. 288;
Ely to Robert Hunter, 25 April 1903, Ely Papers, reel 25 (cited in Leon Fink,
" 'Intellectuals' versus 'Workers': Academic Requirements and the Creation
of Labor History," *American Historical Review* 96, no. 2 [April 1991]: 408).

28. See e.g. the outline Commons used in a lecture from 1891 that treated the
advantages and disadvantages of socialism. Commons' discussion appears to
have stressed the advantages. The outline may be found in John R. Commons,
Political Economy and Labor, Syllabus of Lectures, University Extension,
Oberlin College, 1891, Commons Papers, reel 15, frs. 27–28.

29. Ralph Easley, a journalist and social reformer, organized the National Civic
Federation (NCF) in 1900–01 to foster cooperation between representatives
of capital, labor, and the public. Gabriel Kolko describes the NCF as the
"pro-conservative union, pro-big business, welfare-oriented National Civic
Federation." The group's membership included big business leaders such as
Marcus Hanna, Seth Low, George Perkins, and August Belmont, and labor
leaders such as Samuel Gompers, John Mitchell, and Warren Stone. During
the progressive era, the NCF promoted a variety of mechanisms to improve
relations between capital and labor, including collective bargaining, employ-
ment-based welfare work, and workers' compensation. Federation leaders
also devoted considerable attention to the question of the state's role in economic affairs and ended up supporting the public regulation of utilities as an
alternative to public ownership. See Gordon Maurice Jensen, "The National
Civic Federation: American Business in an Age of Social Change and Social
Reform" (Ph.D. diss., Princeton University, 1956); Gabriel Kolko, *The Tri-*

umph of Conservatism: A Reinterpretation of American History, 1900–1916 (New York: Free Press, 1963), esp. p. 66; Robert H. Wiebe, *Businessmen and Reform* (Chicago: Ivan R. Dee, 1989 [1962]).

30. Dorfman, *Economic Mind,* vol. 3, p. 292; Harter, *John R. Commons,* pp. 23–24; "Report of Commissioners John R. Commons and Florence J. Harriman," *Final Report of the Commission on Industrial Relations* (Washington, 1915), p. 308; "[Commons] Warns Labor to Avoid Socialism; Noted Economist Speaks to Workers," *Milwaukee Journal,* 21 February 1916, Commons Papers, reel 17, fr. 335; Harold L. Miller, ed., *Wisconsin Progressives: The John R. Commons Papers, Guide to a Microfilm Edition* (Madison: State Historical Society of Wisconsin, 1986), p. 14.

31. John R. Commons, "The Labor Problem," address, Freie Gemeinde Hall, Milwaukee, 20 February 1916, Commons Papers, reel 17, fr. 694; Dorfman, *Economic Mind,* vol. 3, p. 291; Adams, "Relation of the State to Industrial Action," pp. 503–511; Ely, *Socialism and Social Reform,* pp. 316–318. The ethical-plane argument is relevant not only to competing firms but also to competing states. Suppose that legislators in twenty competing states are considering a new safety regulation. Even though a majority in each state might think the regulation beneficial, it is possible (in fact likely) that no state legislature will enact it. The reason is that legislators everywhere are afraid of putting industries in their states at a disadvantage relative to competitors in other states that choose not to enact the regulation. As noted in the introduction, I refer to this dynamic between the states as degenerative competition. Leading AALL reformers recognized that the degenerative competition problem was perhaps the most formidable obstacle they faced, and Commons correctly observed in 1915 that it was conceptually comparable to the problem of the twentieth man ("Report of Commissioners Commons and Harriman," p. 395). The leaders of the AALL thus sought to raise the plane of competition not only for firms within states but also for states within the nation.

32. "American Association for Labor Legislation Report of the General Administrative Council Meeting," Chicago, 10 April 1909, *Publications—American Association for Labor Legislation,* nos. 1–11, 1907–1910, p. 11.

33. See John R. Commons, *Industrial Goodwill* (New York: McGraw-Hill, 1919), p. 129; Henry W. Farnam, "Some Fundamental Distinctions in Labor Legislation," *Proceedings of the Second Annual Meeting—American Association for Labor Legislation* (Madison: AALL, 1909), esp. pp. 40–42; Ely, "Conservation and Economic Theory," esp. pp. 27–46; Samuel P. Hays, *Conservation and the Gospel of Efficiency: The Progressive Conservation Movement, 1890–1920* (Cambridge: Harvard University Press, 1959), esp. pp. 122–146. For an example of the AALL's wartime letterhead slogan, see John B. Andrews to Thomas Chadbourne, 25 September 1918, AALL Papers, reel 18.

34. John R. Commons, "Industrial Government," *Railway Expressman,* June 1922, Commons Papers, reel 19, fr. 299. See also John R. Commons, *Indus-*

trial Government (New York: Macmillan, 1921), pp. 268–69. Eugene V. Debs, the Socialist candidate for president, received 402,283 votes in 1904, 420,793 in 1908, and 900,672 in 1912. A. L. Bensen took 585,113 votes as the Socialist candidate in 1916, and Debs secured 919,799 votes when he returned as the party's nominee in 1920. The progressive era marked the high point of Socialist Party strength in American presidential elections.

35. Ely, *Socialism and Social Reform*, pp. 259–260. See also e.g. "Capitalism not doomed—Commons," *Eau Claire Leader,* 26 June 1925, Commons Papers, reel 19, frs. 1004–05.

36. Commons, "Labor Problem," fr. 691.

37. Henry Rogers Seager, *Economics* (New York: Columbia University Press, 1908), p. 24.

38. "Report of Commissioners Commons and Harriman," p. 391. The context for this statement about insecurity was an extremely unusual proposal by Commons and Harriman for the creation of a Federal Fund for Social Welfare to be financed mainly out of a new, national inheritance tax. The Federal Fund for Social Welfare never appeared as an item on the AALL's legislative agenda.

39. Andrews to "Dear Sir" (membership circular), 19 September 1911, AALL Papers, reel 6.

40. John R. Commons, "Social Economics and City Evangelization," *The Christian City,* December 1898, p. 772, Commons Papers, reel 15, fr. 335.

2. Charging up the Middle

1. John Maynard Keynes, *The General Theory of Employment, Interest, and Money* (New York: Harcourt Brace Jovanovich, 1964 [1936]), p. 383. For an intriguing critique of Keynes's pronouncement on the great political influence of economists, see Paul A. Samuelson, "Economists and the History of Ideas," *American Economic Review* 52, no. 1 (March 1962): 17.

2. Richard Hofstadter, *The Age of Reform: From Bryan to F.D.R.* (New York: Vintage, 1955), chap. 4, pp. 131–173.

3. Although Hofstadter's status-anxiety thesis remains a prominent fixture within the historiography of the progressive era, it has faced a barrage of criticism. A number of historians have argued persuasively that the thesis is not particularly useful since, in many cases, it appears just as applicable to middle-class conservatives as to middle-class progressives. See e.g. David P. Thelen, "Social Tensions and the Origins of Progressivism," *Journal of American History* 56, no. 2 (1969): 323–341; Jack Tager, "Progressives, Conservatives and the Theory of the Status Revolution," *Mid-America* 48, no. 3 (1966): 162–175; Richard B. Sherman, "The Status Revolution and Massachusetts Progressive Leadership," *Political Science Quarterly* 78 (1963): 59–65. Another group of historians has challenged Hofstadter's thesis because it suggests (wrongly, they contend) that the middle class was the only important source of reform during the progressive period. See e.g. John D.

Buenker, "The Progressive Era: A Search for Synthesis," *Mid-America* 51, no. 3 (1969): 175–193; J. Joseph Huthmacher, "Urban Liberalism and the Age of Reform," *Mississippi Valley Historical Review* 49, no. 2 (1962–63): 231–241. Both of these criticisms, highlighting Hofstadter's proclivity for overgeneralization, are valid. Still, the characterization of progressive reformers motivated, at least in part, by status anxiety is useful here because it captures an important personality trait of the AALL's leadership. For more sympathetic treatments of Hofstadter's thesis, see Jerome M. Clubb and Howard W. Allen, "Collective Biography and the Progressive Movement: The 'Status Revolution' Revisited," *Social Science History* 1, no. 4 (1977): 518–534; Alan Brinkley, "In Retrospect: Richard Hofstadter's The Age of Reform: A Reconsideration," *Reviews in American History* 13, no. 3 (1985): 462–480.

4. Richard T. Ely, *Ground Under Our Feet* (New York: Macmillan, 1938), p. 196. On Commons' belief that economic theory should be developed with the goal of solving practical problems, see Lafayette G. Harter Jr., *John R. Commons: His Assault on Laissez-Faire* (Corvallis: Oregon State University Press, 1962), p. 205. See also Robert L. Church, "Economists as Experts: The Rise of an Academic Profession in the United States, 1870–1920," in Lawrence Stone, ed., *The University in Society*, vol. 2 (Princeton: Princeton University Press, 1974), pp. 571–609.

5. Charles R. Henderson, "Recent Advances in the Struggle Against Unemployment," *ALLR* 2, no. 1 (February 1912): 110.

6. Ernst Freund to John B. Andrews, 12 June 1915, AALL Papers, reel 14.

7. Cited in John B. Andrews, "Secretary's Report 1915," *ALLR* 6, no. 1 (1916): 109.

8. See Robert H. Bremner, *American Philanthropy* (Chicago: University of Chicago Press, 1988), pp. 7–15, 42–43, 47–48, 106–108.

9. A number of scholars, especially Robert Wiebe and Samuel Hays, have identified the emergence during the progressive era of a "new middle class," whose membership sought social cohesion (or group membership) across geographic space. See Robert H. Wiebe, *The Search for Order, 1877–1920* (New York: Hill and Wang, 1967), esp. chap. 5 ("A New Middle Class"); Samuel P. Hays, *The Response to Industrialism, 1885–1914* (Chicago: University of Chicago Press, 1957), esp. chap. 4 ("The Individual in an Impersonal Society"). The distinguishing characteristics of this "new middle class" include a commitment to specialization and professionalization as well as a profound faith in the promise of science. Wiebe describes members of the new class as "[a]lmost worshipful of a nebulous, exhilarating something they called 'science' " (*Search for Order*, p. 132), while Hays uses the term "scientific humanitarianism" in depicting middle-class efforts at social reform during the progressive period (*Response to Industrialism*, p. 82). From this perspective, one might understand the leaders of the AALL as members of the "new middle class" who successfully derived political influence from their professional, scientific credentials.

10. R.G. Hazard to Irving Fisher, 17 January 1916, AALL Papers, reel 16; " 'Intellectuals,' Please Note," *American Federationist* 23, no. 3 (March 1916):

199. See also "Advice Welcome—Intrusion Never," *American Federationist* 22, no. 11 (November 1915): 974; Samuel Gompers, "Labor vs. Its Barnacles," *American Federationist* 23, no. 4 (April 1916): 272.

11. A few scholars have resurrected the suggestion that the AALL might have been controlled by prominent corporate capitalists, based primarily on the fact that several capitalists helped to finance the organization. Irwin Yellowitz notes that the "Association's big contributors included John D. Rockefeller; Elbert Gary of the United States Steel Corporation; Felix Warburg, a leading banker and philanthropist; Mrs. Madeline Astor; V. Everitt Macy . . . and Mrs. Anne Morgan, the daughter of the financier." Based on this reading, James Weinstein dismisses the AALL in his book on corporate liberalism as "an organization of middle class reformers financed by such men as John D. Rockefeller, Elbert H. Gary, and V. Everitt Macy." Trade unionists, Weinstein adds, "had little use for the AALL." Yellowitz's and Weinstein's references to Rockefeller and other major capitalists who contributed to the AALL are somewhat misleading. Rockefeller, for example, appears to have contributed $1,000 a year between 1911 and 1914, but he was never the largest contributor and, according to Andrews, did not contribute to the AALL's vital health insurance campaigns. The Association's biggest contributor during the progressive period was the Yale professor of economics, Henry W. Farnam, who served as the Association's second president. Farnam's name is not mentioned in either Yellowitz's or Weinstein's account of AALL finances. Nor do these accounts take note of any of the labor activists who contributed (including Mrs. Raymond Robins, whose annual contributions were substantial). Yellowitz's reference to Anne Morgan is also slightly misleading. Her participation in and contributions to reform organizations such as the AALL were about as likely calculated to spite her father as to please him. She became estranged from him in her adult life and managed to be a constant source of embarrassment to him. Other members of the Morgan circle, including Thomas Lamont, supported the Association, but never J. P. Morgan himself. See Irwin Yellowitz, *Labor and the Progressive Movement in New York State* (Ithaca: Cornell University Press, 1965), pp. 72–73; James Weinstein, *The Corporate Ideal in the Liberal State* (Boston: Beacon Press, 1968), p. 48; Andrews to James Lynch, 3 July 1918, AALL Papers, reel 18; Andrews to Editor, *New York Times,* 17 February 1917, AALL Papers, reel 17; Ron Chernow, *The House of Morgan* (New York: Simon and Schuster, 1990), pp. 140–142.

12. Andrews to William F. Cochran, 27 July 1915, AALL Papers, reel 14; Andrews to R. Clipston Sturgis, 14 November 1918, AALL Papers, reel 18.

13. See Farnam to Andrews, 10 March 1909, AALL Papers, reel 1; Andrews to Seager, 26 December 1911, AALL Papers, reel 6.

14. See Luke Grant to Osgood, 26 June 1909; George H. Ellis to AALL, 24 June 1909; Commons to Farnam, 26 June 1909; Commons to John Mitchell, 26 June 1909; Farnam to Commons, 28 June 1909; Mitchell to Commons, 28 June 1909; Commons to Ellis, 28 June 1909, AALL Papers, reel 2.

15. Ferd C. Schwedtman to Andrews, 17 April 1911, AALL Papers, reel 5. Robert Wuest, the commissioner of the National Metal Trades Association, once offered to help Andrews with a membership drive by sending him some names, but noted that he "could not possibly think of using stationery on which that un-American insignia 'The Union Label' appears." See Robert Wuest to Andrews, 2 September 1911, AALL Papers, reel 6.

16. Otto Nicols to Andrews, 14 March 1916, AALL Papers, reel 16. See also Jack Karpf to AALL, 22 April 1916, AALL Papers, reel 17.

17. Andrews to John D. Hubbard, 25 February 1914, AALL Papers, reel 11.

18. Andrews to Wm. Standcumbe, 29 April 1912, AALL Papers, reel 7; Reubin A. Meyers to L. P. Sanders, 27 September 1911, AALL Papers, reel 6.

19. See Theda Skocpol, *Protecting Soldiers and Mothers: The Political Origins of Social Policy in the United States* (Cambridge: Harvard University Press, 1992), pp. 188–193.

20. John R. Commons, *Industrial Goodwill* (New York: McGraw-Hill, 1919), p. 177.

21. "Organized Labor and Organized Employers Hold Conference on Proposed Legislation Laying 'Cards Face Up on the Table'," *Monitor* 2, no. 8 (January 1916): 2.

22. "Administration Ripper Bill Is Introduced," *Legislative Labor News* 4, no. 80 (15 March 1915): [1]. Prior to their acceptance of public appointments, Lynch had served as president of the International Typographical Union and Mitchell as president of the United Mine Workers.

23. See Andrews, "Secretary's Report 1915," pp. 106–111; "Labor Opposes Consolidation," *Legislative Labor News* 4, no. 83 (9 April 1915): [1]; Yellowitz, *Labor and the Progressive Movement*, pp. 119–121; *Journal of the Senate* (New York State), 1915, pp. 470, 951–952, 954, 1012–13, 1149, 1420–23, 1695.

24. Andrews to H. J. Wright, 16 April 1915, AALL Papers, reel 14; "Labor Legislation of 1915," *ALLR* 5, no. 4 (December 1915): 690–691; *Laws of New York,* 1915, chap. 674, pp. 2260–61; Andrews, "Secretary's Report 1915," p. 108; John R. Commons, *Myself* (New York: Macmillan, 1934), p. 72; John R. Commons, "A New Way of Settling Labor Disputes," *American Monthly Review of Reviews,* March 1901, pp. 328–333; Commons to Andrews, 11 October 1915, AALL Papers, reel 15; John R. Commons, "Industrial Government," *Railway Expressman,* June 1922, Commons Papers, reel 19, frs. 296–299; Commons, *Industrial Goodwill,* p. 183. See also John B. Andrews, "An Industrial Commission for the State of New York," *Survey* 34, no. 5 (1 May 1915): 101–102.

25. "17 Bills Affecting Labor Are Signed by Governor; 19 Vetocd," *Legislative Labor News* 4, no. 86 (June 1915): [4–5]; *Laws of New York,* 1915, chap. 674, pp. 2259–72; Andrews to Margaret Loomis Stecker, 14 May 1915, AALL Papers, reel 14; [E.J. Barcolo] to Andrews, 11 June 1915, AALL Papers, reel 14.

26. Andrews, "Secretary's Report, 1915," pp. 109–110.

27. "Direct Commission Reports on New Workmen's Compensation Law," *New York Times,* 24 August 1915, p. 12.

28. [E.J. Barcolo] to Andrews, 11 June 1915, AALL Papers, reel 14.

29. "Mr. Gompers Opposes Enemies of Labor Legislation," *Legislative Labor News* 4, no. 86 (June 1915): [5]; Milton Fairchild to Seager, [c. June 1915], AALL Papers, reel 14.

30. Andrews to William Cochran, 27 July 1915, AALL Papers, reel 14; Andrews to H. E. Hoagland, 7 July 1915, AALL Papers, reel 14.

31. See esp. Roy Lubove, *The Struggle for Social Security, 1900–1935* (Pittsburgh: University of Pittsburgh Press, 1986), chap. 1 ("The Constraints of Voluntarism").

32. John R. Commons, "Health Insurance," *Wisconsin Medical Journal,* November 1918, Commons Papers, reel 17, frs. 437–438.

33. Transcript of the New York State Senate Judiciary Committee Hearing on the Mills Health Insurance Bill (Senate Print no. 365), 7 March 1917, reprinted in "Convincing and Effective Opposition to Health Insurance Bill Takes Proponents Off Their Feet," *Monitor* 3, no. 10 (March 1917): 13.

34. For a discussion of employment policies designed to minimize labor turnover in the 1920s, see Laura Jane Owen, "The Decline in Turnover of Manufacturing Workers: Case Study Evidence from the 1920s," (Ph.D. diss., Yale University, May 1991), esp. chap. 5. See also Sanford M. Jacoby, *Employing Bureaucracy: Managers, Unions, and the Transformation of Work in American Industry, 1900–1945* (New York: Columbia University Press, 1985), esp. pp. 196–199.

35. See e.g., Olga S. Halsey to Ralph S. Easley, 24 March 1916, AALL Papers, reel 16.

36. John R. Commons, "Social Insurance," address delivered to Civics Club, Madison, 1 April 1916, Commons Papers, reel 17, frs. 698–710, pp. 11–12.

37. Frederick E. Hoffman to Irving Fisher, 5 February 1917, AALL Papers, reel 17.

38. Ralph Easley to Olga Halsey, 25 April 1916, AALL Papers, reel 17.

39. Noting that both Easley and Gompers were attacking health insurance, Andrews joked to Commons in 1916, "Now if the Catholic Church gets busy we will have the opposition all lined up and know just where we stand." Andrews to Commons, 21 March 1916, AALL Papers, reel 16.

40. See Gompers, "Labor vs. Its Barnacles," esp. p. 270. The AFL's official preference for voluntary union benefit plans over compulsory social insurance is quite clear in the organization's annual proceedings. The entry on "Social Insurance" in the 1916 proceedings concludes, "We strongly recommend that the subject of social insurance in all its phases be given greater consideration and extension by the unions and preferentially by the national and international unions, as well as by the local unions, and in any event, in so far as social insurance by the state and national governments is concerned, if established at all, shall be voluntary and not compulsory." *Report of Proceedings of the Thirty-Sixth Annual Convention of the American Federation of Labor* (Washington: Law Reporter Printing Co., 1916), p. 145.

41. See William E. Forbath, *Law and the Shaping of the American Labor Movement* (Cambridge: Harvard University Press, 1991).

42. Gompers, "Labor vs. Its Barnacles," p. 271.

43. In 1894 Commons had written that "the wage-working classes do need intelligent and friendly counsel. They need powerful influences to be brought to bear for their benefit upon legislatures, courts, and executives [by educated men]." See John R. Commons, *Social Reform and the Church* (New York: Crowell, 1894), p. 55.

44. Gompers wrote that "the men in control of the so-called American Association for Labor Legislation are respectfully but insistently advised that in any struggle which that association may desire to inaugurate or maintain, they will find the American labor movement an adversary worthy of any combatant, and that after the smoke of battle shall have cleared away, the American labor movement will still be marching along the road to triumph in the protection and promotion of the rights, interests, welfare, and freedom of the toilers." Gompers, "Labor vs. Its Barnacles," p. 272.

45. By the end of 1918, some 18 state federations of labor, 21 internationals, and many other labor organizations (including the National Women's Trade Union League and the Southern Labor Congress) had endorsed health insurance against the wishes of Samuel Gompers. The New York State Federation of Labor, moreover, had joined the AALL in its campaign for a health insurance bill in New York. The general secretary-treasurer of the Brotherhood of Painters, Decorators and Paperhangers of America tactfully acknowledged: "In urging that we work toward our desired ends through the trade union rather than through political action, President Gompers probably voices the sentiments of the majority of the active workers in the labor movement. Many, however, feel that he is somewhat prejudiced on this subject." Such prominent labor leaders as John Mitchell and William Green dissented from Gompers—Mitchell writing for the AALL that experience with workers' compensation "indicates the need of some system of insurance protecting workmen during periods of incapacity due to sickness." See "Prominent Labor Organizations Already on Record for Health Insurance," *ALLR* 8, no. 4 (December 1918): 319; "Recent American Opinion in Favor of Health Insurance," *ALLR* 6, no. 4 (December 1916): 348; J. C. Skemp to Andrews, 13 April 1916, AALL Papers, reel 16; William Green to Andrews, 12 December 1916, AALL Papers, reel 17; statement signed by John Mitchell, 19 January 1916, AALL Papers, reel 16.

46. Andrews to Nicholas Klein, 26 May 1916, AALL Papers, reel 17.

47. A column in the *New Republic* ("A Government Plea for Health Insurance," 20 May 1916, p. 57) described the number of union leaders who opposed Gompers' position on compulsory health insurance as "large and growing."

48. William F. Cochran to John B. Andrews, 7 December 1914, and Andrews to Cochran, 5 January 1915, AALL Papers, reel 13.

49. Andrews to Cochran, 5 January 1915, AALL Papers, reel 13.

50. Commons, *Industrial Goodwill*, p. 90.

3. Security Floors and Opportunity Ceilings

1. Robert H. Bremner, *From the Depths: The Discovery of Poverty in the United States* (New York: New York University Press, 1964).

2. In fact, it was not unusual for progressive reformers to mix together new and old approaches to problems. In a synthetic essay on progressivism and its legacy, Thomas K. McCraw describes the progressives as having "one foot stuck firmly in the nineteenth century, the other striding overconfidently into the twentieth . . . Habituated to outmoded patterns of thought, they nonetheless sensed that the impersonal, cosmopolitan, ultimately post-industrial twentieth century was, without question, a new type of world." McCraw, "The Progressive Legacy," in Lewis L. Gould, ed., *The Progressive Era* (Syracuse: Syracuse University Press, 1974), p. 199.

3. This point, and much of the discussion that follows, is based on David A. Moss, "The Political Economy of Insecurity: The American Association for Labor Legislation and the Crusade for Social Welfare Reform in the Progressive Era" (Ph.D. diss., Yale University, 1992), chap. 2 ("The American Experience With Poverty: New Ideas and Old Values"), pp. 54–96.

4. See e.g. Charles R. Lee, " 'This Poor People': Seventeenth-Century Massachusetts and the Poor," *Historical Journal of Massachusetts* 9 (January 1981): 42–43.

5. David M. Schneider, *The History of Public Welfare in New York State, 1609–1866* (Chicago: University of Chicago Press, 1938), esp. p. 61. See also Eleanor Parkhurst, "Poor Relief in a Massachusetts Village in the Eighteenth Century," *Social Service Review* 11, no. 3 (September 1937): 446–464.

6. See e.g. "Report of the Secretary of State in 1824 on the Relief and Settlement of the Poor," delivered to the New York Assembly and Senate by J.V.N. Yates, reprinted in David J. Rothman, ed., *The Almshouse Experience* (New York: Arno, 1971), p. 963.

7. The editor of a Baltimore newspaper explained in 1820 that the purpose of the Baltimore Society for the Prevention of Pauperism was "not indeed to prevent a man from being poor, but to prevent him if possible from becoming a degraded object of public bounty." This editorial, which appeared in the *Morning Chronicle and Baltimore Advertiser,* 15 April 1820, is quoted in Blanche D. Coll, "The Baltimore Society for the Prevention of Pauperism, 1820–1822," *American Historical Review* 61, no. 1 (October 1955): 83.

8. M. J. Heale, "The New York Society for the Prevention of Pauperism, 1817–1823," *New York Historical Society Quarterly* 55, no. 2 (April 1971): 163; Raymond A. Mohl, *Poverty in New York, 1783–1825* (New York: Oxford University Press, 1971), pp. 245–246.

9. For a broader commentary on the decline of individualism in American social thought during the late nineteenth and early twentieth centuries, see R. Jackson Wilson, *In Quest of Community: Social Philosophy in the United States, 1860–1920* (New York: Wiley, 1968), esp. chap. 1 ("The Plight of the Transcendent Individual").

10. *ALLR* 5, no. 4 (December 1915).

11. Commons had written in 1894: "True, there are natural conditions, but natural conditions have become of inferior significance. A century ago, or among uncivilized tribes, they were all-important. But the machinery and inventions, the aids to production, all that go to make up the wealth of our country, are so abounding that if the American people seriously wished it, there would not be an able-bodied pauper or tramp among us." John R. Commons, *Social Reform and the Church* (New York: Crowell, 1894), p. 15.

12. William F. Willoughby, "The Problem of Social Insurance: An Analysis," *ALLR* 3, no. 2 (June 1913): 156.

13. Ibid., 157.

14. John R. Commons, "The Right to Work," *The Arena* 21, no. 2 (February 1899): 141.

15. See Susan Lehrer, *Origins of Protective Labor Legislation for Women, 1905–1925* (Albany: State University of New York Press, 1987), pp. 80–84; Louise B. More, *Wage-Earners' Budgets* (New York: Holt, 1907); Robert C. Chapin, *The Standard of Living among Workingmen's Families in New York City* (New York: Russell Sage Foundation, 1909). Chapin cautiously noted that although "wise use of the family income" may be more important than the total amount earned in warding off poverty, "there are limits to what can be done by thrift and economy" (p. 248). Investigators disagreed about what level of income would provide a minimally adequate standard of living for a typical family, but Chapin identified a figure of $800 per year for a family of five living in New York City. As a matter of fact, a large segment of the unskilled working population in New York had annual family incomes under $800. Of the 391 New York families interviewed in Chapin's study, 45 percent lived on less than $800 per year (p. 40). See also Martha May, "The 'Good Managers': Married Working Class Women and Family Budget Studies, 1895–1915," *Labor History* 25, no. 3 (Summer 1984): 351–372. Writing in 1904, Robert Hunter estimated that at least 10 million (and perhaps as many as 15 to 20 million) Americans lived in poverty—that is, were unable "to obtain those necessaries which will permit them to maintain a state of physical efficiency." Since the total population of the United States was 82 million in 1904, the poverty rate (as defined by Hunter) was somewhere between 12 and 24 percent. See Robert Hunter, *Poverty* (New York: Macmillan, 1907 [1904]), pp. 5, 11.

16. Henry R. Seager, "Outline of a Program of Social Legislation with Special Reference to Wage Earners," *American Association for Labor Legislation: Proceedings of the First Annual Meeting,* Madison, April 1908, pp. 85–86.

17. Ibid., p. 91.

18. Willoughby, "Problem of Social Insurance," p. 159.

19. As a result of focusing on worker security and ignoring the very poor who were not members of the regular workforce, the leaders of the AALL—whether consciously or unconsciously—failed to address special problems of black Americans in their reform agenda. I do not develop connections between issues of poverty and issues of race in this book primarily because

references to race are rare in the AALL papers, and references to blacks in particular are virtually nonexistent. Although John Commons was an adherent of scientific racism and wrote extensively on the subject of racial and ethnic differences, he never directly linked his theories about race to his social reform work at the AALL. It seems obvious, however, that an agenda biased against individuals on the periphery of the workforce would implicitly discriminate against many African Americans, who were economically margin alized because of systematic racial bias against them. The fact that Commons (and probably others at the Association) ascribed to a philosophy of scientific racism does not prove that the AALL as a reform organization cared less about blacks than about other disadvantaged groups, but it does help to explain why the AALL's insensitivity to the plight of black Americans was so unremarkable at the time. See my discussion at the end of this chapter on the effective exclusion of blacks from social insurance programs in the United States. See also John R. Commons, *Races and Immigrants in America* (New York: Macmillan, 1907), which offers the best expression of Commons' ideas about race. Finally, it should be noted that the AALL's racial "blind spot" was not atypical. One historian of the progressive era wrote in the late 1960s that "the supreme blind spot of the progressives, North and South alike, was the Negro problem." David W. Southern, *The Malignant Heritage: Yankee Progressives and the Negro Question, 1901–1914* (Chicago: Loyola University Press, 1968), p. 85. See also Dewey W. Grantham Jr., "The Progressive Movement and the Negro," *South Atlantic Quarterly* 65, no. 4 (October 1955): esp. 472–474.

20. On scientific charity, see esp. Robert Bremner, " 'Scientific Philanthropy,' 1873–93," *Social Service Review* 30, no. 2 (June 1956): 168–173; Nathan Irvin Huggins, *Protestants Against Poverty—Boston's Charities, 1870–1900* (Westport: Greenwood, 1971).

21. Hunter, *Poverty*, pp. 62, 105.

22. Ibid., p. 108.

23. Mary Van Kleeck to Andrews, 6 January 1915, AALL Papers, reel 13.

24. *ALLR* 4, no. 2 (May 1914): 218.

25. According to Alexander Keyssar, the word "unemployed" underwent a change of meaning in the 1870s and 1880s and crept into common usage over the next few decades. For a long time, the word remained vague and little used, referring generally to persons with no occupations. But by 1878, the Massachusetts Bureau of Statistics of Labor had inverted the word's meaning, now using it to describe those who had occupations but had no work. Keyssar explains that "between 1875 and 1885, the word ['unemployed'] was sloughing off its once primary and potentially pejorative meaning, while acquiring the status of a recognized and official label for 'honest, industrious workers' who were 'involuntarily without employment.' " Alexander Keyssar, *Out of Work: The First Century of Unemployment in Massachusetts* (Cambridge, Eng.: Cambridge University Press, 1986), pp. 3–4.

26. Andrews to Henry Bruere, 13 October 1915, AALL Papers, reel 15. See also [Andrews] to Dr. [Graham?] Taylor, 8 November 1915, AALL Papers, reel 15.

27. "Unemployment Survey," *ALLR* 5, no. 3 (November 1915): 538–539.
28. Charles Henderson, "Recent Advances in the Struggle Against Unemployment," reprinted in *ALLR* 2, no. 1 (February 1912): 107.
29. "The Men We Lodge," reprinted in *ALLR* 5, no. 3 (November 1915): 616–617, 622. Although the average for 1914 was about a thousand per night, the winter months were the heaviest period for homeless men, who made up the vast majority of applicants. The number of women lodgers, interestingly, was higher in summer than in winter (p. 616, n. 13).
30. Ibid., pp. 599–600.
31. Ibid., p. 598.
32. Ibid., p. 602. The population of New York City in 1915 was just over 5 million. If the police estimates were accurate, the homeless population represented about one-half of 1 percent of the total.
33. Ibid., p. 604. Of the 1,448 who stated their places of birth, 621 (or 43 percent) were foreign-born. Another 304 applicants to the Lodging House were excluded from the investigation because they could not speak English (p. 611).
34. Ibid., p. 604.
35. Ibid.
36. Ibid., pp. 604–605. The report notes that the investigation upon which these figures were based occurred *before* the "abnormal period of unemployment in the winter of 1914–15."
37. Ibid., p. 605.
38. Ibid., p. 607.
39. Ibid., pp. 607–610.
40. Ibid., p. 608. Data on alcoholism within the general public during the progressive era (for purposes of comparison) are unavailable. But E. M. Jellinek (writing in 1947) estimated rates of chronic alcoholism in 1915 at 2.068 percent for adult males, 0.355 percent for adult females, and 1.202 percent for all adults, dramatically lower than the 39 percent figure for Municipal Lodging House clients in March 1914. See Jellinek, "Recent Trends in Alcoholism and in Alcohol Consumption," *Quarterly Journal of Studies on Alcohol* 8, no. 1 (June 1947): 19–20.
41. "The Men We Lodge," p. 609.
42. Ibid., pp. 614–615.
43. John A. Garraty, *Unemployment in History: Economic Thought and Public Policy* (New York: Harper and Row, 1978), pp. 112–113, 140, 120.
44. *ALLR* 1, no. 3 (October 1911): 138.
45. See extracts from New York Law, 1911, C. 812, reprinted in *ALLR* 1, no. 3 (October 1911): 141–142.
46. "General Discussion," *ALLR* 5, no. 2 (June 1915): 455–456.
47. Robert G. Valentine, "What the Awakened Employer Is Thinking on Unemployment," *ALLR* 5, no. 2 (June 1915): 426–427.
48. Andrews to Michael Drummond, 15 February 1915, AALL Papers, reel 13; [Director, Investigation and Industrial Organization, Mayor's Committee on

Unemployment] to Seager, 2 February 1915, AALL Papers, reel 13; John R. Shillady to Seager, 18 March 1915, AALL Papers, reel 14; Seager, "Outline of a Program of Social Legislation," p. 100; "Unemployment Survey," *ALLR* 5, no. 3 (November 1915): 594.

49. Irene Osgood Andrews, "The Relation of Irregular Employment to the Living Wage for Women," *ALLR* 5, no. 2 (June 1915): 308–309.

50. Ibid., p. 293.

51. Ibid., pp. 313, 332, 357. As of 1900, 5,329,000 women (as against 8,550,000 in 1920) were gainfully employed in the United States, 25.8 (23.8) percent of whom were involved in manufacturing, mining, or construction. Over half of all gainfully employed women—53.6 (60.7) percent—worked in the service sector; but of those women employed in manufacturing, 73.1 (54.2) percent were engaged the textile industry or in the apparel and kindred trades. See A. T. Mallier and M. J. Rosser, *Women and the Economy: A Comparative Study of Britain and the USA* (New York: St. Martin's Press, 1987), table 3.3 (p. 37). On the highly seasonal nature of women's work, see also Leslie Woodcock Tentler, *Wage-Earning Women: Industrial Work and Family Life in the United States, 1900–1930* (New York: Oxford University Press, 1979), pp. 35–38.

52. Osgood Andrews, "Relation of Irregular Employment to the Living Wage for Women," pp. 306–308.

53. Ibid., p. 310.

54. "Woman's Work," *ALLR* 2, no. 3 (October 1912): 495.

55. "Legislation for Women in Industry," *ALLR* 6, no. 4 (December 1916): 383–384; Hoffman to H. B. Wooston, 10 December 1913, AALL Papers, reel 10; Lehrer, *Origins of Protective Labor Legislation for Women*, pp. 67, 71. The eight additional states that enacted minimum-wage laws for women in 1913 were California, Colorado, Minnesota, Nebraska, Oregon, Utah, Washington, and Wisconsin.

56. Henry R. Seager, "The Theory of the Minimum Wage," address before a joint session of the AALL and the American Economic Association, 28 December 1912, *ALLR* 3, no. 1: 85. For similar arguments, see John R. Commons, "The Minimum Wage," *Independent*, 2 October 1902, p. 2375, Commons Papers, reel 16, fr. 64; testimony of I. M. Rubinow before the New York State Factory Investigating Commission in *Fourth Report of the [New York State] Factory Investigating Commission, 1915*, vol. 5 (Albany: J. B. Lyon, 1915), p. 2843. For a contemporary academic discussion of the problem by a member of the AALL, see F. W. Taussig, *Principles of Economics*, vol. 2 (New York: Macmillan, 1911), pp. 300–302. The effect of minimum-wage requirements on employment is an issue of some contention in the modern literature. On the adverse effects of minimum-wage laws on "inefficient" workers, see esp. Peter Linneman, "The Economic Impacts of Minimum Wage Laws: A New Look at an Old Question," *Journal of Political Economy* 90, no. 3 (June 1982): 443–469; Charles Brown, Curtis Gilroy, and Andrew Kohen, "The Effect of the Minimum Wage on Employment and Unemployment," *Journal*

of Economic Literature 20, no. 2 (June 1982): 487–528. For studies that challenge the traditional view, see Alison J. Wellington, "Effects of the Minimum Wage on the Employment Status of Youths: An Update," *Journal of Human Resources* 26, no. 1 (Winter 1991): 27–46; William T. Alpert and John B. Guerard Jr., "Employment, Unemployment and the Minimum Wage: A Causality Model," *Applied Economics* 20, no. 11 (November 1988): 1453–64; David Card, "Do Minimum Wages Reduce Employment? A Case Study of California, 1987–89," *Industrial and Labor Relations Review* 46, no. 1 (October 1992): 38–54, and "Using Regional Variation in Wages to Measure the Effects of the Federal Minimum Wage," 22–37.

57. Henry R. Seager, "The Minimum Wage as Part of a Constructive Program for Social Insurance," address at American Academy of Political and Social Science, Philadelphia, 5 April 1913, AALL Papers, reel 67, p. 8. This speech is reprinted as "The Minimum Wage as Part of a Program for Social Reform," in Seager, *Labor and Other Economic Essays*, ed. Charles A. Gulick Jr. (New York: Harper, 1931), pp. 214–226.

58. Ibid., p. 10.

59. Thirty-nine states enacted mothers' pension laws during the progressive period, but the legislation typically was restrictive (often covering only widows) and poorly implemented. In addition, the cash allowances generally were very low. See Theda Skocpol, *Protecting Soldiers and Mothers: The Political Origins of Social Policy in the United States* (Cambridge: Harvard University Press, 1992), pp. 439–479; Roy Lubove, *The Struggle for Social Security, 1900–1935* (Pittsburgh: University of Pittsburgh Press, 1986), chap. 4 ("Mothers' Pensions and the Renaissance of Public Welfare"), pp. 91–112.

60. Seager, "Theory of the Minimum Wage," p. 89.

61. Willoughby, "Problem of Social Insurance," p. 158. See also John R. Commons and John B. Andrews, *Principles of Labor Legislation* (New York: Harper, 1920), p. 447; Edward T. Devine, "Pensions for Mothers," *ALLR* 3, no. 2 (June 1913): 191–201; Katherine Coman's statement in "General Discussion," *ALLR* 3, no. 2 (June 1913): 237–239.

62. See Michael Katz, *In the Shadow of the Poorhouse: A Social History of Welfare in America* (New York: Basic Books, 1986), pp. 180–181; James T. Patterson, *America's Struggle Against Poverty, 1900–1985* (Cambridge: Harvard University Press, 1986), p. 76; Theda Skocpol and John Ikenberry, "The Political Formation of the American Welfare State in Historical and Comparative Perspective," *Comparative Social Research* 6 (1983): 134–139; Linda Gordon, "Social Insurance and Public Assistance: The Influence of Gender in Welfare Thought in the United States, 1890–1935," *American Historical Review* 97, no. 1 (February 1992): esp. 28–29, 47–48.

63. Nearly all of the workers' compensation laws passed during the teens as well as the Social Security Act of 1935 excluded domestic and agricultural workers from coverage. According to Michael Katz, fully two-thirds of black workers were left out of Social Security (that is, unemployment and old-age insurance) on account of these exclusions. Domestic and agricultural workers were ex-

cluded ostensibly because of concerns regarding erratic labor force participation and the potential costs of administering contributions and benefits for
such workers. In fact, the exclusions were more likely the product of political
and racial motivations. See Lee J. Alston and Joseph P. Ferrie, "Labor Costs,
Paternalism, and Loyalty in Southern Agriculture: A Constraint on the
Growth of the Welfare State," *Journal of Economic History* 45, no. 1 (March
1985): 95–117; Katz, *In the Shadow of the Poorhouse,* p. 211; Jill Quadagno, "From Old-Age Assistance to Supplemental Security Income: The Political Economy of Relief in the South, 1935–1972," in Margaret Weir, Ann
Shola Orloff, and Theda Skocpol, eds., *The Politics of Social Policy in the
United States* (Princeton: Princeton University Press, 1988), especially p. 238.

4. Internalizing Industrial Externalities

1. AALL pamphlet, January 1914, AALL Papers, reel 61.
2. Andrews to Olga Halsey, 27 January 1915, AALL Papers, reel 13.
3. William Franklin Willoughby, an early authority on social insurance and later
   a president of the AALL, wrote in 1905: "The purpose of workingmen's
   insurance is to make provision for the assistance of workingmen when
   through any incapacity they are unable to earn their usual wages." Willoughby, "Insurance Against Unemployment," in John R. Commons, ed.,
   Trade Unionism and Labor Problems (New York: Ginn, 1905), p. 589.
4. Henry R. Seager, "Outline of a Program of Social Legislation with Special
   Reference to Wage Earners," *American Association for Labor Legislation:
   Proceedings of the First Annual Meeting* (Madison, 1908), p. 100.
5. Charles Richmond Henderson, "Insurance Against Unemployment," *ALLR*
   3, no. 2 (June 1913): 178.
6. John R. Commons and John B. Andrews, *Principles of Labor Legislation*
   (New York: Harper, 1920 [1916]), p. 448.
7. John R. Commons, "Unemployment—Prevention and Insurance," *The Stabilization of Business,* ed. Lionel D. Edie (New York: Macmillan, 1923),
   p. 190.
8. Presumably, many accident cases never went to court. But Lawrence M.
   Friedman and Jack Ladinsky suggest that, of those that did, plaintiffs won
   more frequently than has traditionally been thought. Even they acknowledge,
   however, that recovery amounts were usually small and that litigation costs
   "consumed much of whatever was recovered." See Friedman and Ladinsky,
   "Social Change and the Law of Industrial Accidents," *Columbia Law Review*
   67, no. 1 (January 1967): 60–61, 66.
9. Charles Richmond Henderson, *Industrial Insurance in the United States*
   (Chicago: University of Chicago Press, 1909), pp. 243–244.
10. John R. Commons, review of Charles Henderson's *Industrial Insurance in
    the United States,* in *Economic Bulletin* 2, no. 1 (April 1909): 57.
11. See e.g. Wallace D. Yaple, "Administration by Courts or by Commission?"
    ALLR 5, no. 1 (March 1915): 118.

12. Henry R. Seager, "The Constitution and Social Progress in the State of New York," in *Labor and Other Economic Essays,* ed. Charles A. Gulick Jr. (New York: Harper, 1931), p. 264.

13. Seager, "Outline of a Program of Social Legislation," pp. 92–93; Henry R. Seager, "Outline of a Program of Social Reform" (1907), reprinted in *Labor and Other Economic Essays,* pp. 82–83. See also Henry Rogers Seager, *Economics* (New York: Columbia University Press, 1908), pp. 22–23.

14. "Report of Commissioners John R. Commons and Florence J. Harriman," *Final Report of the Commission on Industrial Relations* (Washington, 1915), p. 391; John R. Commons, *Industrial Goodwill* (New York: McGraw-Hill, 1919), p. 56; Adna F. Weber, "Employers' Liability and Accident Insurance," originally in *Political Science Quarterly* 17 (1902): 256–283, reprinted in Commons, ed., *Trade Unionism and Labor Problems* (1905), pp. 548–549.

15. On the existence of compensating wage differentials for hazardous and otherwise disagreeable work during the late nineteenth and early twentieth centuries in the United States, see Price V. Fishback and Shawn Everett Kantor, " 'Square Deal' or Raw Deal? Market Compensation for Workplace Disamenities, 1884–1903," *Journal of Economic History* 52, no. 4 (December 1992): 826–848; Timothy J. Hatton and Jeffrey G. Williamson, "Unemployment, Employment Contracts, and Wage Differentials: Michigan in the 1890s," *Journal of Economic History* 51, no. 3 (September 1991): 605–632; Price V. Fishback, "Liability Rules and Accident Prevention in the Workplace: Empirical Evidence from the Early Twentieth Century," *Journal of Legal Studies* 16, no. 2 (June 1987): 305–328; Price V. Fishback, "Workplace Safety during the Progressive Era: Fatal Accidents in Bituminous Coal Mining, 1912–1923," *Explorations in Economic History* 23, no. 3 (July 1986): 269–298.

16. Seager, "Outline of a Program of Social Reform," p. 83.

17. For a textbook definition, see Hal R. Varian, *Microeconomic Analysis* (New York: Norton, 1984), p. 259. An externality may be positive or negative. A positive externality involves a consequence of production that benefits other agents but offers no additional profits to the producer. For the purposes of this chapter, however, the term "externality" will be understood to mean "negative externality"—that is, a consequence of production that *adversely* affects other agents (or society generally) but that does not show up as a cost to the producer.

18. Commons, *Industrial Goodwill,* p. 129. The AALL reformers found the concept of conservation intriguing. Beginning in 1909 they placed the motto "Conservation of Human Resources" atop their letterhead. Significantly, their emphasis on conservation is consistent with the pollution metaphor.

19. See A. C. Pigou, *Wealth and Welfare* (London: Macmillan, 1912), pp. 162–165.

20. The first careful, although rather brief, expression of the externality concept dates to 1887, when the British political economist Henry Sidgwick discussed potential divergences between individual and social utility. See his *The Principles of Political Economy* (London: Macmillan, 1887), p. 410.

21. Pigou, *Wealth and Welfare,* p. 163. The AALL reformers would later use just such an argument to justify the inclusion of maternity insurance in their proposals for health insurance; see Chapter 6 on the AALL campaigns for protective labor legislation for women. Louis D. Brandeis and Josephine Goldmark employed a similar argument in their 1908 brief on the constitutionality of the Oregon ten-hour law for women; see "Brandeis Brief," reprinted in Brandeis and Goldmark, *Women in Industry* (New York: Arno and *New York Times,* 1969).

22. Ibid., p. 164.

23. Ibid., p. 165.

24. John R. Commons, "Industrial Relations," address at the International Convention of Government Labor Officials, Madison, Wisconsin, 3 June 1919, Commons Papers, reel 17, fr. 820. Commons was not alone in interpreting workers' compensation as a tax on accidents. See e.g. Alpheus H. Snow, "Social Insurance," *University of Pennsylvania Law Review and American Law Register* 59, no. 5 (February 1911): 288–289.

25. John R. Commons, "Social Insurance and the Medical Profession," *Wisconsin Medical Journal* (January 1915): 303, Commons Papers, reel 17, fr. 312.

26. Wesley C. Mitchell, "Commons on the Legal Foundations of Capitalism," *American Economic Review* (June 1924), Commons Papers, reel 19, fr. 671.

27. John R. Commons, *Myself* (New York: Macmillan, 1934), p. 28.

28. See Lafayette G. Harter, *John R. Commons: His Assault on Laissez-Faire* (Corvallis: Oregon State University Press 1962), pp. 41–42, 166; Commons, *Industrial Goodwill,* p. 177; John R. Commons, "The Passing of Samuel Gompers," *Current History* (February 1925): 675; Commons, *Myself,* p. 87.

29. Commons, *Myself,* pp. 43–44; John R. Commons, *Social Reform and the Church* (New York: Thomas Y. Crowell, 1894), pp. 46, 58–62.

30. John R. Commons, "Social Economics and City Evangelization," *The Christian City* (December 1898): 770, 772, Commons Papers, reel 15, frs. 332 335.

31. Commons, *Myself,* p. 143.

32. Ibid., pp. 8–9, 21.

33. John R. Commons, *The Distribution of Wealth* (New York: Macmillan 1893), pp. 68–69.

34. Henry W. Farnam advanced a similar argument about slavery and individual welfare in *The Economic Utilization of History and Other Economic Studies* (New Haven: Yale University Press, 1913), pp. 62–63.

35. Commons, *Distribution of Wealth,* p. 80.

36. Ibid., pp. 82–83.

37. To supplement the common-law proposal, which would remedy some but not all forms of unemployment, Commons suggested workingmen's insurance, extensive public works, and labor exchanges. See his "The Right to Work," *Arena* 21, no. 2 (February 1899): 140–141; Commons, *Distribution of Wealth,* p. 80.

38. For contemporary statements on the inadequacy of employers' liability law, see Snow, "Social Insurance," pp. 280–281; Henderson, *Industrial Insurance*

in the United States, p. 288. See also Lawrence M. Friedman, "Civil Wrongs: Personal Injury Law in the Late 19th Century," *American Bar Foundation Research Journal* 1987, nos. 2–3 (Spring-Summer 1987): 369.

39. John R. Commons, discussion at Meeting of American Association for Labor Legislation, *City Club Bulletin* (1909): 378, Commons Papers, reel 16, fr. 837. Interestingly, Commons never applied this distinction between the legal hazard and the actual hazard to his earlier proposal for a common-law right to work.

40. Commons, *Myself,* p. 141.

41. Ibid, pp. 141–142.

42. Ibid., pp. 162–163. Several years later, when the AALL was pressing Congress to enact a new, model workers' compensation bill for federal employees, Andrews asserted the same point—that even intoxicated workers should be covered—to a congressman with whom he was working. See Andrews to Daniel J. McGillicuddy, 7 February 1916, AALL Papers, reel 16.

43. Ezra Ripley Thayer, "Liability Without Fault," *Harvard Law Review* 29, no. 8 (June 1916): 802–803. This article is cited in George L. Priest, "The Invention of Enterprise Liability: A Critical History of the Intellectual Foundations of Modern Tort Law," *Journal of Legal Studies* 14 (December 1985): 466. Priest traces the transformation of product-liability law during the mid-twentieth century, and he observes that the internalization concept, which was employed during the debate over workers' compensation in the progressive era, was also utilized later in the century to justify a standard of strict liability for the producer in product-liability cases.

44. The question of whether the existence of workers' compensation contributes to the prevention of on-the-job accidents continues to call forth empirical studies by economists. The results are mixed. See esp. Fishback, "Workplace Safety During the Progressive Era" and "Liability Rules and Accident Prevention"; James R. Chelius, "Liability for Industrial Accidents: A Comparison of Negligence and Strict Liability Systems," *Journal of Legal Studies* 5, no. 2 (June 1976): 293–309; James R. Chelius, "The Influence of Workers' Compensation on Safety Incentives," *Industrial and Labor Relations Review* 35, no. 2 (January 1982): 235–242; Michael J. Moore and W. Kip Viscusi, "Promoting Safety through Workers' Compensation: The Efficacy and Net Wage Costs of Injury Insurance," *RAND Journal of Economics* 20, no. 4 (Winter 1989): 499–515; John W. Ruser, "Workers' Compensation and Occupational Injuries and Illnesses," *Journal of Labor Economics* 9, no. 4 (October 1991): 325–350.

45. Commons, "Social Insurance and the Medical Profession," p. 303.

46. Commons, *Myself,* p. 143.

47. See John B. Andrews, "A Practical Program for the Prevention of Unemployment," *ALLR* 5, no. 2 (June 1915): 189–191; Commons and Andrews, *Principles of Labor Legislation,* p. 448. Unemployment insurance was in fact only one component of Andrews' and Commons' program to prevent unemployment. In the mid-teens, they regarded efficiently run labor exchanges as the

most effective means of preventing unemployment. They also endorsed public works, job training, and the regularization of work by employers as measures to remedy unemployment.

48. Commons to Andrews, 23 August 1915, AALL Papers, reel 15.

49. Andrews to Mrs. Raymond [Margaret Dreier] Robins, 10 March 1915, AALL Papers, reel 14. See also Andrews to William P. Capes, 4 December 1915, AALL Papers, reel 15.

50. In 1919 Commons criticized the English system of unemployment insurance for emphasizing relief over prevention. The incentives it provided to employers to reduce unemployment, he thought, were too limited. See "Industrial Relations," Commons Papers, reel 17, frs. 821–822. On the theoretical connection between unemployment insurance and unemployment prevention, see also John Maurice Clark, *Studies in the Economics of Overhead Costs* (Chicago: University of Chicago Press, 1923), pp. 370–385, esp. 381.

51. Commons, "Unemployment—Prevention and Insurance," pp. 166–167.

52. Ibid., p. 181. Clearly, in this instance, Commons conceived of the business cycle as a supply-side phenomenon and ignored the role of aggregate demand. Commons had made almost the same point in 1921; see "To Prevent Unemployment," *New York Times,* 10 October 1921, Commons Papers, reel 19, fr. 246.

53. When asked in April 1909 which subject was of greatest importance to the AALL, the Association's first president, Richard Ely, responded: "Industrial Hygiene, without question." In 1910 the second president, Henry Farnam, appointed a committee of experts to draft a "Memorial on Occupational Diseases" to be presented to the president of the United States. That committee estimated the total social and economic cost of sickness in the United States at $772,892,860. They thought, moreover, that $193,223,215 (or a fourth of the total) could be saved annually through active preventive efforts. See "Report of the General Administrative Council Meeting of the AALL," Chicago, 10 April 1909, AALL Papers, reel 61; John B. Andrews, "Report of Work, 1909," *American Association for Labor Legislation—Third Annual Meeting—Proceedings, Reports, Addresses—Labor and the Courts* (New York, 1910), Publication 9, p. 21; "Memorial on Occupational Diseases," *ALLR* 1, no. 1 (January 1911): 127–128.

54. Andrews to J. Hopkins, 5 September 1918, AALL Papers, reel 18.

55. See e.g. John B. Andrews, "Compensation for Occupational Diseases," *Survey* 30, no. 1 (5 April 1913): 15–19.

56. See Andrews to James Lynch, 1 November 1916, AALL Papers, reel 17; John R. Commons and A. J. Altmeyer, "The Health Insurance Movement in the United States," in Ohio Health and Old Age Insurance Commission, *Health, Health Insurance, Old Age Pensions* (Columbus: F. J. Heer, 1919), p. 290.

57. Andrews to Lynch, 1 November 1916, AALL Papers, reel 17.

58. Andrews to Eugene L. Fisk, 16 November 1915, Andrews to Lillian D. Wald, 16 November 1915, AALL Papers, reel 15.

59. John R. Commons, "Health Programs," address at 15th annual meeting of National Tuberculosis Association, Atlantic City, 16 June 1919, Commons Papers, reel 17, fr. 843.

60. Henry R. Seager, "Plan for a Health Insurance Act," *ALLR* 6, no. 1 (1916): 23; William Hard, "Is Health Insurance 'Paternalism'?" *ALLR* 6, no. 2 (June 1916): 125–126. See also "Brief for Health Insurance," *ALLR* 6, no. 2 (June 1916): 230–236.

61. Commons, "Health Programs," frs. 842–843.

62. Commons, "Unemployment—Prevention and Insurance," p. 188.

63. "General Discussion," *ALLR* 3, no. 2 (June 1913): 280–281. See also I. M. Rubinow, "First American Conference on Social Insurance," *Survey* 30, no. 14 (5 July 1913): 479.

64. Epstein changed the organization's name to the American Association for Social Security in 1933.

65. See Lubove, *Struggle for Social Security*, pp. 173–174.

66. "The Common Welfare," *Charities and the Commons*, 10 October 1908, Commons Papers, reel 16, fr. 694.

67. Commons, *Social Reform and the Church*, pp. 37–38.

68. Commons, "Industrial Relations," p. 4 (fr. 818).

69. Commons, "Unemployment—Prevention and Insurance," p. 202.

5. Kindling a Flame Under Federalism

1. Because so many different reforms were enacted in so many different places and at all levels of government, there is little agreement among scholars as to the precise nature of the progressive-reform movement. One prominent historian has even questioned whether a unified movement ever existed at all. See Peter G. Filene, "An Obituary for the 'Progressive Movement,' " *American Quarterly* 22, no. 1 (Spring 1970): 20–34.

2. There are three main schools of thought on the subject. One highlights the critical role of middle-class reformers. Early historians of the progressive era generally advanced an "enlightened reformer" interpretation. In their view, the driving force behind progressive reforms were benevolent (mainly middle-class) activists who despised the trusts and who cared deeply about the working classes and the poor. See e.g. Harold U. Faulkner, *The Quest for Social Justice, 1898–1914* (New York: Macmillan, 1931). Subsequent generations of historians, however, have proved more skeptical. Although many scholars have continued to focus on the role of middle-class (especially professional-class) reformers, increasingly since the 1940s they have underscored motivations arising out of self-interest rather than simple benevolence. Two of the earliest and most influential historians to advance this position were Richard Hofstadter and George Mowry, who argued that middle-class professionals desired reform both to enhance their own status and to minimize the risk of disorder from below. See Hofstadter, *The Age of Reform: From Bryan to F.D.R.* (New York: Vintage Books, 1955); Mowry, *The Era of Theodore Roosevelt and the Birth of Modern America, 1900–1912* (New York: Harper and Row, 1962).

The most radical reinterpretation of progressive-era history belongs to the so-called corporate liberal school. Emerging out of the pathbreaking work of Gabriel Kolko, the corporate liberal thesis asserts (1) that business people were often deeply involved in the reform process and (2) that economic and social reforms typically ended up serving the interests of corporate capital. According to the school's proponents, these facts indicate that the true driving force behind most of the period's economic and social reforms were not enlightened reformers but far-seeing corporate capitalists. See Gabriel Kolko, *The Triumph of Conservatism: A Re-interpretation of American History, 1900–1916* (New York: Free Press, 1963). In general, proponents of the corporate liberal thesis maintain that corporate elites sought reforms that would help rationalize society and minimize competition.

Adherents of a pluralist perspective have carved out a third school, insisting that neither devoted middle-class reformers nor conspiring corporate elites deserve top billing. Rather, the pluralists argue, economic and social reforms during the progressive era were products of intense conflict between numerous competing interest groups. If there was any dominant source of reform, it was the democratic process in an age of increasingly well-organized interest groups. For examples of pluralist interpretations of progressive-era reform, see John D. Buenker, John C. Burnham, and Robert M. Crunden, *Progressivism* (Rochester, Vermont: Schenkman Books, 1986 [1977]); Peter Temin, *Taking Your Medicine: Drug Regulation in the United States* (Cambridge: Harvard University Press, 1980). On the dramatic rise of special interest groups during the progressive era, see Samuel P. Hays, *The Response to Industrialism, 1885–1914* (Chicago: University of Chicago Press, 1957), esp. chap. 3 ("Organize or Perish"); Richard L. McCormick, *From Realignment to Reform: Political Change in New York State, 1893–1910* (Ithaca: Cornell University Press, 1979), esp. pp. 151–155. The three schools identified here roughly correspond to those distinguished by Thomas K. McCraw ("public interest," "capture," and "pluralist") in his "Regulation in America: A Review Article," *Business History Review* 49, no. 2 (Summer 1975): 159–183.

3. For an intriguing discussion of boundary setting as an expression of power, see Steven Lukes, *Power: A Radical Critique* (London: Macmillan, 1974), esp. pp. 21–25.

4. See Arthur S. Link and Richard L. McCormick, *Progressivism* (Arlington Heights: Harland Davidson, 1983), p. 65.

5. Although there are no definite rules regarding which interests, if any, dominate each of the four phases of reform, a few basic patterns are discernible. Very often, the corporate liberal thesis is useful in characterizing phases one and four, boundary setting and implementation. The pluralist interpretation nearly always proves valuable in explaining the legislative phase. And, particularly with regard to the progressive period, an emphasis on the role of middle-class reformers is often reasonable in interpreting the policy-initiation phase. An entire volume, or perhaps several, would be required to demonstrate these patterns convincingly across a variety of campaigns for economic and social change. The main purpose for raising them here is that they are broadly applicable to progressive-era social welfare reform and exceedingly helpful in delineating the precise role of the AALL.

6. It should be noted that this book focuses mainly on phases one through three and, consequently, does not examine policy implementation in detail.

7. John B. Andrews to Henry W. Farnam, 16 November 1910, AALL Papers, reel 4.

8. "President's Annual Message," *Congressional Record,* vol. 46, part 1, 61st Cong., 3rd sess., 6 December 1910, p. 29.

9. The two letters are dated 11 January 1911 and 22 December 1910. Both are reprinted in House Committee on Ways and Means, *White Phosphorus Matches,* 61st Cong., 3rd sess., 16 December 1910 and 20 January 1911, pp. 309–310 and 328–330.

10. R. Alton Lee, "The Eradication of Phossy Jaw: A Unique Development of the Federal Police Power," *Historian* 29, no. 1 (November 1966): 2; Herbert Manchester, *The Diamond Match Company* (New York: The Diamond Match Co., 1935), pp. 14–62; Alfred D. Chandler, *The Visible Hand: The Managerial Revolution in American Business* (Cambridge: Harvard University Press, 1977), pp. 292–293; John B. Andrews, "Phosphorus Poisoning in the Match Industry in the United States," *Bulletin of the Bureau of Labor* 20 (1910): 42–47.

11. Andrews, "Phosphorus Poisoning in the Match Industry," pp. 59, 39; Manchester, *Diamond Match Company,* pp. 35–47. Another associated hazard was that children occasionally died (or became severely ill) by innocently sucking on the heads of matches. Cases of such tragic deaths were documented in the United States even before 1855. See e.g. "Death from Eating Loco Foco Matches," *New York Daily Tribune,* 25 June 1846, p. 1.

12. Andrews, "Phosphorus Poisoning in the Match Industry," p. 40.

13. Ibid., pp. 106, 90. In fact, women workers were exposed to phosphorus in match factories much more commonly than men. Andrews' 1910 study of 3,591 workers in fifteen match factories identified 2,024 men, 1,253 women, 121 boys, and 193 girls (children being those under 16 years of age). Overall, 65 percent of the workers were exposed to phosphorus in some way; but 95 percent of the women and 83 percent of the children suffered exposure, leaving the male exposure rate at a comparatively low 44 percent (p. 33). Perhaps it was more than coincidence that the very first match worker diagnosed with phosphorus necrosis was a woman.

14. Manchester, *Diamond Match Company,* pp. 35–36, 70.

15. Andrews, "Phosphorus Poisoning in the Match Industry," pp. 86–140.

16. Manchester, *Diamond Match Company,* pp. 35–36, 70; Andrews, "Phosphorus Poisoning in the Match Industry," pp. 41–42. A copy of the original U.S. patent is exhibited in House Committee on Ways and Means, *White Phosphorus Matches,* 61st Cong., 3rd sess., 16 December 1910 and 20 January 1911, p. 340.

17. Andrews, "Phosphorus Poisoning in the Match Industry," pp. 37–8; Ernest Mahaim, "The Historical and Social Importance of International Labor Legislation," in James T. Shotwell, ed., *The Origins of the International Labor Organization* (New York: Columbia University Press, 1934), vol. 1, pp. 10–11.

18. In instructing the German ambassadors and ministers who were to extend invitations to the other European powers, Chancellor Otto von Bismarck wrote: "The competition of nations in the trade of the world, and the community of interests proceeding therefrom, makes it impossible to create successful institutions for the benefit of working men of one country without curtailing that country's power of competing with other countries. Such institutions can only be established on a basis adopted in common in all countries concerned." See "Instructions of Prince Bismarck to the German Ambassadors and Ministers, February 8, 1890, Inviting the Powers to a Conference at Berlin, March, 1890," reprinted in James T. Shotwell, ed., *Origins of the International Labor Organization,* vol. 1, p. 471.

19. Mahaim, "Historical and Social Importance of International Labor Organization," p. 8; Malcolm Delevingne, "The Pre-War History of International Labor Legislation," in Shotwell, ed., *Origins of the International Labor Organization,* vol. 1, p. 33.

20. Delevingne, "Pre-War History of International Labor Legislation," pp. 31–42, 47; Mahaim, "Historical and Social Importance of International Labor Legislation," pp. 10–12. The signatories to the Phosphorus Match Convention of 1906 were Germany, the Netherlands, Switzerland, France, Luxembourg, Italy, and Denmark. See "International Convention Respecting the Prohibition of the Use of White (Yellow) Phosphorus in the Manufacture of Matches, Berne, September 26, 1906," reprinted as appendix 14 in Shotwell, ed., *Origins of the International Labor Organization,* vol. 1, pp. 495–497; John R. Commons, "The International Association for Labor Legislation," *Charities and the Commons* (12 September 1908): 689, Commons Papers, reel 16, fr. 683.

21. The U.S. government was not one of the signatories to the IALL's phosphorus match convention.

22. See Andrews to Commons, 31 May 1909, AALL Papers, reel 2.

23. The one match factory not investigated in the study was located in Chico, California. See Andrews to Constance D. Leupp, 11 September 1911, AALL Papers, reel 6.

24. Andrews, "Phosphorus Poisoning in the Match Industry," esp. pp. 32–36. As Andrews' report for the Bureau of Labor demonstrates, it was not uncommon for AALL leaders to intertwine their work with that of public agencies. The Association's investigation of the match industry began in 1909 with modest funding from the Minnesota and Wisconsin commissioners of labor. The U.S. Bureau of Labor had begun its own investigation in 1908 but turned it over to Andrews (along with $1,000 to cover expenses) as soon as the bureau's commissioner learned of the AALL's work. See David A. Moss, "The Political Economy of Insecurity: The American Association for Labor Legislation and the Crusade for Social Welfare Reform in the Progressive Era" (Ph.D. diss., Yale University, 1992), pp. 214–220. According to Michael Lacey and Mary Furner, such close interaction between public agencies and private organizations appears frequently in the history of social investigation, not only in

the United States but also in Great Britain. See their "Social Investigation, Social Knowledge, and the State: An Introduction," in Michael J. Lacey and Mary O. Furner, eds., *The State and Social Investigation in Britain and the United States* (Cambridge, Eng: Cambridge University Press, 1993), pp. 3–62.

25. See Lee, "Eradication of Phossy Jaw," p. 7. According to Wiebe, John Andrews' "exposure of 'phossy jaw' among the workers in phosphorus match factories remains a classic in the history of industrial health." Robert H. Wiebe, *The Search for Order, 1877–1920* (New York: Hill and Wang, 1967), pp. 128–129.

26. Miles Dawson to Charles D. Norton (secretary to President Taft), 3 June 1910, reprinted in House Committee on Interstate and Foreign Commerce, *Health Activities of the General Government*, part 6, 1910, p. 394.

27. House Committee on Ways and Means, *White Phosphorus Matches*, 62nd Cong., 2nd sess., 10 January 1912, p. 73.

28. Dawson to Andrews, 17 May 1910, AALL Papers, reel 3.

29. Ibid. See also *McCray V. United States*, 195 U.S. 27 (1904); *Veazie Bank v. Fenno*, 8 Wallace 533 (1869); *McCulloch v. Maryland*, 4 Wheaton 316 (1819).

30. *De Geofroy v. Riggs*, 133 U.S. 258 (1890), p. 297; Dawson to Andrews, 17 May 1910, AALL Papers, reel 3.

31. *White Phosphorus Matches*, p. 5. On Dawson's reasoning, see also Miles M. Dawson, "Brief upon the Bill to Tax Matches Manufactured by the Use of White or Yellow Poison Phosphorus," New York, 30 December 1910, Farnam Papers, Yale University Manuscripts and Archives, group 203, series 2, box 252, fdr. 3266.

32. When describing the history of the bill on the House floor the following February, Esch openly admitted that AALL reformers had drafted the bill and that he had introduced it at their request. *Congressional Record*, vol. 46, part 4, 27 February 1911, p. 3629.

33. At the time, a box of matches (ranging in quantity from 500 to 1,000 matches) typically cost about 5 cents.

34. Andrews to John J. Esch, 3 June 1910, Esch to Andrews, 4 June 1910, Andrews to Farnam, 3 June 1910, Esch to Dawson, 11 June 1910, [Irene Osgood?] to Andrews, 16 June 1910, Andrews to Farnam, 21 June 1910, AALL Papers, reel 3.

35. O. C. Barber to Charles E. McKenna, 15 March 1909, reprinted in House Committee on Interstate and Foreign Commerce, *Health Activities of the General Government*, part 4, p. 390.

36. According to Farnam, Diamond Match only began to cooperate in the legislative campaign after the AALL had documented cases of workers with phosphorus necrosis, cases which Diamond previously had denied existed. Apparently, Diamond's dentist had overlooked cases of the disease in order to maintain his position with the company. See Farnam to Irving Fisher, 19 January 1916, AALL Papers, reel 16.

37. See E. R. Stettinius (president, Diamond Match Company) to Ways and Means Committee, 18 January 1911, reprinted in *White Phosphorus Matches*, 16 December 1910 and 20 January 1911, pp. 332–333.
38. W. A. Fairburn (superintendent, Diamond Match Company) to Andrews, 15 July 1910, Andrews to Fairburn, 18 July 1910, Andrews to Stephen Bauer, 25 July 1910, AALL Papers, reel 3; Andrews to Farnam, 2 December 1910, AALL Papers, reel 4.
39. The licensing agreement also required the licensees to pack their sesquisulphide matches in a very specific manner, ostensibly for safety purposes. The agreement and a letter from Stettinius to the Committee on Ways and Means explaining the agreement are reprinted in *White Phosphorus Matches*, 16 December 1910 and 20 January 1911, pp. 332–336.
40. At a subsequent congressional hearing, a representative of the independent match manufacturers was asked whether he and the other independents acceded to the agreement with Diamond because they viewed it as a sound business proposition or because they felt compelled to do so. The witness responded pointedly, "Through fear of impending legislation." *White Phosphorus Matches*, 16 December 1910 and 20 January 1911, pp. 301–302.
41. The 11 December 1910 letter from Stettinius to the independents as well as the revised agreement of 22 December 1910 are reprinted in ibid., pp. 336–338.
42. One significant change in the new version was that all importation and exportation of white phosphorus matches would be prohibited as of 1 July 1911. H.R. 29469 is reprinted in ibid., pp. 349–351.
43. Ibid., p. 286.
44. Ibid., pp. 287–291, 289.
45. Ibid., pp. 292–301.
46. Ibid., pp. 303–305.
47. Andrews to Esch, 26 December 1910, [Joseph P. Chamberlain?] to Charles P. Neill, 29 December 1910, Neill to Chamberlain, 3 January 1911, Andrews to Osgood Andrews, 6 January 1911 (telegram), Andrews to Anne Morgan, 9 January 1911, AALL Papers, reel 4. A copy of Diamond Match's indenture assigning its patent to the trustees is reprinted in *White Phosphorus Matches*, pp. 338–339. See also Counsel, AALL to Metropolitan Match Company, 5 January 1911, Andrews to Charles D. Norton, 13 January 1911, AALL Papers, reel 4. For copies of a letter from the trustees to President Taft asking him to call on Diamond to abandon its patent, Taft's reply, and the certificate from the commissioner of patents canceling Diamond's sesquisulphide patent, see *White Phosphorus Matches*, pp. 347–349.
48. Minutes of Executive Committee Meeting, 25 January 1911, AALL Papers, reel 61; notes on talk with Sereno E. Payne and E. J. Hill, 29 January 1911, Farnam Papers, group 203, series 2, box 252, fdr. 3266; Seager to Andrews, 10 February 1911, AALL Papers, reel 4.
49. On congressional treatment of the match bill in 1911, see Moss, "Political Economy of Insecurity," pp. 248–251.

50. On endorsements, see Andrews to Samuel Gompers, 17 January 1911, Gompers to Andrews, 10 February 1911, AALL Papers, reel 4; Minutes of Executive Committee Meeting, 8 February 1911, AALL Papers, reel 61; Farnam to Hill, 13 January 1911, AALL Papers, reel 4. A good example of copy provided to a journal is John B. Andrews, "Industrial Diseases and Physicians," *Journal of the American Medical Association* 56, no. 15 (15 April 1911): 1132–34. For examples of direct AALL correspondence with Ways and Means members, see circular from Andrews to members of the committee, 13 January 1911, AALL Papers, reel 4; Seager to Andrews, 8 April 1911, circular letter (on infant deaths due to phosphorus poisoning), 30 June 1911, AALL Papers, reel 5. Regarding Andrews' direct-mail campaign, see AALL circular to members, 30 January 1911, Farnam Papers, group 203, series 2, box 252, fdr. 3266; Andrews to D. C. Lewis, 13 March 1911, AALL Papers, reel 5 (documents the sizes of AALL mailing lists); Andrews to W. C. Warner, 17 February 1911, AALL Papers, reel 4. Examples of correspondence in which Esch reported on the success of the AALL's direct-mail campaign include Esch to Andrews, 23 January 1911, 4 December 1911, and 29 February 1912, AALL Papers, reels 4, 6, 7; Farnam, talk with [E. J.] Hill, 19 February 1911, Farnam Papers, group 203, series 2, box 252, fdr. 3266.
51. *White Phosphorus Matches*, 10 January 1912, pp. 37–38, 49–50, 89–92.
52. Ibid., pp. 16–17.
53. Ibid., p. 88.
54. Seager to Farnam, 23 January 1912, AALL Papers, reel 6.
55. Esch to Andrews, 28 February 1912, AALL Papers, reel 7; *Congressional Record*, vol. 48, part 3, 26 February 1912, p. 2489; Esch to Andrews, 29 February 1912, AALL Papers, reel 7.
56. Telegram, Esch to Andrews, 4 March 1912, AALL Papers, reel 7; *Congressional Record*, vol. 48, part 4, 11 March 1912, p. 3148.
57. House Committee on Ways and Means, *Taxing White Phosphorus Matches*, 62nd Cong., 2nd sess, H. Rept. no. 406, 11 March 1912, p. 2.
58. Ibid., pp. 1–8.
59. *Congressional Record*, vol. 48, part 4, 28 March 1912, pp. 3967–68.
60. Ibid., p. 3971.
61. Ibid.
62. Ibid., pp. 3974–75.
63. Andrews to Esch, 16 March 1912, AALL Papers, reel 7; Senate Committee on Finance, *Tax upon White Phosphorus Matches*, 62nd Cong., 2nd sess., S. Rept. No. 541, 2 April 1912; *Congressional Record*, vol. 48, part 5, 3 April 1912, pp. 4234–41.
64. *Congressional Record*, 3 April 1912, pp. 4234, 4235, 4238.
65. Ibid., p. 4236.
66. Ibid., p. 4240.
67. Ibid., pp. 4241, 4240.
68. Ibid., 12 April 1912, p. 4679; Andrews to Seager, 12 April 1912, AALL Papers, reel 7.

69. Manchester, *Diamond Match Company*, p. 81.
70. Alice L. Hainen to Andrews, 2 August 1912, AALL Papers, reel 7; Farnam to Irving Fisher, 19 January 1916, AALL Papers, reel 16.
71. James Weinstein, *The Corporate Ideal in the Liberal State, 1900–1918* (Boston: Beacon Press, 1968), p. ix.
72. See e.g. Richard L. McCormick, "The Discovery that Business Corrupts Politics: A Reappraisal of the Origins of Progressivism," *American Historical Review* 86, no. 2 (1981): 246–274.
73. The interpretation offered here might be classified as a "weak" version of the corporate liberal thesis. In contrast to "strong" versions, in which business elites are portrayed as hegemonic forces in the reform process, the "weak" version highlights not only the important role of business leaders but also their genuine dependence on the initiative and support of academic and middle-class reformers. For classic renditions of the "strong" corporate liberal thesis, see Gabriel Kolko, *The Triumph of Conservatism: A Reinterpretation of American History, 1900–1916* (New York: Free Press, 1963); Gabriel Kolko, *Railroads and Regulation, 1877–1916* (Princeton: Princeton University Press, 1965); Weinstein, *Corporate Ideal in the Liberal State*. For further discussion of the "weak" thesis, see Moss, "Political Economy of Insecurity," pp. 50–52.
74. Frances Perkins, *The Roosevelt I Knew* (New York: Viking, 1946), p. 286. Arthur Altmeyer observed in 1966 that if he and the other framers of Social Security had not felt so bound by constitutional constraints in the mid-thirties, they "undoubtedly would have made radically different recommendations in a number of respects." See Altmeyer, *The Formative Years of Social Security* (Madison: University of Wisconsin Press, 1966), pp. 14–15. See also Wilbur J. Cohen, "The Development of the Social Security Act of 1935: Reflections Some Fifty Years Later," *Minnesota Law Review* 68, no. 2 (December 1983): 399.

6. The Gendered Politics of Protection

1. Leading AALL reformers stated explicitly that although they viewed hour and wage legislation as essential, they preferred not to duplicate the work of other reform organizations, especially the National Consumers' League. See "Woman's Work," *ALLR* 4, no. 4 (December 1914): 633; Andrews to Freund, 1 November 1910, AALL Papers, reel 4; Seager to Florence Kelley, 31 May 1912, AALL Papers, reel 7.
2. See esp. Louis Lee Athey, "The Consumers' Leagues and Social Reform, 1890–1923," Ph.D. diss. University of Delaware, 1965; Diane Kirkby, " 'The Wage-Earning Woman and the State': The National Women's Trade Union League and Protective Labor Legislation, 1903–1923," *Labor History* 28, no. 1 (Winter 1987): 54–74; Diane Kirkby, *Alice Henry: The Power of Pen and Voice* (New York: Cambridge University Press, 1991); Nancy Schrom Dye, *As Equals and as Sisters: Feminism, the Labor Movement, and the*

Women's Trade Union League of New York (Columbia: University of Missouri Press, 1980), esp. chap. 7; Theda Skocpol, *Protecting Soldiers and Mothers: The Political Origins of Social Policy in the United States* (Cambridge: Harvard University Press, 1992), esp. chaps. 6 and 7.

3. For an insightful treatment of this issue, see Judith Sealander, "Feminist Against Feminist: The First Phase of the Equal Rights Amendment Debate, 1923–1963," *South Atlantic Quarterly* 81, no. 2 (Spring 1982): 147–161.

4. Ernst Freund, *The Police Power: Public Policy and Constitutional Rights* (Chicago: University of Chicago Press, 1904), p. 17. See also the definition in John R. Commons and John B. Andrews, *Principles of Labor Legislation* (New York: Harper, 1927 [1916]), p. 13.

5. Freund, *Police Power*, pp. 141–142.

6. On the emergence of the liberty-of-contract doctrine, see Roscoe Pound, "Liberty of Contract," originally in *Yale Law Review* 18 (1909): 454–487, reprinted in John R. Commons, ed., *Trade Unionism and Labor Problems*, 2nd ser. (Boston: Ginn, 1921), pp. 579–613; Susan Lehrer, *Origins of Protective Labor Legislation for Women, 1905–1925* (Albany: State University of New York Press, 1987), pp. 42, 48–54.

7. Freund, *Police Power*, p. 142; see also pp. 537–539.

8. *Holden v. Hardy*, 169 U.S. 366 (1898).

9. Ibid., pp. 395–396.

10. *Lochner v. New York*, 198 U.S. 45 (1905).

11. Henry Rogers Seager, "Outline of a Program of Social Legislation with Special Reference to Wage-Earners," *American Association for Labor Legislation: Proceedings of the First Annual Meeting* (Madison, 1908), pp. 101–102. See also Henry Rogers Seager, "Adaptation of Written Constitutions to Changing Economic and Social Conditions," reprinted in Seager, *Labor and Other Economic Essays*, ed. Charles A. Gulick Jr. (New York: Harper, 1931), p. 197.

12. See Henry Rogers Seager, "American Labor Legislation," *ALLR* 6, no. 1, (1916): 89.

13. See Elizabeth Faulkner Baker, *Protective Labor Legislation, with Special Reference to Women in the State of New York* (New York, 1925), pp. 34–51. See also Freund, *Police Power*, p. 537.

14. Henry R. Seager, "Outline of a Program of Social Reform," [February 1907], reprinted in *Labor and Other Economic Essays*, p. 82.

15. Freund, *Police Power*, p. 299; see also pp. 721–725.

16. Ibid., pp., 57–61, 300.

17. *Commonwealth v. Hamilton Mfg. Co.*, 120 Mass. 383 (1876); *Ritchie v. People*, 155 Ill. 98 (1895); *Commonwealth v. Beatty*, 15 Pa. Super. Ct. 5 (1900); *Wenham v. State*, 65 Neb. 394 (1902); *State v. Buchanan*, 29 Wash. 602 (1902); *Muller v. Oregon*, 208 U.S. 412 (1908). For a good discussion of these cases, see Baker, *Protective Labor Legislation*, pp. 59–71.

18. *Muller v. Oregon*, 208 U.S. 412 (1908); Felix Frankfurter, "Hours of Labor and Realism in Constitutional Law," originally in *Harvard Law Review* 29,

(1916): 353–373, reprinted in Commons, ed., *Trade Unionism and Labor Problems*, 2nd ser., p. 625; Commons to John M. Glenn, 24 February 1908, Glenn to Commons, 29 February 1908, and Commons to Glenn, 2 March 1908, AALL Papers, reel 1. For a contrary view of the Brandeis-Goldmark brief and the *Muller v. Oregon* decision, see Nancy S. Erickson, "Muller v. Oregon Reconsidered: The Origins of a Sex Based Doctrine of Liberty of Contract," *Labor History* 30 (1989): 228–250.

19. See *Ritchie v. Wayman*, 244 Ill. 509 (1910); *Riley v. Mass.*, 232 U.S. 671 (1914); *Hawley v. Walker*, 232 U.S. 718 (1914); *Miller v. Wilson*, 236 U.S. 373 (1915).

20. See Alice Kessler-Harris, *Out to Work: A History of Wage-Earning Women in the United States* (New York: Oxford University Press, 1982), p. 191.

21. Baker, *Protective Labor Legislation*, pp. 133, 140.

22. *People v. Williams*, 189 N.Y. 131 (1907); *People v. Charles Schweinler Press*, 214 N.Y. 395 (1915); *Radice v. People*, 264 U.S. 292 (1924).

23. See *Stettler v. O'Hara et al., Industrial Welfare Commission*, 69 Ore. 519 (1914); *Simpson v. O'Hara et al.*, 70 Ore. 261 (1914); *Stettler v. O'Hara*, 243 U.S. 629 (1917); *State v. Crowe*, 130 Ark. 272 (1917); *Williams v. Evans et al.*, 139 Minn. 32 (1917); *Larson v. Rice*, 100 Wash. 642 (1918); *Holcombe v. Creamer*, 231 Mass. 99 (1918); *Spokane Hotel v. Younger*, 113 Wash. 359 (1920); *G.O. Miller Telephone Co. v. Min. Wage Commission*, 145 Minn. 262 (1920); *Children's Hospital v. Adkins*, 284 Fed. 613 (1922); *Adkins v. Children's Hospital, Adkins v. Lyons*, 261 U.S. 525 (1923). For discussions of these minimum-wage cases, see Baker, *Protective Labor Legislation*, pp. 79–99; and U.S. Department of Labor, Women's Bureau, *The Development of Minimum-Wage Laws in the United States, 1912 to 1917*, Bulletin no. 61 (1928), pp. 316–325.

24. See e.g. "Legislation for Women in Industry," *ALLR* 6, no. 4 (December 1916): 360–361. See also Carroll Smith-Rosenberg and Charles Rosenberg, "The Female Animal: Medical and Biological Views of Woman and Her Role in Nineteenth-Century America," *Journal of American History* 60, no. 2 (September 1973): 334; Rosalind Rosenberg, "In Search of Woman's Nature, 1850–1920," *Feminist Studies* 3, no. 1/2 (Fall 1975): 141–154, esp. 152.

25. John R. Commons, *Proposed Minimum Wage Law for Wisconsin* (Wisconsin Consumers' League, 1911), p. 5, in Commons Papers, reel 17, fr. 57; see also Elizabeth Brandeis, "Labor Legislation," in Commons, ed., *History of Labor in the United States, 1896–1932* (New York: Macmillan, 1935), vol. 3, pp. 507, 512–513. Although Commons drafted a gender-neutral bill in 1911, he was aware of the growing public interest in minimum-wage laws for women. He wrote two years later: "The question of the minimum wage, especially for women, is now recognized as one of great public interest and public policy." See his "A Living Wage for Women Workers," 18 January 1913, Commons Papers, reel 17, fr. 185.

26. Katherine Lenroot, "Constitutionality of the Proposed Law," in Commons, *Proposed Minimum Wage Law for Wisconsin*, p. 18.

27. See Commons to Andrews, 2 July 1915, AALL Papers, reel 14; Commons and Andrews, *Principles of Labor Legislation,* p. 32.
28. Commons and Andrews, *Principles of Labor Legislation,* pp. 26–27.
29. On their opinions regarding the adverse effects of long hours on workers, see ibid., p. 233.
30. Freund, *Police Power,* pp. 299–300.
31. Ernst Freund, "Constitutional Aspects of Hour Legislation for Men," *ALLR* 4, no. 1 (March 1914): 129–131.
32. Seager, "American Labor Legislation," pp. 93–94.
33. Dorothy W. Douglas, "American Minimum-Wage Laws at Work," originally in *American Economic Review* 9 (1919): 701–738, reprinted in Commons, ed., *Trade Unionism and Labor Problems,* 2nd ser., pp. 741–744. Many reformers had sought a mandatory law with an effective enforcement mechanism. They only reluctantly accepted the optional law, Elizabeth Brandeis explained, and regarded it "as an entering wedge and hoped that the publicity as to wages which it would provide would lead to the enactment of a more effective law" ("Labor Legislation," p. 510). In its first decree issued in 1914, the Massachusetts commission set a minimum-wage scale for the brush industry at 15.5 cents per hour for experienced workers and 10.08 cents per hour for inexperienced workers. Although this and many subsequent scales raised average weekly earnings for the women workers affected, 40 percent of the wage-board recommendations over the next fourteen years involved rates below what the boards themselves estimated as the minimum cost of living. According to Elizabeth Brandeis, Massachusetts was not atypical in its failure to mandate adequate minimum rates. See *Development of Minimum-Wage Laws,* pp. 474, 140; Douglas, "American Minimum-Wage Laws at Work," *Trade Unionism,* pp. 743–744; Brandeis, "Labor Legislation," p. 530.
34. See Douglas, "American Minimum-Wage Laws at Work," pp. 745–751; Brandeis, "Labor Legislation," pp. 506–522.
35. James T. Patterson, "Mary Dewson and the American Minimum Wage Movement," *Labor History* 5, no. 2 (Spring 1964): 143n26. See also Kessler-Harris, *Out to Work,* p. 196.
36. *Preliminary Report of the [New York State] Factory Investigating Commission, 1912* (hereafter cited *Preliminary Report*), vol. 1 (Albany: Argus, 1912), pp. 11–16; David R. Colburn, "Al Smith and the New York State Factory Investigating Commission, 1911–1915," in David R. Colburn and George E. Pozetta, eds., *Reform and Reformers in the Progressive Era* (Westport: Greenwood Press, 1983), pp. 26–27; *Fourth Report of the [New York State] Factory Investigating Commission, 1915* (hereafter cited *Fourth Report*), vol. 1 (Albany: J.B. Lyon, 1915), pp. 1–8.
37. *Fourth Report,* vol. 1, pp. 8–10.
38. Ibid., pp. 33–34.
39. Ibid., pp. 34–38. See also the reports on wage investigations by industry reprinted in vol. 2, the statistical appendix to the wage investigations pro-

vided in vol. 3, and the report on the New York State cost of living study in vol. 4 (pp. 1461–1844).

40. F. W. Taussig, "Minimum Wages for Women," originally in *Quarterly Journal of Economics* 30 (1916): 411–422, reprinted in Commons, ed., *Trade Unionism and Labor Problems*, 2nd ser., p. 719.

41. *Fourth Report, vol. 1, p. 657.*

42. Ibid., p. 639. Of 1,300 working women surveyed in the Commission's wage investigation, 65 percent lived with their nuclear families and only 15 percent lived alone. The remainder lived with friends or relatives. Of those living with their families, 75 percent contributed all of their wages to the family budget, and some served as primary wage earners (pp. 36–38, and vol. 5, pp. 2651–62).

43. See e.g. the statement of Paul U. Kellogg, editor of *The Survey*, in "General Discussion [on the Minimum Wage]," *ALLR* 3, no. 1 (February 1913): 102.

44. As I have mentioned, Commons proposed a gender-neutral bill for Wisconsin in 1911, but it did not get very far in the state legislature. Reformers in Ohio secured an amendment to the state constitution in 1912 permitting the enactment of a minimum-wage law covering all workers. But despite the best efforts of the Ohio Minimum Wage League, a law covering both men and women was never enacted there. By the end of 1919, fourteen states had enacted minimum-wage laws, and none of these laws applied to men. See Commons and Andrews, *Principles of Labor Legislation*, p. 207; Thomas Gilbert to Osgood Andrews, 3 February 1914, AALL Papers, reel 11.

45. See Abram I. Elkus to Andrews, 26 January 1915, AALL Papers, reel 13.

46. *Fourth Report*, vol. 5, p. 2793.

47. See Brandeis, "Labor Legislation," pp. 508–510.

48. *Fourth Report*, vol. 1, pp. 291–298.

49. Seager, "The Constitution and Social Progress in the State of New York," p. 261. The Factory Investigating Commission acknowledged in its report that the decision not to give the proposed wage commission enforcement powers was a direct result of concern that such a law would be found unconstitutional. See *Fourth Report*, vol. 1, p. 48.

50. *Fourth Report*, vol. 1, pp. 769–786. See also Irwin Yellowitz, *Labor and the Progressive Movement in New York State, 1897–1916* (Ithaca: Cornell University Press, 1965), pp. 135–136; Thomas J. Kerr IV, "The New York Factory Investigating Commission and the Minimum Wage Movement," *Labor History* 2, no. 3 (Summer 1971): 382.

51. See Kerr, "The New York Factory Investigating Commission," pp. 382, 385; "Many Minds on the Minimum Wage," *Survey* 33, no. 17 (23 January 1915): 435; *Fourth Report*, vol. 5, p. 2724; "Fixing Wages by Law or Unionism," *American Federationist* 22, no. 5 (May 1915): 363–367. For the position of the AFL Executive Council on wage legislation, see *Report of Proceedings of the Thirty-Fifth Annual Convention of the American Federation of Labor* (Washington: Law Reporter, 1915), pp. 63–64; and for the opinions of labor leaders who shared Gompers' aversion to wage legislation, see *Fourth Report*, vol. 1, pp. 774–776, 778–779.

52. A representative of the National City Bank explained to the Factory Investigating Commission that his firm employed over 60 women and paid each of them at least $12 per week. He claimed that National City derived great advantages from paying relatively high wages, and he supported a minimum-wage law. *Fourth Report,* vol. 1, p. 792.

53. See e.g. *Fourth Report,* vol. 1, pp. 808, 810–811.

54. Ibid., p. 806.

55. "General Discussion," *ALLR* 3, no. 1 (February 1913): 100.

56. Paul J. Watrous to Irene Osgood Andrews, 13 March 1914, AALL Papers, reel 11; *Fourth Report,* vol. 1, p. 656.

57. Most students of protective labor legislation in the United States have recognized the pervasiveness of the interstate competition argument. See e.g. Douglas, "American Minimum Wage Laws at Work," p. 755; Lehrer, *Origins of Protective Labor Legislation for Women,* p. 79; Kessler-Harris, *Out to Work,* pp. 198–199.

58. Robert F. Wesser, *A Response to Progressivism: The Democratic Party and New York Politics, 1902–1918* (New York: New York University Press, 1986), pp. 21–160.

59. Kerr, "The New York Factory Investigating Commission," pp. 377, 383–386; *The Work of the Consumers' League of the City of New York, 1915* (New York, 1916), p. 16. For a brief discussion of the "political overturn" in New York in 1914, see also John B. Andrews, "Secretary's Report 1915," *ALLR* 6, no. 1 (1916): 106.

60. Baker, *Protective Labor Legislation,* pp. 145, 253–257; *Fourth Report,* vol. 1, pp. 3–4; Commons and Andrews, *Principles of Labor Legislation,* pp. 385–386. For the text of the New York Factory Investigating Commission's bill, see *Preliminary Report,* vol. 1, p. 833.

61. "Legislation for Women in Industry," p. 405.

62. Andrews to Rudolph Hering, 13 March 1913, AALL Papers, reel 9; "Woman's Work," *ALLR* 4, no. 4 (December 1914): 638; Olga Halsey to Secretary of the National Association for the Study and Prevention of Infant Mortality, 13 May 1916, AALL Papers, reel 17; Olga Halsey to Florence Kelley, 23 December 1915, AALL Papers, reel 15.

63. "Brief for Health Insurance," *ALLR* 6, no. 2 (June 1916): 221.

64. "Health Insurance: Tentative Draft of an Act," *ALLR* 6, no. 2 (June 1916): pp. 249–250, 246.

65. Andrews to Richard M. Neustadt, 19 November 1915, AALL Papers, reel 15; [Neustadt?], secretary to Edwin C. Shaw, second vice president, B.F. Goodrich Co., to Andrews, 14 December 1915, AALL Papers, reel 15; Andrews to Neustadt, 23 December 1915, AALL Papers, reel 15.

66. See Andrews to Commons, 16 March 1916, AALL Papers, reel 16; Henry R. Seager, "Plan for a Health Insurance Act," *ALLR* 6, no. 1 (1916): 25.

67. See Florence Kelley, "Memorandum on the Maternity Features of the Proposed Health Insurance Act," December 1915, AALL Papers, reel 62. Kelley wrote in the memorandum that good policy should "discourage in every

possible way the wage-earning employment of mothers of young children. The tendency of [the maternity provisions of the health insurance bill] appears to be to put a premium on employing them."

68. Ibid.

69. Andrews to Sophy Sanger, 24 March 1916, AALL Papers, reel 16.

70. Seager, "Plan for a Health Insurance Act," p. 25; "General Discussion," *ALLR* 6, no. 1 (1916): 34; Seager to Andrews, 27 February 1916, AALL Papers, reel 16.

71. See Sophy Sanger to Andrews, [?] 1916, [Murial Ritson] to Andrews, 11 December 1916, Mary R. MacArthur to Olga Halsey, 14 December 1916, AALL Papers, reel 17.

72. Olga Halsey to Florence Kelley, 23 December 1915, AALL Papers, reel 15; [LCL], AALL Staff, to Kelley, 5 January 1916, Halsey to Kelley, 22 January 1916, Halsey to Josephine Baker, 27 January 1916, Andrews to Alice Henry, 23 February 1916, AALL Papers, reel 16. While presumably politically necessary, the omission of maternity benefits from the New York health insurance bill proved unpopular with many progressive reformers, including many women reformers. See e.g. Alice Stone Blackwell, "Married Women Left Out," *Woman's Journal and Suffrage News* (19 February 1916): 60; Andrews to Commons, 16 March 1916, AALL Papers, reel 16; "Maternity Benefits and the Health Insurance Bill: A Vital Issue for Socialists," *New York Call* (13 February 1916): 11.

73. "Legislation for Women in Industry," p. 402.

74. Kelley, "Memorandum," AALL Papers, reel 62.

75. "Legislation for Women in Industry," p. 410; Olga S. Halsey, "Maternity Benefits under Health Insurance," January 1917, AALL Papers, reel 62. For documentation of the AALL view that the entrance of married women into the workforce was an unstoppable trend, see Claudia Goldin, *Understanding the Gender Gap: An Economic History of American Women* (New York: Oxford University Press, 1990), pp. 16–42; Susan Householder Van Horn, *Women, Work, and Fertility, 1900–1986* (New York: New York University Press, 1988), esp. chap. 5. By 1920, the proportion of working women who were married reached 23 percent, and the proportion of married women who were working reached 9 percent. See U.S. Department of Commerce, Bureau of the Census, *Historical Statistics of the United States: Colonial Times to 1970,* part 1 (Washington: GPO, 1975), series D-55, D-60, p. 133.

76. Baker, *Protective Labor Legislation,* pp. 189–190; "Women Who Work Say They Are Protected Too Much; Driven from Good Jobs," *Monitor* 6, no. 1 (June 1919): 5. Members of the League for Equal Opportunity vigorously expressed their opinions at a hearing before the labor and industry committees of the New York State Assembly and Senate on March 5, 1919. The transcript of this hearing offers a fascinating window onto the views and politics of equal-rights feminists regarding protective labor legislation for women. The transcript, heretofore considered lost, is reprinted in "Hearing

on Labor Bills Develops an Unexpected Opposition of Women to Passage of Proposed Acts," *Monitor* 5, no. 10 (March 1919): 1–40.

77. Lehrer, *Origins of Protective Labor Legislation for Women,* p. 107.

78. Baker, *Protective Labor Legislation,* pp. 191–201; Lehrer, *Origins of Protective Labor Legislation for Women,* pp. 95–107. On the NWP after 1920, see also William H. Chafe, *The American Woman* (New York: Oxford University Press, 1972), chap. 5; Susan D. Becker, *The Origins of the Equal Rights Amendment: American Feminism Between the Wars* (Westport: Greenwood Press, 1981); Peter Geidel, "The National Woman's Party and the Origins of the Equal Rights Amendment, 1920–1923," *Historian* 42, no. 4 (August 1980): 557–582; Nancy F. Cott, "Feminist Politics in the 1920s: The National Woman's Party," *Journal of American History* 71, no. 1 (June 1984): 43–68.

79. Lehrer, *Origins of Protective Labor Legislation,* pp. 103–104; Baker, *Protective Labor Legislation,* p. 192.

80. Maud Younger to Ethel Smith, 19 December 1921, copy, AALL Papers, reel 25; Maud Younger to Andrews, 24 January 1922, AALL Papers, reel 25. Some of the attorneys who questioned the efficacy of explicitly exempting "welfare legislation" from equal-rights laws or from an equal-rights amendment were Felix Frankfurter, Ernst Freund, and Roscoe Pound. See George Gordon Battle to Ethel Smith, 16 December 1921, copy, AALL Papers, reel 25. On the general issue of exempting labor legislation from equal-rights laws, see also Cott, "Feminist Politics," pp. 56–59.

81. J. P. Chamberlain to Andrews, 8 March 1922, AALL Papers, reel 26.

82. Baker, *Protective Labor Legislation,* pp. 193–202; Lehrer, *Origins of Protective Labor Legislation,* pp. 107–114; Cott, "Feminist Politics," pp. 59–61. According to Peter Geidel, both equal-rights and protective feminists were "partly to blame for the split, but the Social feminists [protective feminists] were more uncompromising." See "The National Woman's Party and the Origins of the Equal Rights Amendment," p. 581.

83. *Adkins v. Children's Hospital,* 261 U.S. 525 (1923), p. 553.

84. See Alice Paul's statement on the decision in "The Minimum Wage—What Next?" *Survey* 50, no. 4 (15 May 1923): 222, 256; Lehrer, *Origins of Protective Labor Legislation for Women,* pp. 74–75.

85. *Adkins v. Children's Hospital,* pp. 569–570.

86. "The Minimum Wage—What Next?" pp. 215–216, 261, 263. The AALL's proposed constitutional amendment requiring a two-thirds Supreme Court majority may be found under the title "Suggested 20th Amendment to the Constitution of the United States," AALL Papers, reel 62 (under the division "General Social Insurance—Undated").

87. Significantly, Commons was elected president of the National Consumers' League in 1923. During his tenure over the next few years, one of the league's top priorities was to oppose the NWP's proposed equal-rights amendment to the Constitution. See Lafayette G. Harter Jr., *John R. Commons: His Assault on Laissez Faire* (Corvallis: Oregon State University Press, 1962), p. 73;

"Equal Rights Law Opposed by Consumers," *Christian Science Monitor,* 19 November 1925, p. 1.

7. In Search of Security

1. William F. Willoughby, "The Problem of Social Insurance: An Analysis," *ALLR* 3, no. 2 (June 1913): 158, 154–155.
2. Adna F. Weber, "Employers' Liability and Accident Insurance," originally in *Political Science Quarterly* 27 (1902), reprinted in John R. Commons, *Trade Unionism and Labor Problems* (Boston: Ginn, 1905), p. 548.
3. H. P. Webster to John B. Andrews, 2 July 1913, AALL Papers, reel 9.
4. Paul U. Kellogg, "Editor's Forward," in Crystal Eastman, *Work-Accidents and the Law* (New York: Charities Publication Committee, 1910), p. v. For more on American distinctiveness within the context of the social insurance debate, see John R. Commons, "Unemployment—Prevention and Insurance," in Lionel D. Edie, ed., *The Stabilization of Business* (New York: Macmillan, 1923), pp. 182–185; John R. Commons, "Unemployment Insurance," Economic Series Lecture 24, delivered 9 April 1932 over NBC radio, in Commons Papers, reel 21, frs. 488–497; and John R. Commons, "What Is the Difference Between Unemployment Insurance and Unemployment Reserves?" *State Government* 5, no. 5 (May 1932), Commons Papers, reel 21, frs. 498–500.
5. Henry W. Farnam, "Some Fundamental Distinctions in Labor Legislation," *Proceedings of the Second Annual Meeting—American Association for Labor Legislation* (Princeton University Press, 1909), pp. 38–39.
6. Henry R. Seager, "The Constitution and Social Progress in the State of New York," reprinted in *Labor and Other Economic Essays,* ed. Charles A. Gulick Jr. (New York: Harper, 1931), pp. 262, 260.
7. Frederick L. Hoffman, "Industrial Accident Statistics," *Bulletin of the U.S. Bureau of Labor Statistics,* no. 157 (March 1915): esp. 6, 121; Frederick L. Hoffman, "Industrial Accidents," *Bulletin of the Bureau of Labor* 17, no. 78 (September 1908): 417–465; Gilbert Lewis Campbell, *Industrial Accidents and Their Compensation* (Boston: Houghton Mifflin, 1911), esp. pp. 15–17; Henry W. Farnam, *The Economic Utilization of History and Other Economic Studies* (New Haven: Yale University Press, 1913), p. 172.
8. See Roy Lubove, "Workmen's Compensation and the Prerogatives of Voluntarism," *Labor History* 8, no. 3 (Fall 1967): 258–259.
9. Henry R. Seager, "The Compensation Amendment to the New York Constitution," in *Labor and Other Economic Essays,* pp. 155–157. All of Seager's colleagues at the AALL shared this belief. Adna F. Weber wrote in 1902: "It must be clear, upon reflection, that the conditions under which modern industry is carried on preclude the possibility of explaining every accident by somebody's negligence." Weber, "Employers' Liability and Accident Insurance," p. 569.
10. Weber, "Employers' Liability and Accident Insurance," p. 573 (1905 postscript to 1902 article).

11. The AALL later led a campaign for a new, more generous and far-reaching workers' compensation program for federal employees, which Congress enacted in 1916. For a description of the 1916 program, see *ALLR* 6, no. 3 (1916): 317–320. See also note 47 below.

12. See Robert Asher, "Failure and Fulfillment: Agitation for Employers' Liability Legislation and the Origins of Workmen's Compensation in New York State, 1876–1910," *Labor History* 24, no. 2 (Spring 1983): 202.

13. Many states and territories appointed such commissions: three in 1909, eight in 1910, twelve in 1911, and eleven between 1913 and 1919. See Elizabeth Brandeis, "Labor Legislation," in John R. Commons, ed., *History of Labor in the United States, 1896–1932* (New York: Macmillan, 1935), vol. 3 p. 572.

14. See Robert F. Wesser, "Conflict and Compromise: The Workmen's Compensation Movement in New York, 1890s–1913," *Labor History* 11, no. 3 (Summer 1971): 350–351.

15. The commission's other members were Senators Frank C. Platt and Howard R. Bayne; Assemblymen Alfred D. Lowe, George A. Voss, Frank B. Thorn, Cyrus W. Phillips, and Edward D. Jackson; and gubernatorial appointees George W. Smith (Lackawanna Steel Company), Philip Titus (president of the Railway Trainmen's Association), Otto M. Eidlitz (governor of the Building Trades Employers Association of the City of New York), and John Mitchell (vice-president of the American Federation of Labor).

16. *Report to the Legislature of the State of New York by the Commission Appointed under Chapter 518 of the Laws of 1909 to Inquire into the Question of Employers' Liability and Other Matters,* First Report, 19 March 1910 (Albany: J. B. Lyon, 1910), p. 5; hereafter cited *First Wainwright Report.* The figures presented are for the year ending 30 September 1909.

17. Ibid., pp. 7, 13, 26–27.

18. Ibid., p. 7.

19. The fellow-servant rule was modified slightly in New York by the state's Employers' Liability Act of 1902. The act held that the defense was not applicable if the fellow-servant who caused the accident was a superintendent.

20. Eastman, *Work-Accidents and the Law,* pp. 86–87. The sum of the figures identifying responsibility for accidents exceeds the total number of accidents because responsibility was assigned when a party was found to be *either* partly or solely responsible, thus allowing for overlap in blame.

21. Ibid., pp. 121, 192. Eastman also noted that she could find no compensating wage differentials for hazardous work (pp. 129–130).

22. Seager, "The Compensation Amendment to the New York Constitution," p. 156; John R. Commons and John B. Andrews, *Principles of Labor Legislation* (New York: Harper, 1927 [1916]), p. 430. See also Andrews to Adolph Lewisohn, 19 May 1916, AALL Papers, reel 17.

23. *First Wainwright Report,* pp. 31, 19–33.

24. Ibid., p. 7.

25. Ibid., pp. 50–66.

26. Ibid., p. 46.
27. Ibid., pp. 50–54.
28. Ibid., pp. 57–66.
29. Asher, "Failure and Fulfillment," p. 203; Wesser, "Conflict and Compromise," pp. 357–358, 353–354; *First Wainwright Report,* pp. 109–110.
30. Wesser, "Conflict and Compromise," p. 358.
31. *Ives v. South Buffalo Railway Company,* 201 N.Y. 271, 272, 285, 284, 294 (1911). Ironically, the New York Court of Appeals handed down the *Ives* decision just one day before the infamous Triangle Shirtwaist fire of 25 March 1911.
32. Seager, "Constitution and Social Progress," p. 260.
33. See Lubove, "Workmen's Compensation and the Prerogatives of Voluntarism," p. 269; Wesser, "Conflict and Compromise," p. 360; Seager, "Compensation Amendment to the New York Constitution," p. 162; "Three Years under the New Jersey Workmen's Compensation Law," *ALLR* 5, no. 1 (March 1915): 31–102; Ernst Freund, "Constitutional Status of Workmen's Compensation," *ALLR* 2, no. 1 (February 1912): 51–55. Washington was the only state to enact a compulsory workers' compensation law in 1911 that was upheld in the courts. The Washington law, significantly, also mandated an exclusive state insurance fund. See "Employers' Liability, Workmen's Compensation and Insurance," *ALLR* 1, no. 3 (October 1911): 96–114.
34. Seager, "Compensation Amendment to the New York Constitution," pp. 163–165. Seager acknowledged that amending the state constitution would not eliminate the due-process requirements defined in the fourteenth amendment to the federal Constitution. But he believed that the U.S. Supreme Court would interpret that restriction less narrowly than had the New York State Court of Appeals. He also thought that making the U.S. Supreme Court the only interpreter of due process in the arena of social insurance would promote uniformity among the states (see pp. 166–167).
35. Paul Kennaday to Mary E. Dreier, 7 December 1911, AALL Papers, reel 6; Richard Martin Lyon, "The American Association for Labor Legislation and the Fight for Workmen's Compensation Laws" (M.S. thesis, Cornell University, 1952), pp. 105–106.
36. The procedure for ratifying a constitutional amendment in New York state at that time required majority approval of the amendment by two consecutive state legislatures and majority approval by the electorate in a state-wide referendum.
37. Wesser, "Conflict and Compromise," pp. 362–366.
38. William F. Willoughby to Andrews, 18 March 1913, Andrews to Charles M. Cabot, 19 March 1913, Paul Kennaday circular to members of New York Legislative Committee, New York Association for Labor Legislation, 27 March 1913, and Andrews to J. H. Thom, 3 April 1913, AALL Papers, reel 9. The decision of the AALL leadership to support the exclusion of casualty companies alienated many of the Association's most conservative members and friends, especially those associated with the insurance industry. See David

Van Schaak to Andrews, 18 April 1913, P. T. Sherman to Andrews, 13 June 1913, Otto M. Eidlitz to Andrews, 5 July 1913, AALL Papers, reel 9; William Brosmith to Andrews, 20 April 1914, AALL Papers, reel 11; Walter G. Cowles to Andrews, 2 November 1914, AALL Papers, reel 13.

39. See e.g. circular letter to New York members, 5 April 1913, AALL Papers, reel 9.

40. Andrews to Emile E. Watson, 15 May 1913, and Andrews to Paul Kennaday, 17 May 1913, AALL Papers, reel 9; Wesser, "Conflict and Compromise," p. 367.

41. Robert F. Wesser, *A Response to Progressivism: The Democratic Party and New York Politics, 1902–1918* (New York: New York University Press, 1986), pp. 112–133; Wesser, "Conflict and Compromise," pp. 367–368.

42. Seager to Andrews, 23 November 1913, AALL Papers, reel 10; Wesser, "Conflict and Compromise," pp. 368–370. On the AALL's evolving position on the issue of excluding casualty companies from workers' compensation coverage after 1913, see David A. Moss, "The Political Economy of Insecurity: The American Association for Labor Legislation and the Crusade for Social Welfare Reform in the Progressive Era" (Ph.D. diss., Yale University, 1992), p. 369n47.

43. Andrews, "Memoranda: Workmen's Compensation" (notes from meetings with lawmakers in Albany), 25 November 1913; Andrews to O.G. Villard, 28 November 1913; Andrews to Governor Martin H. Glynn, telegram, 9 December 1913; "Dear Sir" circular to employers from Henry Seager, part of Andrews' release, 9 December 1913, AALL Papers, reel 10.

44. Andrews, circular letter to New York members, 17 December 1913, AALL Papers, reel 10.

45. "Dear Sir" circular to employers from Henry Seager, part of Andrews' release, 9 December 1913, AALL Papers, reel 10.

46. E. E. Pratt to Andrews, 28 January 1914, AALL Papers, reel 11.

47. AALL reformers helped to draft the Federal Employees' Compensation Act of 1916 and lobbied aggressively for it for nearly four years, sending out over 100,000 letters and buttonholing and petitioning congressmen on a regular basis. Commonly known as Kern-McGillicuddy, the new law (which superseded the much less comprehensive Federal Employers' Liability Act of 1908) offered generous benefits to federal workers who were injured or killed on the job or who were the victims of occupational disease. It covered all medical, surgical, and hospital expenses and provided substantial wage replacement: survivors of a deceased worker could receive up to two-thirds of wages (35 percent for the widow and 10 percent for each child) for as long as they remained dependents; totally disabled workers were to receive two-thirds of wages for the duration of their disability; and partially disabled workers were entitled to two-thirds of their lost earning power. The maximum benefit was $66.67 per month. Soon after it was enacted, Andrews described Kern-McGillicuddy as "the most scientific and the most liberal compensation act in any country." See Statement for Social Insurance Committee, 22 August

1916, AALL Papers, reel 17; John B. Andrews, "New Federal Workmen's Compensation Law," *Survey* 36 (23 September 1916): 617–618; Willis J. Nordlund, "The Federal Employees' Compensation Act," *Monthly Labor Review* (September 1991): 3–14.

48. Andrews to Commons, 16 March 1916, AALL Papers, reel 16; "American Association for Labor Legislation, Memorandum of Some of Its Activities during February, 1916," enclosure in Andrews circular to Executive Committee, 6 March 1916, AALL Papers, reel 16; Andrews, "New Federal Workmen's Compensation Law," pp. 617–618; Lyon, "American Association for Labor Legislation and the Fight for Workmen's Compensation Laws," pp. 78–168; Lloyd F. Pierce, "The Activities of the American Association for Labor Legislation in Behalf of Social Security and Protective Labor Legislation" (Ph.D. diss., University of Wisconsin, 1953), pp. 159–239; Roy Lubove, *The Struggle for Social Security* (Pittsburgh: University of Pittsburgh Press, 1986), pp. 53–61; "Standards for Workmen's Compensation Laws," *ALLR* 4, no. 4 (December 1914): 585–594.

49. John Nelson, "New Menace of Higher Manufacturing Costs," *Iron Age* 98, no. 2 (13 July 1916): 87.

50. Although degenerative competition between the states appears not to have played a major role in blocking the enactment of workers' compensation statutes (because of the preexistence of employers' liability law), it subsequently constrained legislatures in determining the size of workers' compensation benefits. See Harry Weiss, "Employers' Liability Law and Workmen's Compensation," in John R. Commons, ed., *History of Labor in the United States* (New York: Macmillan, 1935), vol. 3, p. 600.

51. Lubove, "Workmen's Compensation and the Prerogatives of Voluntarism," p. 268.

52. James Weinstein, *The Corporate Ideal in the Liberal State, 1900–1918* (Boston: Beacon Press, 1968), p. 61.

53. Lubove, "Workmen's Compensation and the Prerogatives of Voluntarism," p. 259; Wesser, "Conflict and Compromise," p. 346; Weinstein, *Corporate Ideal,* p. 45; James Weinstein, "Big Business and the Origins of Workmen's Compensation," *Labor History* 8, no. 2 (Spring 1967): 156; Yellowitz, *Labor and the Progressive Movement,* p. 110.

54. James Weinstein would probably disagree with this point. Like most writers on the history of American workers' compensation laws, Weinstein highlights developments in New York. Yet he neglects to mention a number of important details that might qualify his argument about the role of big business. He overlooks, for example, Governor Sulzer's 1913 veto of the bill that business leaders from the Civic Federation endorsed. His implication, moreover, that labor's defeat on the issue of state-fund exclusivity was somehow more fundamental than was its victory on compensation scales is open to question. "The business unionists sacrificed the principle of state insurance in return for immediately higher benefits," he writes. "It was not the last time trade unionists and big business would reach a compromise of this kind" (*The

Corporate Ideal, p. 60). But one could just as easily come to the opposite conclusion about who got the upper hand, and at least one careful student of the subject has. Referring to the final workers' compensation law enacted in New York in 1913, Robert F. Wesser writes, "As a 'compromise' measure, it undoubtedly favored the workingman, for compensation rates were high and a powerful commission supervised the dispensation of payments from private sources as well as from the state fund" ("Conflict and Compromise," p. 370).

55. P. T. Sherman to Andrews, 13 June 1913, AALL Papers, reel 9; Sherman to Andrews, 16 December 1913, Andrews to Sherman, 8 January 1914, Sherman to Andrews, 9 January 1914, AALL Papers, reel 10.

56. Andrews to Fisher, 31 March 1916, AALL Papers, reel 16.

8. Legislative Limits

1. John B. Andrews, "Social Insurance," n.d., AALL Papers, reel 62. According to a federal study cited in AALL documents, 38.3 percent of all charity cases resulted from illness of the breadwinner, whereas poverty associated with industrial accidents accounted for only 3.8 percent of the total. Even at the peak of the economic crisis of 1914–15, the Buffalo Charity Organization Society reported that it spent twice as much on relief for families victimized by illness as for those suffering unemployment. See "Brief for Health Insurance," *ALLR* 6, no. 2 (June 1916): 178–180; John B. Andrews, "Human Conservation through Health Insurance," 5 May 1917, AALL Papers, reel 62. See also "California Commission Favors Compulsory Contributory System," *ALLR* 7, no. 1 (March 1917): 206.

2. Andrews to John A. Voll, 7 April 1916, AALL Papers, reel 16. The phrase "biggest next step in labor legislation" anticipated the slogan "next great step in social legislation," which Rupert Blue, surgeon-general of the U.S. Public Health Service and president of the American Medical Association, uttered at the AMA's annual meeting in June 1916. As early as January 1915, Commons described health insurance as "the next great step in preventive medicine." See John R. Commons, "Social Insurance and the Medical Profession," *Wisconsin Medical Journal,* January 1915, p. 304, reprinted in Commons Papers, reel 17, frs. 310–315.

3. "Unemployment Survey," *ALLR* 5, no. 3 (November 1915): 479. See also *Report of the [Massachusetts] Special Commission on Social Insurance,* House Document 1850, February 1917 (Boston: Wright and Potter, 1917), p. 294; John B. Andrews, "Introductory Note—Organization to Combat Unemployment," *ALLR* 4, no. 2 (May 1914): 211–212; handwritten reports describing the severity of the economic crisis, in AALL Papers, reel 66.

4. See Henry R. Seager, "Unemployment: Problem and Remedies," Reprints of Reports and Addresses of the National Conference of Charities and Correction, 1915 meeting at Baltimore, no. 42, pp. 1, 3.

5. "Reports of Official Delegates on the State of Employment," *ALLR* 4, no. 2 (May 1914): 246; "Unemployment in the United States during the Winter of

1913–14" and "Unemployment in 1914," AALL Papers, reel 66. The national unemployment rate has been estimated (retrospectively) at 4.3 percent in 1913, 7.9 percent in 1914, 8.5 percent in 1915, and 5.1 percent in 1916. See *Historical Statistics of the United States: Colonial Times to 1970*, part 1 (Washington: GPO 1975), series D-85, p. 135.

6. John B. Andrews, "Outline of Work [of the American Section of the International Association on Unemployment] 1914," [4 August 1914], AALL Papers, reel 12.

7. John B. Andrews, "Introductory Note," *ALLR* 5, no. 3 (November 1915): 469. William H. Beveridge published *Unemployment: A Problem of Industry* in 1909. See also Irene Osgood Andrews, review of Beveridge's *Unemployment*, in *Economic Bulletin*, 2, no. 2 (June 1909): 141–144.

8. William M. Leiserson, "Public Employment Offices in Theory and Practice," *ALLR* 4, no. 2 (May 1914): 326. Leiserson and those who echoed this notion in the United States borrowed it from Beveridge. One historian of unemployment has described Leiserson as an American "carbon copy" of Beveridge. See John A. Garraty, *Unemployment in History* (New York: Harper and Row, 1978), pp. 139–140.

9. John B. Andrews, "Introductory Note—Organization to Combat Unemployment," pp. 212–214; John B. Andrews, "A Practical Program for the Prevention of Unemployment in America," *ALLR* 5, no. 2 (June 1915): 174–175. Andrews' "Practical Program" was first published as a pamphlet in December 1914, and the AALL quickly distributed 22,000 copies. See John B. Andrews, "Introductory Note," *ALLR* 5, no. 2 (June 1915): 168–169. The Association reprinted a revised "Practical Program," along with the proceedings of the Second National Conference on Unemployment, as the second number of the *ALLR*'s fifth volume.

10. Andrews, "Practical Program," p. 176; Henry R. Seager, "Introductory Address," *ALLR* 4, no. 2 (May 1914): 311; "Resolutions," *ALLR* 4, no. 2 (May 1914): 353–354; Andrews, "Introductory Note—Organization to Combat Unemployment," pp. 209–210; "New Legislation on Employment Exchanges," *ALLR* 4, no. 2 (May 1914): 391–399; Andrews, "Introductory Note," *ALLR* 4, no. 3 (October 1914): 427–428; [Seager] to Honorable David J. Lewis, 4 June 1914, AALL Papers, reel 11; John Andrews, "Introductory Note," *ALLR* 5, no. 2 (June 1915): 169.

11. Andrews, "Practical Program," pp. 182–183. See also "Reports of Official Delegates on the State of Employment," *ALLR* 4, no. 2 (May 1914): 251; Morris L. Cooke, "Responsibility and Opportunity of the City in the Prevention of Unemployment," *ALLR* 5, no. 2 (June 1915): 436; "General Discussion," *ALLR* 5, no. 2 (June 1915): 451–452.

12. See "Unemployment Survey," *ALLR* 5, no. 3 (November 1915): 564–581; "Relief Employment—Public Works," draft report, AALL Papers, reel 66; Frank O'Hara, "Redistribution of Public Work in Oregon," *ALLR* 5, no. 2 (June 1915): 238–244; F. Ernest Richter, "Seasonal Fluctuation in Public Works," *ALLR* 5, no. 2 (June 1915): 245–264; Andrews to Father Edwin V.

O'Hara, 28 May 1914, AALL Papers, reel 11; Andrews to Sarah Whitney, 22 June 1914, AALL Papers, reel 12; F. Ernest Richter to Andrews, 12 July 1914, AALL Papers, reel 12; Andrews to William Hard, 29 May 1916, AALL Papers, reel 17. See also John B. Andrews, "Introductory Note," *ALLR* 5, no. 4 (December 1915): 637–638; Andrews to George W. Rabinoff, 25 August 1915, AALL Papers, reel 15; John T. Ryan to AALL, 28 April 1916, and Andrews to Hard, 29 May 1916, AALL Papers, reel 17.

13. On the popularity of regularization among proponents of scientific management, see esp. Sanford M. Jacoby, *Employing Bureaucracy: Managers, Unions, and the Transformation of Work in American Industry, 1900–1945* (New York: Columbia University Press, 1985), pp. 105–115.

14. Andrews, "Practical Program," pp. 184, 175, 189–191; John R. Commons, *Industrial Goodwill* (New York: McGraw-Hill, 1919), p. 65. See also Seager, "Unemployment: Problem and Remedies," pp. 4, 10. In commenting on the expected gains in efficiency that would result from employers regularizing their output, the AALL reformers appear to have overlooked the important issue of inventory costs.

15. J. E. Cunningham to Andrews, 12 April 1915, AALL Papers, reel 14; Andrews to David C. Adie, 27 April 1916, AALL Papers, reel 17; "Unemployment Survey," *ALLR* 5, no. 3 (November 1915): 582–588; Andrews to Mrs. Raymond Robins, 10 March 1915, AALL Papers, reel 14; Andrews to William P. Capes, 4 December 1915, AALL Papers, reel 15.

16. On the issue of private, firm-originated unemployment insurance, see Andrews to Henry Dennison, 1 March 1915, and Dennison to Andrews, 1 March 1915, AALL Papers, reel 13.

17. The MCU was a virtual blood relative of the AALL. In 1911, one year after European reformers founded the International Association on Unemployment (IAU), AALL president Henry Seager appointed an American Committee on Unemployment, which later became the IAU's official American section. The American Committee remained tightly affiliated with the AALL and ultimately spawned the MCU. See Andrews, "Introductory Note—Organization to Combat Unemployment," pp. 214–217; circular letter from the IAU, 20 November 1910, AALL Papers, reel 4; Robert G. Valentine to Andrews, 19 November 1914, AALL Papers, reel 13; pamphlet, Massachusetts Committee on Unemployment, 1915, AALL Papers, reel 15; Joseph L. Cohen, *Insurance Against Unemployment* (London: P. S. King and Son, 1921), p. 492.

18. *Journal of the House of Representatives of the Commonwealth of Massachusetts*, 1916, p. 91; John B. Andrews, "Report of Work, 1916," *ALLR* 7, no. 1 (March 1917): 191; Daniel Nelson, *Unemployment Insurance: The American Experience, 1915–1935* (Madison: University of Wisconsin Press, 1969), pp. 17–18. On the disagreement over who would take control of the drafting process, see Andrews to Mary K. Hale, 17 April 1915, and Hale to Andrews, 26 April 1915, AALL Papers, reel 14.

19. Mary K. Hale to Andrews, 11 April 1915, AALL Papers, reel 14; Massachusetts Committee on Unemployment, *Unemployment Insurance for Massa-*

chusetts, bulletin no. 2, January 1916, p. 10; Andrews to Ordway Tead, 25 October 1915, AALL Papers, reel 15. Massachusetts Committee on Unemployment, *Unemployment Insurance,* pp. 11–26. Ironically, one of the early shipments of copies of the National Insurance Act was lost at sea on its way to America. Stephen Bauer informed Andrews, "I am just told by Miss Sanger that copies of the *National Insurance Act*' by a most cruel irony of tragic fate have sunk with the 'Titanic'. The parcel (value of 9£) was not insured." See Bauer to Andrews, 20 April 1912, AALL Papers, reel 7.

20. *National Insurance Act [of Britain], 1911* [1&2 Geo. 5. Ch. 55], part 2; Massachusetts Committee on Unemployment, *Unemployment Insurance,* pp. 12–14, 19–20; Massachusetts Committee on Unemployment, *England Provides Out-of-Work Benefits for Three Million Workers; Why Not Massachusetts?,* n.d., AALL Pamphlet Collection, Labor Management Documentation Center, Cornell University; Cohen, *Insurance Against Unemployment,* pp. 465–492.

21. See Andrews to J. W. Magruder, 18 November 1915, AALL Papers, reel 15; Andrews to Eleanor Arms Kiler, 25 January 1916, AALL Papers, reel 16; Andrews, "Report of Work, 1916," p. 191. See also Irwin Yellowitz, "The Origins of Unemployment Reform," *Labor History,* 9, no. 3 (Fall 1968): 359; Lloyd F. Pierce, "The Activities of the American Association for Labor Legislation" (Ph.D. diss., University of Wisconsin, 1953), p. 295. On the economic recovery beginning in 1915, see Melvyn Dubofsky, *Industrialism and the American Worker, 1865–1920* (New York: Crowell, 1975), p. 111.

22. I. M. Rubinow wrote in 1934 that when the progressive reformers came together in 1915 "to consider the question: 'What next?' the inevitable conclusion was that health insurance logically came next." See his *The Quest for Security* (New York: Holt, 1934), p. 207. See also Andrews to John Martin, 2 December 1915 [at 2 November 1915 on film], AALL Papers, reel 15; Andrews' letter "To the Editor," 15 January 1917, AALL Papers, reel 17; I.M. Rubinow, "Health Insurance through Local Mutual Funds," *ALLR* 7, no. 1 (March 1917): 69.

23. See "General Discussion," *ALLR* 7, no. 1 (March 1917): 125. See also "Brief for Health Insurance," *ALLR* 6, no. 2 (June 1916): 227; Andrews to Elizabeth M. Fielder, 19 June 1916, AALL Papers, reel 17; Andrews' testimony in "Public Hearing before the [Massachusetts] Special Commission on Social Insurance, held at Room 436, State House, Boston, Mass.," 3 October 1916, AALL Papers, reel 62, pp. 44–45, 52.

24. "Brief for Health Insurance," pp. 231–232, 230. The only difference with respect to the internalization principle was that illness, unlike accidents, was regarded by AALL reformers as the joint responsibility of employers, employees, and the state. As a result, they recommended levying health insurance taxes on all three parties rather than on employers alone. See John B. Andrews, "Human Conservation through Health Insurance," 5 May 1917, AALL Papers, reel 62, p. 3; John B. Andrews, "Social Insurance," n.d., AALL Papers, reel 62, p. 9; "Brief for Health Insurance," pp. 223–230.

25. "Health Insurance: A Positive Statement in Answer to Opponents," *ALLR* 7, no. 4 (December 1917): 685.

26. "Public Hearing before the [Massachusetts] Special Commission on Social Insurance," pp. 55, 125; Andrews to Mary Simkhovitch, 16 November 1915, AALL Papers, reel 15. See also Paul Starr, *The Social Transformation of American Medicine* (New York: Basic Books, 1982), pp. 236, 238.

27. See e.g. Alexander Lambert, "Medical Organization under Health Insurance," *ALLR* 7, no. 1 (March 1917): 36, 37. See also Michael M. Davis Jr., "Organization of Medical Service," *ALLR* 6, no. 1 (1916): 16–20; Andrews, "Human Conservation through Health Insurance," p. 2; Frederick D. Green to H. Edmond Machold, 14 March 1917, AALL Papers, reel 17; "Brief for Health Insurance," pp. 165–169.

28. Lee K. Frankel and Louis I. Dublin, "Community Sickness Survey, Rochester, N.Y., September 1915," *Public Health Reports* 31, no. 8 (25 February 1916): 434.

29. See e.g. John R. Commons and A. J. Altmeyer, "The Health Insurance Movement in the United States," in Ohio Health and Old Age Insurance Commission, *Health, Health Insurance, Old Age Pensions* (Columbus: F.J. Heer, 1919), p. 295.

30. Louise Bolard More, *Wage-Earners' Budgets: A Study of Standards and Cost of Living in New York City* (New York: Holt, 1907), pp. 55, 267–270; Robert Coit Chapin, *The Standard of Living among Workingmen's Families in New York City* (New York: Charities Publication Committee, 1909), pp. 191–197, 245–250; Henry Rogers Seager, *Social Insurance: A Program of Social Reform* (New York: Macmillan, 1910), p. 12; B. S. Warren, "Sickness Insurance: A Preventive of Charity Practice," *Journal of the American Medical Association* 65, no. 24 (11 December 1915): 2057; New York City Bureau of Standards, *Report on the Cost of Living for an Unskilled Laborer's Family in New York City* (1915), pp. 6, 11, 15, 41; "Health Insurance: A Positive Statement," pp. 627–648; Andrews, "Human Conservation through Health Insurance," p. 5.

31. Anna Kalet, "Voluntary Health Insurance in New York City," *ALLR* 6, no. 2 (June 1916): 142–154; *Commission to Study Social Insurance and Unemployment,* Hearings before the Committee on Labor, House of Representatives, 64th Cong., 1st sess. (on H.J. Res. 159), 6 and 11 April 1916 (Washington: GPO, 1918), p. 9; John R. Commons, "Health Insurance," *Wisconsin Medical Journal,* November 1918, in Commons Papers, reel 17, fr. 441; "Health Risk Coming Says Professor Commons," *Capital Times,* 4 October 1918, in Commons Papers, reel 17, fr. 434; Henry R. Seager, "Plan for Health Insurance Act," *ALLR* 6, no. 1 (1916): 21. See also Ronald Numbers, *Almost Persuaded: American Physicians and Compulsory Health Insurance, 1912–1920* (Baltimore: Johns Hopkins University Press, 1978), pp. 5–6; Starr, *Social Transformation,* pp. 241–242.

32. John B. Andrews, "Progress Toward Health Insurance," n.d., AALL Papers, reel 18, pp. 1–2; Andrews, "Introductory Note," *ALLR* 6, no. 2 (June 1916):

121–122; Minutes, AALL Committee on Social Insurance, 24 November 1913, AALL Papers, reel 61; "Standards for Sickness Insurance," 30 October 1914, Chamberlain to Andrews, 11 December 1914, AALL Papers, reel 12; "Preliminary Standards for Sickness Insurance," *ALLR* 4, no. 4 (December 1914): 595–596; "Health Insurance—Tentative Draft of an Act," *ALLR* 6, no. 2 (June 1916): 239–268. The original members of the AALL's Committee on Social Insurance were Edward T. Devine (chairman), Miles M. Dawson, Carroll W. Doten, Henry J. Harris, Charles R. Henderson, Frederick L. Hoffman, I. M. Rubinow, Henry R. Seager, and John B. Andrews (secretary). Joseph P. Chamberlain, of the Columbia Legislative Drafting Research Fund, also played an active role in drafting the AALL's sickness insurance standards and model bill.

33. Workers who earned less than $9 per week would pay less than 40 percent, according to a sliding scale. The scale reduced the contributions of workers earning less than $5 per week to zero; employers of these workers were required to make up the difference.

34. See "Health Insurance—Tentative Draft of an Act."

35. John R. Commons and John B. Andrews, *Principles of Labor Legislation* (New York: Harper, 1927), pp. 459–460; Olga S. Halsey, "Compulsory Health Insurance in Great Britain," *ALLR* 6, no. 2 (June 1916): 130–134; "Brief for Health Insurance," pp. 199–202; "Health Insurance—Tentative Draft of an Act," pp. 255–259.

36. See e.g. Frederick Hoffman to Irving Fisher, 5 February 1917, AALL Papers, reel 17; Frederick L. Hoffman, *Facts and Fallacies of Compulsory Health Insurance* (Newark: Prudential Press, 1917), pp. 7, 88; Frederick L. Hoffman, *More Facts and Fallacies of Compulsory Health Insurance* (Newark: Prudential Press, 1920), p. 5. For examples of like-minded critics attacking compulsory health insurance as "un-American," see L. D. Burlingame to Olga Halsey, 14 February 1916, AALL Papers, reel 16; Mark A. Daly circular letter, 23 February 1918, AALL Papers, reel 18; A. Parker Nevin, "Un-American Tendencies of Compulsory Health Insurance," *American Industries* 17, no. 7 (February 1917): 13.

37. In addition to the activities described here, the leaders of the AALL launched a preemptive assault in New York State on the ever troublesome constitutionality barrier. Mindful of the *Ives* fiasco, they proposed a broad authorizing amendment at the state constitutional convention in 1915 which would have empowered the legislature to enact any form of social insurance it chose. This, they thought, would help to insure legislative success and prevent subsequent invalidation by the courts. To their great surprise and consternation, however, the amendment was summarily rejected by the Republican-dominated convention, and it quickly faded into oblivion. The AALL reformers might have interpreted this defeat as a bad omen or at least a sign of the difficulties that lay ahead. Instead they chose publicly to ignore it and to initiate without delay the legislative phase of their campaigns for unemployment and health insurance, even in the absence of the constitutional trump

card they had hoped to hold. See Andrews to Seager, 26 July 1915, AALL Papers, reel 17; *Constitutional Amendments Relating to Labor Legislation and Brief in Their Defense,* submitted to the Constitutional Convention of New York State by a Committee Organized by the American Association for Labor Legislation, 9 June 1915; *New York Evening Post,* 11 June 1915, p. 8; Henry R. Seager, "A Labor Amendment" (letter to the editor), *New York Evening Post,* 19 June 1915, p. 6; John B. Andrews, "Secretary's Report, 1915," *ALLR* 6, no. 1 (1916): p. 111; Robert F. Wesser, *A Response to Progressivism: The Democratic Party and New York Politics, 1902–1918* (New York: New York University Press, 1986), pp. 167–179.

38. Andrews to Katherine Coman, 7 August 1914, Andrews to Frederick R. Green (secretary, AMA), 11 August 1914, Andrews to Editor, *Medical Record, Medical Times,* 11 August 1914. See also Andrews to Green, 24 September 1914, AALL Papers, reel 12.

39. Numbers, *Almost Persuaded,* p. 29.

40. Green to Andrews, 11 November 1915, AALL Papers, reel 15.

41. Andrews to Henry B. Favill, 7 December 1915, Andrews to Carroll W. Doten, 11 December 1915, AALL Papers, reel 15; Andrews to H.M. Bracken, 7 January 1916, Alexander R. Craig to Andrews, 12 January 1916, AALL Papers, reel 16; Numbers, *Almost Persuaded,* pp. 33–42; Forrest A. Walker, "Compulsory Health Insurance: 'The Next Great Step in Social Legislation,' " *Journal of American History* 56, no. 2 (1969): 301; Gary Land, "American Images of British Compulsory Health Insurance," in Ronald L. Numbers, ed., *Compulsory Health Insurance: The Continuing American Debate* (Westport: Greenwood Press, 1982), pp. 57–58; Andrews to Sophy Sanger, 4 February 1916, AALL Papers, reel 16.

42. The drafts of both circular letters are dated December 1915, addressed "Dear Sir," and located at the end of December 1915 in AALL Papers, reel 15. See also Andrews to William Green, 9 February 1916, Andrews to Magnus W. Alexander, 17 January 1916, AALL Papers, reel 16.

43. See e.g. "Health Insurance Conference Did Not Come to Any Definite Agreement," *Monitor* 3, no. 2 (July 1916): 18–20.

44. See [F.C. Schwedtman ?] to Andrews, 11 June 1914, AALL Papers, reel 11; Andrews to Schwedtman, 23 June 1914 and 10 August 1914, Schwedtman to Andrews, 10 August 1914, AALL Papers, reel 12; transcript of F.C. Schwedtman's address to the National Association of Manufacturers, 19 May 1914, AALL Papers, reel 11; Andrews to William Lander, 18 May 1916, AALL Papers, reel 17; Osgood Andrews to Andrews, 24 February 1916, AALL Papers, reel 16; Andrews to Irving Fisher, 16 May 1916, AALL Papers, reel 17; Commons and Altmeyer, "Health Insurance Movement in the United States," p. 305; Anderson, "Health Insurance in the United States, 1910–1920," pp. 386–387.

45. The AALL bill contained a provision prohibiting workers who insured in multiple ways (such as fraternal and trade union funds as well as the compulsory system) from receiving benefits in excess of their weekly earnings.

The reformers wrote this provision against overinsurance to prevent a high rate of unnecessary (or fraudulent) claims. Presumably, labor leaders feared that this restriction would impinge on the prerogatives of unions to offer special forms of insurance to their members.

46. Irene Sylvester to Andrews, 4 January 1916, AALL Papers, reel 16; Andrews circular to Massachusetts State Federation of Labor members, 29 December 1916, AALL Papers, reel 17; "Health Insurance Approved in Massachusetts," at 29 December 1916 on film, AALL Papers, reel 17; Transcript of the New York State Senate Judiciary Committee Hearing on the Mills Health Insurance Bill (Senate Bill 236), 14 March 1916, reprinted in "Hearing on Mills Health Insurance Bill Brings Out Much Opposition from Both Employer and Employee," *Monitor* 2, no. 10 (March 1916): 24–25, hereafter cited Transcript of the New York Judiciary Committee Hearing on Health Insurance, 14 March 1916; Andrews to James Holland, 21 March 1916, Andrews to N.I. Stone, 17 March 1916, Andrews to J.G. Skemp, 17 April 1916, AALL Papers, reel 16. See also "Objections of President Holland of the New York State Federation of Labor to the Mills Health Insurance Bill—Answered," at 23 March 1916 on film, AALL Papers, reel 16.

47. Transcript of New York Judiciary Committee Hearing on Health Insurance, 14 March 1916, p. 27. See also Andrews to Tead, 15 March 1916, AALL Papers, reel 16. Interestingly, the *Monitor*'s commentary on the hearing noted, "The bill was so obviously without influential support that the big guns of the opposition were not fired at all" ("Hearing on Mills Health Insurance Bill Brings Out Much Opposition," p. 19). See also Andrews to C. C. Carstens, 3 March 1916, AALL Papers, reel 16.

48. "Public Hearing before the [Massachusetts] Special Commission on Social Insurance," 3 October 1916, AALL Papers, reel 62, p. 120.

49. See esp. Olga Halsey, "Hearing on Health Insurance Bill (Senate 236), Albany, 14 March 1916," AALL Papers, reel 62.

50. John Nelson, "New Menace of Higher Manufacturing Costs," *Iron Age* 98, no. 2 (13 July 1916): 87. I was first directed to this source by a citation in Yellowitz, "The Origins of Unemployment Reform," p. 355n69. See also "Health Insurance Now a Practical Issue," *Survey* 35, no. 24 (11 March 1916): 691; Edson S. Lott, "Fallacies of Compulsory Social Insurance," *American Industries* 17, no. 6 (January 1917): 18.

51. Transcript of New York Judiciary Committee Hearing on Health Insurance, 14 March 1916, pp. 28, 32. See also Andrews to Commons, 16 March 1916, AALL Papers, reel 16. In estimating the burden on employers at 1 percent of payroll, Rubinow probably was referring only to the direct burden (the employers' 40 percent contribution). Even with this qualification, his estimate was somewhat low. Commons and Altmeyer noted in 1919 that a standard estimate of the total cost of compulsory health insurance was 4 percent of payroll, which would produce a burden of 1.6 percent on employers alone ("Health Insurance Movement in the United States," p. 296).

52. Andrews to Carroll W. Doten, 11 December 1915, AALL Papers, reel 15; Transcript of New York Judiciary Committee Hearing on Health Insurance,

14 March 1916, pp. 22, 25. On the AALL's bargaining-chip strategy, see also Andrews to Ordway Tead, 15 March 1916, Seager to Otto M. Eidlitz, 29 January 1916, Chamberlain to Halsey, 18 February 1916, Andrews to Charles J. Hatfield, 29 March 1916, AALL Papers, reel 16; Andrews to Eugene T. Lies, 27 June 1916, AALL Papers, reel 17.

53. Arthur J. Viseltear, "Compulsory Health Insurance in California, 1915–1918," *Journal of the History of Medicine and Allied Sciences* 24, no. 2 (April 1969): 154; Numbers, *Almost Persuaded*, pp. 47–49; John A. Lapp, "The Findings of Official Health Insurance Commissions," *ALLR* 10, no. 1 (March 1920): 28; *Journal of the House of Representatives of the Commonwealth of Massachusetts, 1916*, pp. 121, 735, 1188, 1199, 1212, 1225, 1232; *Report of the [Massachusetts] Special Commission on Social Insurance*, February 1917 (Boston: Wright and Potter, 1917), p. 7. On the emergence of the Massachusetts Commission and the role of the AALL reformers, see esp. Michael Davis to Andrews, 3 March 1916 and 24 March 1916, AALL Papers, reel 16; Numbers, *Almost Persuaded*, p. 45. On the demise of the investigatory commission proposal in New York, see Andrews to Chamberlain, 31 March 1916, Andrews to Irving Fisher, 13 April 1916 and 21 April 1916, AALL Papers, reel 16.

54. On the governors' endorsements, see "Governor of California Favors Health Insurance," *ALLR* 7, no. 1 (March 1917): 208; "Governor of Massachusetts Urges Legislature to Enact Compulsory Health Insurance," *ALLR* 7, no. 1 (March 1917): 223. On the verdicts of the commissions, see Lapp, "Findings of Official Health Insurance Commissions," pp. 28–29; Commons and Altmeyer, "Health Insurance Movement in the United States," p. 293; Viseltear, "Compulsory Health Insurance in California," pp. 165–168. See also *Report of the [Massachusetts] Special Commission on Social Insurance*, pp. 16, 17, 109.

55. Nearly all of the relevant AALL literature as well as the Commons and Altmeyer 1919 survey of the health insurance movement put the number of state legislatures that considered health insurance bills in 1917 at twelve. Odin W. Anderson, whose 1950 survey article contains several other clearly identifiable factual errors, puts the number at fifteen and names the states (Colorado, Connecticut, Illinois, Maine, Massachusetts, Michigan, Minnesota, New Hampshire, New Jersey, New York, Ohio, Oregon, Pennsylvania, Washington, and Wisconsin). In his study of the health insurance movement, Ronald Numbers cites Anderson's list of fifteen. See John B. Andrews, "Progress Toward Health Insurance," n.d., AALL Papers, reel 18, p. 3; Commons and Altmeyer, "Health Insurance Movement," p. 293; Pierce, "Activities of the American Association for Labor Legislation," p. 274; Anderson, "Health Insurance in the United States," p. 369; Numbers, *Almost Persuaded*, p. 133n1.

56. On the continued belief in inevitability, see John B. Andrews, "Introductory Note," *ALLR* 6, no. 4 (December 1916): 339. While most AALL reformers underestimated the opposition to health insurance, a few were more cognizant of the problem they faced. See e.g. notes on Seager's comments in min-

utes of the Social Insurance Committee, 29 March 1917, AALL Papers, reel 61. On the AALL reformers' conception of their opponents as of February 1916, see "American Association for Labor Legislation Memorandum of Some of its Activities during February, 1916," AALL Papers, reel 16, p. 2.

57. See Numbers, *Almost Persuaded,* pp. 113–114; "Being Educated," *Monitor* 7, no. 10 (March 1971): 16

58. See "Object of 'Sick Insurance' is to Give Medical Profession Assured Income?" *Monitor* 2, no. 9 (February 1916): 22; "Mills Medical Bill Assailed By Easley," *New York Times,* 13 March 1916, p. 18; "Public Hearing Before the [Massachusetts] Special Commission on Social Insurance . . . October 3, 1916," pp. 28–29, 44; Andrews to Chamberlain, 6 October 1916, AALL Papers, reel 17. See also Anderson, "Health Insurance in the United States," p. 384.

59. Rubinow, *Quest for Security,* pp. 210, 214; Rubinow, "Health Insurance through Local Mutual Funds," p. 70.

60. "General Discussion," *ALLR* 7, no. 1 (March 1917): 51, 55, 60; Joseph Mandelbaum to Andrews, 10 February 1917, D.S. Dougherty to Andrews, 16 February 1917, Charles S. Prest to Hon. Gilbert T. Seelye, 17 February 1917, AALL Papers, reel 17. See also Numbers, *Almost Persuaded,* pp. 64, 65–68.

61. Transcript of the New York State Senate Judiciary Committee Hearing on the Mills Health Insurance Bill (Senate Print No. 365), 7 March 1917, reprinted in "Convincing and Effective Opposition to Health Insurance Bill Takes Proponents Off Their Feet," *The Monitor* 3, no. 10 (March 1917): 22–24, 33, 41, hereafter cited Transcript of the New York Judiciary Committee Hearing on Health Insurance, 7 March 1917; "Public Hearing Before the [Massachusetts] Special Commission on Social Insurance . . . October 3, 1916," pp. 26–29; Transcript of the New York State Senate Judiciary Committee Hearing on Senator Nicoll's Health Insurance Bill, 26 March 1918, reprinted in "Health Insurance Hearing," *Monitor* 4, no. 11 (April 1918): 21, hereafter cited Transcript of the New York Judiciary Committee Hearing on Health Insurance, 26 March 1918. See also John B. Andrews, "Human Conservation Through Health Insurance," [5 May 1917], AALL Papers, reel 62, p. 8. Dr. Strauss's frustration with workers' compensation, which many other physicians shared, was the result of insurance companies wresting from employers the responsibility for choosing doctors—a practice that apparently reduced physicians' control over fee schedules. Although well-informed doctors knew that commercial firms would be excluded under the AALL's health insurance bill, they probably assumed that the bill's nonprofit mutual funds would enjoy disproportionate bargaining power over physicians and, like the commercial carriers under workers' compensation, bid down fees.

62. Alexander Lambert to the Editor, 15 January 1917, AALL Papers, reel 17; Andrews to Eugene T. Lies, 5 July 1917, AALL Papers, reel 18; Walker, "Compulsory Health Insurance," p. 301; Starr, *Social Transformation of American Medicine,* pp. 247–249; Frederick R. Green to Andrews, 13 March

1913, AALL Papers, reel 9; Green to Andrews, 18 September 1913, AALL Papers, reel 10; Numbers, *Almost Persuaded,* pp. 83–84. On AALL reformers' persisting belief that physicians could be converted, see e.g. "Statements by Physicians in Favor of Health Insurance," [July 1917], AALL Papers, reel 62; Transcript of New York Judiciary Committee Hearing on Health Insurance, 26 March 1918, p. 20. The AMA House of Delegates finally voted to oppose compulsory health insurance outright in April 1920; see Anderson, "Health Insurance in the United States," pp. 379–380; Numbers, *Almost Persuaded,* pp. 102–105.

63. Paul Starr, *Social Transformation of American Medicine,* p. 250; Anderson, "Health Insurance in the United States," pp. 386–387; Transcript of New York Judiciary Committee Hearing on Health Insurance, 7 March 1917, p. 16.

64. See Lubove, *Struggle for Social Security,* esp. chap. 1 ("The Constraints of Voluntarism").

65. While the Executive Council voiced the official view of the AFL, representatives of 21 labor organizations (including the International Typographical Union, the West Virginia State Federation of Labor, the Arizona State Federation of Labor, the Western Federation of Miners, the Cigar Makers, the United Textile Workers, and the International Ladies Garment Workers Union) formally dissented from the American Federation's 1916 pronouncement on social insurance. See *Report of Proceedings of the Thirty-Sixth Annual Convention of the American Federation of Labor,* 13–25 November 1916, pp. 144–145, 335. For a complete list of AFL resolutions on social insurance, see *Economic Security Act,* Hearings before the Committee on Finance, U.S. Senate, 74th Cong., 1st sess. (on S. 1130), 22 January to 20 February 1935, revised, pp. 1204–17. The AFL did not endorse compulsory unemployment insurance until 1932. For more on Gompers' view, see *Commission to Study Social Insurance and Unemployment,* Hearings before the Committee on Labor, House of Representatives, 64th Cong., 1st sess. (on H.J. Res. 159), 6 and 11 April 1916, p. 153; Samuel Gompers, "Not Even Compulsory Benevolence Will Do," in *Compulsory Health Insurance,* annual meeting addresses, National Civic Federation, 22 January 1917 (New York, 1917), pp. 9–10; Samuel Gompers, "Labor vs. Its Barnacles," *American Federationist* 23, no. 4 (April 1916): 268–274.

66. Ralph M. Easley to Olga Halsey, 25 April 1916, AALL Papers, reel 17.

67. See Gary Land, "American Images of British Compulsory Health Insurance," p. 59. For a concise statement of the NCF's position on health insurance, see Warren S. Stone's circular letter, 17 March 1917 (at 27 January 1916 on film), AALL Papers, reel 16. Stone was chairman of the NCF's Social Insurance Department, and his letter makes clear that the NCF opposed not only state health insurance legislation but federal legislation as well.

68. Circular letter from Louis H. Fibel, president, Great Eastern Casualty Company, "To Our New York Agents" (copy), 27 January 1916, AALL Papers, reel 16. See also identical circular letter on Great Eastern letterhead, 17 February 1916, AALL Papers, reel 16.

69. At a hearing before the Massachusetts Special Commission on Social Insurance in September 1917, W. G. Curtis, president of the National Casualty Company of Detroit, acknowledged only that the enactment of health insurance would remove "some portion" of the industrial insurance companies' business. See "Hearing before the [Massachusetts] Special Commission on Social Insurance, Room 101, State House, Boston, September 12, 1917," AALL Papers, reel 62, p. 3.

70. I.M. Rubinow, "Public and Private Interests in Social Insurance," *ALLR* 21, no. 2 (June 1931): 185; Rubinow, *Quest for Security*, pp. 212, 213.

71. Andrews to Ogden Mills, 17 February 1916, AALL Papers, reel 16. See also Andrews to James R. Young, 31 March 1916, and Andrews to Emery R. Hayhurst, 31 March 1916, AALL Papers, reel 16.

72. Transcript of New York Judiciary Committee Hearing on Health Insurance, 14 March 1917; "Health Insurance Now a Practical Issue," p. 692. See also [Irene Sylvester] to [?] Mortimer, editorial writer, *New York Times*, 9 March 1917, AALL Papers, reel 17, regarding the insurance interests' failure to attend the 1917 hearings in New York.

73. "Hearing before the [Massachusetts] Special Commission on Social Insurance . . . September 12, 1917," first page of Cox testimony. Cox also explained that Metropolitan Life objected to being excluded in any way from life insurance coverage, either directly or indirectly [see second page of Cox testimony].

74. Andrews, "Progress Toward Health Insurance," p. 11.

75. Numbers, *Almost Persuaded,* pp. 60–61.

76. Quoted from the Insurance Economics Society of America, *Bulletin,* no. 2, in Anderson, "Health Insurance in the United States," p. 384.

77. See Hoffman to Fisher, 5 February 1917, AALL Papers, reel 17. Notably, two other leading critics of compulsory health insurance, P. T. Sherman and Lee K. Frankel, were also associated with the insurance industry and also formerly active members of the AALL. See e.g. P. Tecumseh Sherman, *Dangerous Tendencies in the American Social Insurance Movement,* address at the 138th meeting of the Insurance Society of New York, 21 November 1916 (Insurance Society of New York, 1917).

78. Frederick L. Hoffman, *Facts and Fallacies of Compulsory Health Insurance* (Newark: Prudential Press, 1917), pp. 7, 88, 5, 12, 13, 83. *Facts and Fallacies* was based on two addresses Hoffman delivered at the Section on Social and Economic Science of the American Association for the Advancement of Science on 28 December 1916, and the National Civic Federation on 22 January 1917. Three years later, Hoffman published a sequel entitled *More Facts and Fallacies of Compulsory Health Insurance* (Newark: Prudential Press, 1920). See also Hoffman, *Health Insurance and the Public* (c. 1919).

79. "Convincing and Effective Opposition to Health Insurance Bill Takes Proponents Off Their Feet," p. 11.

80. Viseltear, "Health Insurance in California," pp. 171–172; Andrews to Michael M. Davis, Jr., 4 May 1917, AALL Papers, reel 17.

81. Andrews to Will. J. French, 20 January 1916, AALL Papers, reel 16. See also e.g. Andrews to Jessica B. Peixotto, 5 January 1916, AALL Papers, reel 16.
82. Viseltear, "Compulsory Health Insurance in California," pp. 155–156, 157.
83. See "Objections to the California Plan Urged by Mr. Joseph Chamberlain in a Letter to Miss Nachtrieb," 27 March 1917, Andrews to Barbara Nachtrieb, 7 April 1917, AALL Papers, reel 17; Halsey to Barbara Nachtrieb Grimes, 2 November 1917, AALL Papers, reel 18. Barbara Nachtrieb served as executive secretary of the California Social Insurance Commission.
84. Ernestine W. Black to Andrews, 29 June 1918, AALL Papers, reel 18.
85. Ibid.; Ernest Jerome Hopkins, "To Whom it May Concern," 22 May 1919, statement sworn before a notary public on 23 May 1919, AALL Papers, reel 18; Black to Andrews, 5 December 1918, AALL Papers, reel 18.
86. Black to Andrews, 5 December 1918, AALL Papers, reel 18; Anderson, "Health Insurance in the United States," pp. 370–371; Viseltear, "Compulsory Health Insurance in California," pp. 177–178; *Vote NO ..on.. Number 20,* pamphlet (Los Angeles: League for the Conservation of Public Health, [1918]).
87. Black to Andrews, 5 December 1918, AALL Papers, reel 18; *Do You Know This Girl?,* flier printed by California Social Insurance Commission, AALL Papers (at 26 July 1918 on film), reel 18; Viseltear, "Compulsory Health Insurance in California," pp. 179–180.
88. C.A. Storke to [Irene Sylvester] Chubb, 1 September 1918, Ansley K. Salz to Andrews, telegram [12 October 1918?], Will J. French to Andrews, 1 November and 19 November 1918, AALL Papers, reel 18; Viseltear, "Compulsory Health Insurance in California," p. 181; Numbers, *Almost Persuaded,* pp. 79, 81; Starr, *Social Transformation of American Medicine,* p. 253.
89. James Lynch to Andrews, 22 February 1917, AALL Papers, reel 17; Transcript of New York Judiciary Committee Hearing on Health Insurance, 7 March 1917, pp. 37, 48; Andrews to Walter H. Kidder, 14 March 1917, AALL Papers, reel 17; Numbers, *Almost Persuaded,* p. 68.
90. "Health Insurance Bill as Developed from 'Tentative Drafts,' " *ALLR* 9, no. 2 (June 1919): 209; Transcript of New York Judiciary Committee Hearing on Health Insurance, 26 March 1918, p. 18; "New York Federation of Labor Is Back of Health Insurance Bill to be Urged at Present Session of the Legislature," *Monitor* 4, no. 9 (February 1918): 1–3; *Health Insurance: Official Endorsement of the New York State Federation of Labor, with Report of Its Committee on Health* (New York State Federation of Labor, 1918), especially pp. 3, 5, 6, and 16.
91. "Labor and Health Insurance," *Monitor* 4, no. 9 (February 1918): 10; Mark A. Daly, circular "To All Members," 23 February 1918, copy, AALL Papers, reel 18.
92. Andrews to Bailey B. Burritt, 12 March 1918, AALL Papers, reel 18.
93. Andrews to Israel Strauss, 22 March 1918, AALL Papers, reel 18; Numbers, *Almost Persuaded,* pp. 81–82; Transcript of the New York Judiciary Com-

mittee Hearing on Health Insurance, 26 March 1918; Andrews to William J. Fitzgerald, 28 March 1919, AALL Papers, reel 18; "More Health Insurance," *Monitor* 4, no. 11 (April 1918): 30.

94. Samuel McCune Lindsay, "Next Steps in Social Insurance in the United States," *ALLR* 9, no. 1 (March 1919): 110, 107.

95. See "The Story of a Legislative Fight' as Told by Women's Legislative Lobby," *Monitor* 6, no. 1 (June 1919): 71–73.

96. Extract of Governor Alfred E. Smith's 1 January 1919 message to the New York legislature, reprinted in "Health Insurance Will Conserve Human Life," *ALLR* 9, no. 2 (June 1919): 225.

97. See "Reconstruction Commission of the State of New York Urges Compulsory Health Insurance," *ALLR* 9, no. 2 (June 1919): 250–251; Lapp, "Findings of Official Health Insurance Commissions," p. 37.

98. See examples of such editorial support compiled in "Strong Editorial Support for the Health Insurance Bill," *ALLR* 9, no. 2 (June 1919): 252–264.

99. Numbers describes 10 April as the " 'high point' of the American debate over health insurance." *Almost Persuaded,* p. 91.

100. "Health Insurance Bill as Developed from 'Tentative Drafts,' " p. 210. See also "Story of a Legislative Fight," p. 73.

101. "Health Insurance Bill as Developed from 'Tentative Drafts,' " p. 210; "Health Insurance Bill Passes New York State Senate," *ALLR* 9, no. 2 (June 1919): 232–237; "State of New York, No. 1811. Int. 73. In Senate, Introduced by Mr. Davenport—January 15, 1919. An Act To Conserve the Human Resources of the State by Establishing for Employees a System of Mutual Health Insurance Funds," reprinted in *ALLR* 9, no. 2 (June 1919): 211–224; "Insurgents Block Republican Plan," *New York Times,* 11 April 1919, p. 4; *New Republic,* 19 April 1919, p. 362.

102. "Health Insurance Bill as Developed from 'Tentative Drafts,' " p. 210; "Health Insurance Bill Passes New York Senate," p. 237; "Pronounces Doom of Welfare Bills," *New York Times,* 13 April 1919, p. 5; New York State League of Women Voters, "Report and Protest to the Governor, the Legislature and the People of the State of New York," March 1920, reprinted in *ALLR* 10, no. 1 (March 1920): 88–92; "Filibuster Wins Coalition Victory," *New York Times,* 16 April 1919, p. 4; "Story of a Legislative Fight," pp. 73–75; "The Legislature," *Monitor* 5, no. 11 (April 1919): 20. An article in the *Times* remarked: "The 142d annual session of the Legislature will be noted for what it failed to do, rather than for what it did." See "Legislature Noted For Little It Did," *New York Times,* 20 April 1919, p. 10.

103. "The Albany Filibuster," *New York Times,* 16 April 1919, p. 12 (editorial page); *New Republic,* 26 April 1919, p. 395; "Women and Organized Labor Join Forces to Defeat Republican Assemblymen," *Monitor* 6, no. 2 (July 1919): 31; "Organized Labor and Women Declare War on Speaker Sweet and Republicans," *Monitor* 6, no. 4 (September 1919): 30–31; "Right is Might," *Monitor* 6, no. 6 (November 1919): pp. 19–20. For more examples

of editorial opposition to Sweet's stand, see "Opposition to Welfare Bills Called 'Political Folly,' " *ALLR* 9, no. 2 (June 1919): esp. pp. 267, 269–270. Particularly notable was Mary E. Dreier's assault on Speaker Sweet: "What shall we say of the great State of New York when a little paper manufacturer from Oswego holds up legislation which will benefit almost a million workers" (quoted in "The Albany Filibuster").

104. "Report and Protest to the Governor," esp. pp. 83–86, 96, 99, 87, 91–94.

105. "Charges," *Monitor* 6, no. 10 (March 1920): 20; " 'Charges' of the League of Women Voters; Statement by General Secretary Daly; Resolution of Association," *Monitor* 6, no. 10 (March 1920): 36–39; "Dr. Hoffman Gives Governor Real Facts in Answer to Women's League Charges," *Monitor* 6, no. 12 (May 1920): 43–46.

106. Numbers, *Almost Persuaded,* p. 95; "A Vital Question" [extracts from the second report, 12 February 1920, of the Reconstruction Commission of New York State on the issue of health insurance], *ALLR* 10, no. 1 (March 1920): 46; "Health Insurance Not on League Program," *Monitor* 6, no. 8 (January 1920): 42; "Riot of Legislation Proposed But Only Comparatively Minor Amendments to Existing Laws Affect Business," *Monitor* 7, no. 1 (June 1920): 80–81.

107. See e.g. "Dr. Harris' Attack on Pamphlet of the Civic Federation Answered by Sherman," *Monitor* 7, no. 4 (September 1920): 22–26; Frederick MacKenzie, "The Legislative Campaign in New York for the 'Welfare Bills,' " *ALLR* 10, no. 2 (June 1920): 136–149.

108. "More Testimony," *Monitor,* 7, no. 6 (November 1920): 16.

109. See Starr, *Social Transformation of American Medicine,* p. 254; Rubinow, *Quest for Security,* p. 210; Viseltear, "Compulsory Health Insurance in California," p. 179; Numbers, *Almost Persuaded,* pp. 74–78; W. A. Evans to Andrews, 24 September 1917, Henry J. Harris to Andrews, 12 March 1918 (copy), AALL Papers, reel 18.

110. "Insurgents Block Republican Plan," *New York Times,* 11 April 1919, p. 4.

111. See esp. the very careful discussion of degenerative competition by two dissenting members of the Massachusetts Special Commission on Social Insurance. *Report of the [Massachusetts] Special Commission,* pp. 38–42.

112. "Senator Davenport Sets Forth Position on Compulsory Health Insurance Issue; General Secretary Daly gives facts on legislation before meeting of National Civic Federation—Views widely divergent," *Monitor* 6, no. 10 (March 1920): 15.

9. The Progressive Legacy, 1920–1940

1. Early historians of the progressive era typically took for granted that progressive reform died during the "reactionary" 1920s. According to Eric F. Goldman, "Progressivism of the Twenties was a beaten army, muscles aching, its ranks seriously depleted" (*Rendezvous with Destiny* [New York: Knopf, 1952], p. 289). Similarly, Richard Hofstadter wrote, "Progressivism

had been founded on a mood, and with the reaction that followed the war that mood was dissipated" (*The Age of Reform* [New York: Vintage, 1955], p. 282). Nevertheless, some historians have argued persuasively that essential elements of progressivism survived into the twenties. For an early example of this argument, see Arthur S. Link, "What Happened to the Progressive Movement in the 1920's?" *American Historical Review* 64, no. 4 (July 1959): 833–851.

2. James A Losty, "The Soldiers and Sailors Insurance Act" (Ph.D. diss., Catholic University, 1921); U.S. Treasury Department, Bureau of War Risk Insurance, *Military and Naval Insurance and Military and Naval Compensation Claims as a Result of the World War* (Washington, 30 June 1919), esp. pp. 7–14.

3. Samuel McCune Lindsay, "Next Steps in Social Insurance in the United States," *ALLR* 9, no. 1 (March 1919): 111. See also John B. Andrews, "Introductory Note," *ALLR* 7, no. 3 (June 1917): 527, in which he describes the Military and Naval Insurance Act as "the most liberal government system of accident, health, and life insurance that has ever been adopted by any country for its enlisted men." For contemporary descriptions of the war years as a reactionary period, see e.g. John B. Andrews, "Outline of Work 1914," *ALLR* 5, no. 1 (March 1915): 161; Seager to Andrews, 28 July 1915, AALL Papers, reel 14; Henry R. Seager, "American Labor Legislation," *ALLR* 6, no. 1 (1916): 87.

4. Milton Friedman and Anna Jacobson Schwartz characterize the contraction of 1920–21 as "one of the most rapid declines on record." The unemployment rate in 1921 is estimated to have reached 11.9 percent. See their *A Monetary History of the United States, 1867–1960* (Princeton: Princeton University Press, 1971), pp. 231–232; Jonathan Hughes, *American Economic History*, 3rd ed. (Glenview: Scott, Foresman/Little, Brown, 1990), p. 448.

5. "Another New 'Issue,' " *Monitor* 7, no. 8 (January 1921): 28.

6. Henry A. Huber, "Unemployment Prevention," *Official Labor Review*, c. 1921, reprinted in *La Crosse Trades and Labor Council Review*, in Commons Papers, reel 17, frs. 943–945; Harry Malisoff, "The Emergence of Unemployment Compensation, I," *Political Science Quarterly* 54, no. 2 (June 1939): 243–244; Lafayette G. Harter Jr., *John R. Commons: His Assault on Laissez Faire* (Corvallis: Oregon State University Press, 1962), pp. 116–117; Daniel Nelson, *Unemployment Insurance: The American Experience, 1915–1935* (Madison: University of Wisconsin Press, 1969), pp. 108–118, 163. According to Roy Lubove's research, the South Carolina legislature also considered at least one unemployment insurance bill during the twenties. See his *The Struggle for Social Security, 1900–1935* (Pittsburgh: University of Pittsburgh Press, 1986), p. 168.

7. Paul Starr, *The Social Transformation of American Medicine* (New York: Basic Books, 1982), p. 257; Irene Osgood Andrews, "State Legislation for Maternity Protection," *ALLR* 9, no. 1 (March 1921): 82–83; "Labor Leg-

islation of 1921," *ALLR* 9, no. 4 (December 1921): 372; Marjorie Davie, "The Open Door to Maternity Protection," *ALLR* 9, no. 4 (December 1921): 311; Lloyd F. Pierce, "The Activities of the American Association for Labor Legislation in Behalf of Social Security and Protective Labor Legislation" (Ph.D. diss., University of Wisconsin, 1953), p. 377; *Medical Care for the American People: The Final Report of the Committee on the Costs of Medical Care* (U.S. Department of Health, Education, and Welfare, 1970 [1932]). See also Daniel S. Hirshfield, *The Lost Reform: The Campaign for Compulsory Health Insurance in the United States from 1932 to 1943* (Cambridge: Harvard University Press, 1970), pp. 30–41; Ray Lyman Wilbur, *The First Three Years' Work of the Committee on the Costs of Medical Care and Its Plans for the Future* (1930); "Committee on the Costs of Medical Care," *Journal of the American Medical Association* 99, no. 23 (3 December 1932): 1950–52.

8. Workers' compensation laws that were upheld by the courts were enacted as follows (asterisks indicate compulsory laws): federal law covering U.S. government employees (1908); California, Illinois, Kansas, *Massachusetts, *Nevada, *New Hampshire, New Jersey, *Ohio, *Washington, *Wisconsin (1911); *Arizona, *Michigan, Rhode Island (1912); Connecticut, Iowa, *Minnesota, *New York, Oregon, Texas, West Virginia (1913); Louisiana, Nebraska, *Maryland (1914); *Alaska, Colorado, *Hawaii, Indiana, Maine, Montana, *Oklahoma, Pennsylvania, Vermont, *Wyoming (1915); Kentucky, *Puerto Rico, strengthened federal law covering U.S. government employees (1916); *Delaware, *Idaho, New Mexico, South Dakota, *Utah (1917); *Virginia (1918); Alabama, *North Dakota, Tennessee (1919); Georgia (1920); Missouri (1925); federal law covering U.S. longshoremen and harbor workers (1927); *District of Columbia (1928); North Carolina (1929); Florida, South Carolina (1935); *Arkansas (1939); *Mississippi (1948). See Richard Martin Lyon, "The American Association for Labor Legislation and the Fight for Workmen's Compensation Laws, 1906–1942," (M.S. thesis, Cornell University, 1952), pp. 21, 21-a.

9. See Harry Weiss, "Employers' Liability and Workmen's Compensation," in John R. Commons, ed., *History of Labor Legislation in the United States, 1896–1932* (New York: Macmillan, 1935), pp. 564–610; Allen F. Davis, "Welfare, Reform and World War I," *American Quarterly* 19 (1967): 519–520; Thomas I. Parkinson, "Longshoremen's Compensation Upset by Supreme Court," *ALLR* 10, no. 2 (June 1920): 117–120; "Congress Enacts Federal Accident Compensation Law for Harbor Workers!" *ALLR* 17, no. 1 (March 1927): 13–14; Barbara Nachtrieb Armstrong, *Insuring the Essentials* (New York: Macmillan, 1932), esp. pp. 253, 274, 277–78, 574–97.

10. Lubove, *Struggle for Social Security,* pp. 138–143; Pierce, "Activities of the American Association for Labor Legislation," pp. 391–392, 356–357; Nelson, *Unemployment Insurance,* pp. 152, 194–196. See also Leotto Louis, "Abraham Epstein and the Movement for Old Age Security," *Labor History* 16, no. 3 (1975): 359–377; Hirshfield, *Lost Reform,* pp. 75–76.

11. Frances Perkins, *People at Work* (New York: John Day, 1934), p. 177.
12. John R. Commons and John B. Andrews, *Principles of Labor Legislation*, 4th rev. ed. (New York: Augustus M. Kelley, 1967 [1936]), pp. 54–58; Thomas J. Kerr IV, "The New York Factory Investigating Commission and the Minimum Wage Movement," *Labor History* 11, no. 3 (Summer 1971): 389–391. See also chapter on National Recovery Administration in Ellis W. Hawley, *The New Deal and the Problem of Monopoly* (Princeton: Princeton University Press, 1966).
13. *Schechter Poultry Corp. v. United States*, 295 U.S. 495 (1935).
14. *West Coast Hotel Co. v. Parrish*, 300 U.S. 379 (1937).
15. William E. Leuchtenburg, *Franklin D. Roosevelt and the New Deal* (New York: Harper and Row, 1963), pp. 261–263; Kerr, "New York Factory Investigating Commission," pp. 390–391. See also James T. Patterson, "Mary Dewson and the American Minimum Wage Movement," *Labor History* 5, no. 2 (Spring 1964): 134–152.
16. "Progress Means Not Only Sound Business and Agriculture, But Sound Improvement in American Life," address at Atlanta, Georgia, 29 November 1935, in *The Public Papers and Addresses of Franklin D. Roosevelt*, (New York: Random House, 1938), vol. 4, p. 472; presidential statement upon signing the Social Security Act, 14 August 1935, *Public Papers and Addresses of Franklin D. Roosevelt*, vol. 4, p. 325.
17. "The Initiation of Studies to Achieve a Program of National Social and Economic Security," Executive Order no. 6757, 29 June 1934, *Public Papers and Addresses of Franklin D. Roosevelt*, vol. 3, pp. 321–322.
18. *Report to the President of the Committee on Economic Security* (Washington: GPO, 1935), p. 44; Arthur J. Altmeyer, *The Formative Years of Social Security* (Madison: University of Wisconsin Press, 1966), p. 5. See also Eveline M. Burns, *Toward Social Security: An Explanation of the Social Security Act and a Survey of the Larger Issues* (New York: McGraw-Hill, 1936), pp. 202–203; Donald S. Howard, *The WPA and Federal Relief Policy* (New York: Russell Sage Foundation, 1943), pp. 564, 715–716.
19. "American Legislation on Unemployment Compensation," *ALLR* 11, no. 1 (March 1921): 59.
20. Nelson, *Unemployment Insurance*, pp. 118–128; John R. Commons, "Unemployment Insurance," Economic Series Lecture 24, delivered 9 April 1932 over a nationwide network of the National Broadcasting Company, The University of Chicago Press, reprinted in the Commons Papers, reel 21, frs. 490–491. See also Harold M. Groves, "Compensation for Idle Labor in Wisconsin," *ALLR* 22, no. 1 (March 1932): 7; John R. Commons, "The Groves Unemployment Reserves Law," *ALLR* 22, no. 1 (March 1932): 8–10; Paul A. Raushenbush, "Wisconsin's Unemployment Compensation Act," *ALLR* 22, no. 1 (March 1932): 11–18; Kenneth R. Kennedy, "Jobless Insurance Tested in New Plan," *New York Times*, 8 July 1934, reprinted in Commons Papers, reel 21, frs. 628–629.
21. See "An American Plan for Unemployment Reserve Funds; Tentative Draft of an Act," *ALLR* 20, no. 4 (December 1930): 349–356; AALL, *An American*

Plan for Unemployment Reserve Funds with Revised Draft of an Act (New York, June 1933).

22. Nelson, *Unemployment Insurance,* pp. 145–191; Pierce, "Activities of the American Association for Labor Legislation," pp. 348–357; I. M. Rubinow, "Job Insurance—The Ohio Plan," *ALLR* 23, no. 3 (September 1933): 131–136. See also Malisoff, "Emergence of Unemployment Compensation, I," pp. 246–252.

23. It should also be noted that while exclusive employer financing was a conceptual outgrowth of the prevention school and generally opposed by reformers of the American Association for Social Security, it was also a political demand of organized labor, which was nonetheless aligned with the AASS.

24. The best secondary source on the emergence of unemployment insurance laws in the United States during the 1930s is Nelson, *Unemployment Insurance,* chaps. 8 and 9. See also Jill S. Quadagno, "Welfare Capitalism and the Social Security Act of 1935," *American Sociological Review* 49, no. 5 (October 1984): 640. For details on the CES proposals and the actual unemployment insurance provisions in the Social Security Act, see *Report to the President of the Committee on Economic Security,* pp. 10–23; Social Security Act, Public Law no. 271, 74th Congress, title 9.

25. Altmeyer, *Formative Years of Social Security,* pp. 14–15. See also Wilbur J. Cohen, "The Development of the Social Security Act of 1935: Reflections Some Fifty Years Later," *Minnesota Law Review* 68, no. 2 (December 1983): 399.

26. Frances Perkins, *The Roosevelt I Knew* (New York: Viking, 1946), p. 286.

27. Henry R. Seager, "Labor Legislation a National Social Need," remarks at meeting of the Academy of Political Science, 19 April 1912, reprinted in Seager, *Labor and Other Economic Essays,* ed. Charles A. Gulick Jr. (New York: Harper, 1931), p. 172.

28. R. Alton Lee, *A History of Regulatory Taxation* (Lexington: University of Kentucky Press, 1973), pp. 115–121; *United States v. Doremus,* 249 U.S. 86 (1919).

29. *Hammer v. Dagenhart,* 247 U.S. 251 (1918).

30. Elizabeth Brandeis, "Labor Legislation," in John R. Commons, ed., *History of Labor in the United States, 1896–1932* (New York: Macmillan, 1935), vol. 3, pp. 694–695; Commons and Andrews, *Principles of Labor Legislation* (1936), pp. 172–173; Lee, *History of Regulatory Taxation,* pp. 125–138; *Child Labor Tax Case,* 259 U.S. 20, 38; Thomas I. Parkinson, "Child Labor and the Constitution," *ALLR* 12, no. 2 (June 1922): 111. On the same day as the Child Labor Tax decision, the Supreme Court handed down a decision overturning a federal regulatory tax on grain-futures contracts. *Hill v. Wallace,* 259 U.S. 44 (1922).

31. Frederic P. Lee, "Possibilities of Establishing a National Minimum of Safety in the Coal Industry," *ALLR* 14, no. 1 (March 1924): 73–74.

32. *Florida v. Mellon,* 273 U.S. 12, 17. On the intentions of Congress in creating the inheritance-tax offset scheme, see Thomas H. Eliot's discussion in Katie

Louchheim, ed., *The Making of the New Deal: The Insiders Speak* (Cambridge: Harvard University Press, 1983), pp. 160–161.

33. Statement of Thomas H. Eliot in Louchheim, ed., *Making of the New Deal*, pp. 160–161; Paul A. Raushenbush and Elizabeth Brandeis Raushenbush, *Our "U.C." Story, 1930–1967* (Madison, 1979), pp. 38–39. See also Cohen, "Development of the Social Security Act," pp. 401–402.

34. Nelson, *Unemployment Insurance*, pp. 134–135, 198–204; address of John A. Fitch, general session on the AALL, 1907–1942, *John B. Andrews Memorial Symposium on Labor Legislation and Social Security* (1949), p. 88; "New Federal Plan for Unemployment Compensation Legislation," *ALLR* 24, no. 1 (March 1934): 7–8; John B. Andrews, "A National Challenge," *ALLR* 24, no. 1 (March 1934): 3; "Administration Job Insurance Bill 'Side-Tracked' at Washington," *ALLR* 24, no. 2 (June 1934): 53–56.

35. *Report to the President of the Committee on Economic Security*, pp. 17–20; Public Law no. 271, title 9, secs. 901, 902. See also Nelson, *Unemployment Insurance*, pp. 204–219. The Social Security Act was upheld as constitutional by the Supreme Court in two cases decided on 24 May 1937, *Stewart Machine Co. v. Davis*, 301 U.S. 548, and *Helvering v. Davis*, 301 U.S. 619.

36. Testimony of John B. Andrews, *Economic Security Act*, Hearings Before the Committee on Finance, United States Senate, 74th Cong., 1st sess. (on S. 1130), 22 January to 20 February 1935, revised, pp. 441–442. Also in 1935, Elizabeth Brandeis wrote that "the fear of unequal competition" constituted "the main barrier which has retarded state social legislation in the past" ("Economic and Administrative Criteria for a Social Insurance Program," *ALLR* 25, no. 1 [March 1935]: 25). In 1936 Edwin E. Witte wrote, "Prior to this [national Social Security] legislation no state could enact such a law without handicapping its industries in interstate competition" ("The National Social Security Program," *Wisconsin Alumni Magazine*, January 1936, p. 105).

37. Malisoff, "Emergence of Unemployment Compensation, I," p. 252.

38. See Public Law 271, titles 1, 4, 10, and 5; Cohen, "Development of the Social Security Act," pp. 381, 400–401. It is interesting to note what Edward S. Corwin observed in 1934, that "the success of the spending power in eluding all constitutional snares, goes far to envelop the entire institution of judicial review, as well as its product, constitutional law, in an atmosphere of unreality, even of futility." See his *The Twilight of the Supreme Court—A History of Our Constitutional Theory* (New Haven, Yale University Press, 1934), pp. 178–179.

39. The fact that several of the major social welfare programs inaugurated during the New Deal were based on federal-state structures (so as to avoid constitutional challenges on the principle of federalism) has produced problems that remain with us to the present day. A 1990 article in the *Times* about rapidly declining unemployment insurance benefits and eligibility, for example, attributes a substantial part of the problem to an economic dynamic that I have called degenerative competition among the states: "The states

[have tightened eligibility requirements] mostly to avoid raising the taxes they charge employers," the reporter, David E. Rosenbaum, explains. "Businesses argue, and many politicians agree, that a lower unemployment insurance tax improves the business climate of a state and makes it more attractive to companies that might wish to come there." The article notes that, as of late 1990, only one-third of the jobless in the United States were receiving unemployment insurance benefits. See David E. Rosenbaum, "Unemployment Insurance Aiding Fewer Workers," *New York Times,* 2 December 1990, sec. 1, pp. 1, 38. See also "Restore Unemployment Insurance That Works: March of Folly," letter to the editor from Martin J. Morand, *New York Times,* 27 December 1990, p. A18, which elaborates on the interstate competition issue discussed in Rosenbaum's article.

40. See Henry R. Seager, "Outline of a Program of Social Legislation with Special Reference to Wage-Earners," *American Association for Labor Legislation: Proceedings of the First Annual Meeting* (Madison, April 1908), pp. 85–87; Henry R. Seager, "Old Age Pensions," originally in *Charities and the Commons,* 3 October 1908, reprinted in Gulick, ed., *Labor and Other Economic Essays,* pp. 149–154; F. Spencer Baldwin, "Old Age Insurance," *ALLR* 3, no. 2 (June 1913): 202–212; Rubinow's statement, "General Discussion," *ALLR* 3, no. 2 (June 1913): 242–243; Andrews to Ida Tarbell, 7 May 1915, AALL Papers, reel 14; John B. Andrews, "Introductory Note," *ALLR* 5, no. 4 (December 1915): 637–638; John B. Andrews, "Progress in Old Age Pension Legislation," *ALLR* 13, no. 1 (March 1923): 47–48; Pierce, "Activities of the American Association for Labor Legislation," pp. 387, 391–392; Lyon, "The American Association for Labor Legislation and the Fight for Workmen's Compensation Laws, 1906–1942," p. 67; Lubove, *Struggle for Social Security,* chap. 6 ("The Aged and the State").

41. For a reprinted version of the model bill, see "Old Age Pension Bill," *ALLR* 14, no. 4 (December 1924): 307–310.

42. The state pension laws enacted through 1933 that were upheld as constitutional are as follows: Montana, Nevada (1923); Wisconsin (1925); Kentucky (1926); Maryland, Colorado (1927); California, Minnesota, Utah, Wyoming (1929); New York, Massachusetts (1930); Delaware, New Hampshire, Idaho, New Jersey, West Virginia (1931); Arkansas, Maine, North Dakota, Oregon, Indiana, Colorado, Arizona, Washington (1933). See Roy Lubove, *Struggle for Social Security,* pp. 113–143; Elizabeth Brandeis, "Labor Legislation," in Commons, ed., *History of Labor in the United States,* vol. 4, pp. 611–624.

43. See e.g. John B. Andrews, "Old Age Pensions; Their Basis in Social Needs," *ALLR* 19, no. 4 (December 1929): 357.

44. Social Security Act, August 14, 1935, Public Law 74–71, ch. 531, 49 stat. 620.

45. See e.g. Jill Quadagno, *The Transformation of Old Age Security: Class and Politics in the American Welfare State* (Chicago: University of Chicago, 1988), pp. 99–100.

46. See Perkins, *The Roosevelt I Knew,* p. 289; Witte, *Development of the Social Security Act,* p. 174; Cohen, "Development of the Social Security Act," pp. 384, 387; Ronald Numbers, *Almost Persuaded: American Physicians and Compulsory Health Insurance, 1912–1920* (Baltimore: Johns Hopkins University Press, 1978), p. 114; Altmeyer, *Formative Years of Social Security,* p. 267. See also Hirshfield, *Lost Reform.*

47. " 'Prophet of New Deal,' Now Retired, Surveys Fruits of Own Teachings," *Syracuse Herald,* 17 January 1935, reprinted in Commons Papers, reel 21, fr. 647. With regard to economic legislation, Commons wrote in his autobiography in 1934: "In thirty years I have seen little acorns grow to mighty trees whirling in a stratosphere of high wind. Whew! Poor me! I am not in it." *Myself* (New York: Macmillan, 1934), p. 75.

Epilogue

1. The doctrine of federalism as interpreted by the Supreme Court no longer constrains the federal government in the area of social welfare policy as it once did. But many social welfare policies—especially those enacted before World War II—are still run at the state level. Firms continue to feel the effects of state-level differences in regulation and taxation; and the various state governments continue to face strong competitive pressures that militate against program expansion and often encourage downsizing.

2. The states added approximately $10 million in relief appropriations, and the American Red Cross spent almost $20 million out of private funds. Still, the total relief effort amounted to only about 13 percent of total costs in 1927. See Bruce Alan Lohof, "Hoover and the Mississippi Valley Flood of 1927: A Case Study of the Political Thought of Herbert Hoover" (Ph.D. diss., Syracuse University, 1968), esp. pp. 122, 169–170, 185; American National Red Cross, *The Mississippi Valley Flood Disaster of 1927: Official Report of the Relief Operations* (Washington, D.C., n.d.), esp. pp. 11–13.

3. Warren Cohen, "Uncle Sam's Open Wallet," *U.S. News & World Report,* 22 August 1994, p. 54; Edward Walsh, "Missouri Farmers Are Determined to Till in the Flood Plain—Again; One Year After Midwest's Big Flood, Residents Go Back to Old Ways," *Washington Post,* 19 April 1994, p. A6; "Clinton Signs $6.2 Billion Aid Package," *Facts on File World News Digest,* 26 August 1993, p. 624 E3.

4. One question that deserves close study is why some risks are compensated on the basis of public mandate much more than others and why some are not covered at all. In other words, what determines which risks get socialized and by what means (mandatory private insurance, public insurance, noncontributory public coverage, tort liability, etc.)?

5. I emphasize the phrase "in retrospect" because the AALL reformers rarely articulated this logic at the time. Of course, they viewed protective labor legislation and social insurance as responses to industrialization. But instead of explicitly characterizing these policies as necessary to address deviations

from a rising mean, they simply characterized them as necessary to counteract or prevent what appeared to them to be the greatest cause of poverty at the time: industrial hazards. Hazard-based insecurity probably would not have risen to the top of the AALL agenda, however, had industrial wages either been terribly deficient (in terms of a minimally acceptable standard of living) or declining significantly. Although it was widely assumed during the progressive era that real wages were rising, there was by no means universal agreement on this point. I. M. Rubinow, for example, claimed (on the basis of poor retail price data) that increases in the cost of living equaled or exceeded increases in nominal wages after 1900. But even he must have recognized the logical connection between rising wages and social insurance, for after challenging the evidence for rising wages in his book *Social Insurance,* he acknowledged, "It may be argued that all this evidence of the unsatisfactory economic condition of the working class, if correct, proves rather the necessity of a higher wage level than a policy of social insurance." Rubinow escaped from this logical trap by insisting that while he recognized the necessity for higher wages, "the economic and statistical evidence produced seems to force the conclusion, that if the general status of the wage-worker's life is much below the standard of physiological necessity and economic efficiency, surely the wage-worker is seldom in condition to withstand the attack of any cause which produced an interruption of income." See I.M. Rubinow, "The Recent Trend of Real Wages," *American Economic Review* 4, no. 4 (December 1914): 793–817; Rubinow, *Social Insurance, with Special Reference to American Conditions* (New York: Holt, 1916), pp. 44–45. Recent estimates show real wages to have grown by about 1.2 percent per year between 1900 and 1910. For historical real wage data, see Donald R. Adams Jr., "Prices and Wages," in Glenn Porter, ed., *Encyclopedia of American Economic History* (New York: Scribner, 1980), vol. 1, table 5 (p. 244). For labor-productivity data, see Bureau of the Census, *Historical Statistics of the United States, Colonial Times to 1970* (Washington, 1975), part 1, series D-683 (p. 162).

6. Between 1910 and 1973, real per capita GNP grew at a compound annual rate of 1.8 percent, and real wages grew at 2.2 percent. Although the compound annual growth rate of real per capita GNP between 1929 and 1939 was −0.4 percent, real wages grew during those years at 3.6 percent annually. See Adams, "Prices and Wages," table 5 (p. 244); *Economic Report of the President* (Washington, 1994), tables B-45 (p. 320) and B-6 (p. 277); *Historical Statistics of the United States, Colonial Times to 1970,* part 1, series F-4 (p. 224).

7. Between 1973 and 1993, real wages *declined* at a compound annual rate of 0.7 percent. Real per capita GNP, meanwhile, *grew* at a rate of 1.3 percent. The disparity is largely attributable to increasing inequality of income and increasing participation of women in the workforce. See *Economic Report of the President* (1994), tables B-45 (p. 320) and B-6 (p. 277).

8. Of course, there are many different ways to interpret the available data on wages. The trend I have highlighted involves real wages—that is, the hourly

pre-tax take-home pay of wage earners corrected for inflation. If one looks at total compensation per hour (which includes not only take-home pay but also fringe benefits such as pensions, health insurance, and vacation time), the trend has been stagnant rather than declining. Another relevant variable is median family income, which also has been roughly stagnant rather than declining, primarily because of growing participation of women in the workforce. Nevertheless, the most important point, in my opinion, is that most Americans—especially those in the lower portions of the earnings distribution—have had to work harder for their take-home pay since the early 1970s.

9. Ronald Brownstein, "America's Anxiety Attack," *Los Angeles Times Magazine,* 8 May 1994, p. 15.

10. Michael R. Kagay, "From Coast to Coast, From Affluent to Poor, Poll Shows Anxiety Over Jobs," *New York Times,* 11 March 1994, p. A14; Brian O'Reilly, "The New Deal; What Companies and Employees Owe One Another," *Fortune,* 13 June 1994, p. 50; Charles Stein, "The Politics of Security; Americans Are Feeling Nervous About Their Futures," *Boston Globe,* 21 November 1993, p. A1; Robert Reich, "The Fracturing of the Middle Class," *New York Times,* 31 August 1994, p. A19.

11. Dirk Johnson, "Family Struggles to Make Do After Fall From Middle Class," *New York Times,* 11 March 1994, p. A1.

Acknowledgments

In exploring the AALL's role, I relied primarily on the papers and quarterly journal of the Association, the papers of a number of its leading members, state commission reports, and state and federal legislative records. One other source that proved invaluable to me was the *Monitor,* the official organ of the Associated Manufacturers and Merchants of New York State. The journal not only provides a window on the attitudes of upstate employers toward social welfare legislation but also reprints numerous documents that are no longer available in original form, including the transcripts of several very important legislative hearings. To my knowledge, these transcripts have not previously been utilized by social welfare historians.

The human resources on which I depended in writing this book proved equally rich. I am deeply indebted to my doctoral advisers: Howard Lamar, David Weiman, and Steven Gillon, who offered consistently outstanding criticism and encouragement. I owe special thanks to Professor Lamar who, true to form, accepted me as an advisee with little more than a handshake as collateral. I am also grateful to members of the Yale Economic History Workshop and the Harvard Business History Seminar for providing markets for my work; to the Whiting Foundation, the Yale University Graduate School, and the Harvard Business School's Division of Research for their generous financial support; to John Morton Blum, Jonathan Cedarbaum, and Rabbi Jerome D. Folkman for their superb editorial comments and critical suggestions on early drafts of the dissertation; to James Tobin, who disciplined my economic reasoning; to James Patterson, who offered reassurance at a crucial moment; to Thomas McCraw for his impeccable editorial advice on a late version of the book manuscript; to my dear friend James Wooten for his unwavering support and critical commentary throughout the project; to my parents, Joy and Arthur Moss, to whom I owe my love of history and without whom my debts would have been greatly multiplied; and, of course, to my partner in life, Abigail Kischin, who provided me with security of a wholly non-financial sort that made possible this historical study about security and insecurity.

Index